Having lived through these thrilling day
gives an accurate picture, the most ac
gladly endorse *Island Aflame*.

WILLIAM AND MARGARET MACLEOD
Barvas, Isle of Lewis

Numerous books have been written about past revivals in Lewis and across Scotland, containing many stories that have deeply impressed readers with the wonders that God wrought on these remarkable occasions. The most wonderful of all, of course, was the manifestation of God's power in people's lives, leading to a turning from darkness to light.

In *Island Aflame*, Tom Lennie has written a thoroughly researched account of the move of the Spirit in Lewis & Harris between 1949 and '52. Much of the myth and misreporting which arose in succeeding decades has been corrected. He has rightly focused on the revival of hungry hearts through the ministry of God's word and the power of the Holy Spirit, and as a convert of the revival, I can confirm that he has done an excellent job – providing a most accurate account.

DONALD JOHN SMITH
Ballantrushal, Isle of Lewis

With admirable courage and exemplary humility, Tom Lennie carves a clear pathway between cynicism and exaggeration to give the reader a compelling, convincing and captivating account of God's powerful work in Lewis and Harris almost 75 years ago. This books serves as both an accessible introduction to the Revival of 1949–52 and as an important reappraisal of how those famous years should be remembered. This book contains careful research, fascinating history and, above all, a wonderful reminder of the mighty works done by God in the Outer Hebrides.

THOMAS DAVIS
Minister, Carloway Free Church of Scotland, Isle of Lewis

A must read for anyone seeking to understand 'genuine' revival...I pray that *Island Aflame* will set your own heart aflame.

SHANE IDLEMAN
Lead Pastor, Westside Christian Fellowship, Leona Valley, California

Island Aflame is a meticulously researched, comprehensive account of the spiritual movement which swept through the Isle of Lewis between 1949–52, primarily under the preaching of Duncan Campbell. Indeed, I suspect it will be the seminal work on the subject for many years to come.

As an honest historian, Tom Lennie has not shirked his responsibility in drawing the reader's attention to the embellishments, additions and myths surrounding the movement – in particular some of the questionable claims made by Mr Campbell himself. Many will find this shocking – but Tom approaches these issues with compassion and grace, as, with an eye always to the truth, he seeks to understand the motivation and reasons behind such exaggerated claims.

Tom's research, much of it original, reveals, as the subtitle of the book suggests, that this movement needed no exaggeration, and witness after witness whom he has interviewed clearly bears this out.

The story of the 1949–52 Lewis revival has been told many times before – but this book is unique in its depth, attention to detail, statistical analysis, and personal accounts and assessments – much of which have not been published before.

Island Aflame is, in essence, the most comprehensive and honest treatment of a movement which has been made famous in Christian circles throughout the world. It needs to be read by all who want to know and understand the true Lewis revival of 1949–52.

STEVE TAYLOR

Photographer,

Author, *Skye Ablaze: Spiritual Awakening on the Isle of Skye and the Maritimes*

Tom Lennie has accomplished a Herculean task in providing us with a comprehensive and searching examination of the evidence for the Lewis revival of 1949-52. The quality, depth and perception of his research shines through every page of this monumental study.

What Tom has presented us with is the result of high-quality library investigation together with his own field research, interviewing those who could give first-hand accounts of events in the island community, while also offering his own carefully weighed assessment of the evidence. Tom has a particular gift in painting a word picture for us of scenes that bring events alive for the reader in a remarkable way.

I greatly appreciate this study, from which I have learned a lot about the factual situation. But also, I found the journey that Tom takes us on to be a profoundly spiritual one, assembling a vast amount of evidence and carefully sifting it for truth. His treatment of Duncan Campbell is of a high quality; recognising the spiritual characteristics of this great evangelist who ensured that all the glory for the revival went to the Lord, while at the same time giving an honest assessment of Campbell's own accounts of the awakening.

Well done, Tom – the book is truly a great read!

CLIFFORD HILL

Former Senior Lecturer, Sociology of Religion, London University;
Founder and former Editor-in-Chief of *Prophecy Today*

Tom has, I believe, walked a tricky road successfully. In deconstructing some of the embellishments told by Duncan Campbell himself, his account has, nevertheless retained a confidence in the genuineness of the revival, as also plausible reasons as to why Campbell could do this. Many will value this, in addition to the author's conclusion, from a personal knowledge of Campbell, that despite this predisposition, he was a sincere and godly man who was used by the Lord as a channel of blessing to many.

I found Tom's assessment and conclusions about Duncan Campbell's distortions - and indeed lies - most informative. This very much accords with comments I would hear from time to time from Free Church people over the years, and it may well be that a reluctance on the part of some to accept the genuineness of the revival itself stemmed from knowing that some aspects of it had been exaggerated or embellished.

I am pleased that Tom has judiciously compared the 1930s revival with that of 1949-52. I have heard of the former being spoken of more favourably than the latter, possibly because it did not involve any prominent individual at its head or in its spread. As Tom says, the movement in the 1930s has received nothing like the prominence given to the other.

I hope the book will prove a means of correcting the widespread myths about the revival while also reminding people that the glorious power of God was indeed evident in the transformation of many lives. May it be a means of persuading us all that God has not gone away and that it is incumbent upon us to pray, *"Will you not revive us again, that your people may rejoice in you?"*

JAMES MACIVER

Minister, Free Church of Scotland, Stornoway, Isle of Lewis

I have been privileged to have met several converts of the extraordinary move of the Spirit of God that is the subject of this meticulously researched book by Tom Lennie. To look into their eyes, hear their unadorned, unexaggerated reports of what God actually did has been proof enough for me that revival is an undeniable fact. It has brought me to tears more than once, so sweet was the presence of the Lord bearing His own witness to truthful testimony. They are of course by now elderly, with all the frailty that comes from the passing of the years, but when they talk of those former times, it is as though they become young again, and one becomes aware of the presence of unquenchable fire. They are still ablaze not only with precious memories but with faith in what can happen when God rends the heavens and comes down. They still pray for that.

Any book that seeks to genuinely trace the facts of the going forth of God in extraordinary power is worth reading. Tom was a member of my congregation in Edinburgh. I know of few people who long for a day of God's power with such prayerfulness and integrity. May God's blessing attend what he has penned in this honest work.

KENNY BORTHWICK
Former senior pastor, Holy Trinity, Wester Hailes, Edinburgh

Tom Lennie has placed the Scottish Church in his debt with this latest volume chronicling the 1949–52 Lewis and Harris spiritual revival. In this book, he makes use of earlier reliable accounts, plus significant church records, all supplemented with oral testimony from those who lived through these momentous events and times, thus bringing to us the most comprehensive account that I have yet come across, of the scope, size and significance of what is often referred to simply as 'the Lewis revival.'

In addition, in *Island Aflame* Tom Lennie sensitively and fairly handles oppositional accounts and exaggerated claims as he brings together this compelling account of the gracious movement of God's Spirit in the island of Lewis and Harris in the years 1949-52. My prayer is that this volume would lead many of us to cry out for God's gracious blessing to come in these days for the sake of the benighted generations in our land who know nothing of the splendid, glorious, saving and renewing power of the God of all grace.

HECTOR MORRISON
Principal, Highland Theological College, Dingwall,
minister, Barvas Church of Scotland, 1981-90

Island
Aflame

The Famed Lewis Awakening that Never Occurred and the Glorious Revival that Did

(Lewis & Harris 1949–52)

TOM LENNIE

Copyright © Tom Lennie 2023

paperback ISBN 978-1-5271-1051-9
ebook ISBN 978-1-5271-1109-7

First published in 2023
By
Christian Focus Publications Ltd,
Geanies House, Fearn, Ross-shire
IV20 1TW, Scotland

www.christianfocus.com

CIP catalogue record for this book is available from the British Library.

Cover design by Daniel Van Straaten

Cover photo: Sea stacks at Mangersta, Isle of Lewis (fstopphotography)

Other than vintage photographs, landscape photos throughout
the book are courtesy of the author

Printed by Bell & Bain, Glasgow

CONTENTS

Part 6: Post Revival

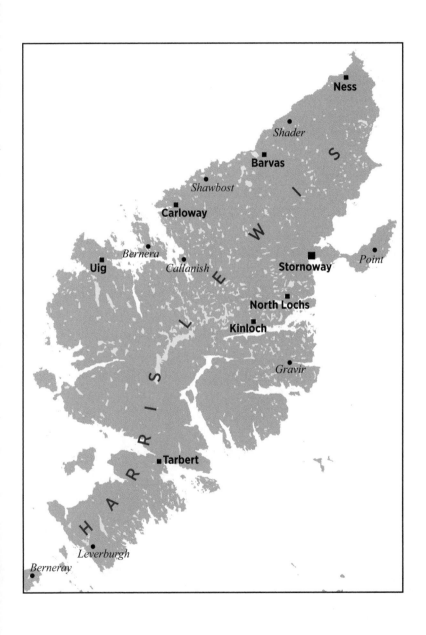

75th Anniversary Edition

The year 2024 marks the 75th anniversary of the beginning of the Lewis revival of 1949-52 – a year that will be accompanied by a heightened interest in all things connected to that stirring movement so famed in revival literature. *Island Aflame* constitutes a rare attempt at setting out the main incidents of that revival in a reasonably chronological order. Our hope is that the book will also go some way to helping set the movement in its historic context, and in so doing provide a fairly reliable account of the events of those exciting days.

Acknowledgements

It would be impractical to list the names of everyone who helped in the research for this book, though I have sought to provide individual credits in the footnotes of the pages that follow.

In particular, I would like to thank those revival converts who provided me with firsthand testimonies of the movement. Chief among their number were William and Margaret Macleod, Donald John Smith and Agnes Morrison, all of whom, given their warmth of personality and sense of graciousness and humility, soon became precious friends.

I am extremely grateful to all those who provided generous endorsements, and to R.T. Kendall for his thoughtful Foreword. I'm hugely indebted to the Rev. Hector Morrison for his enormously helpful feedback, and in particular, the graphs and charts he allowed me to use highlighting church membership increases.

I have very much appreciated the encouragement of Rev. Andrew Woolsey, whose deeply engaging early biography of Duncan Campbell, whom he knew better than almost anyone currently alive, first attracted me to the Lewis revival. Meeting with Sheena Vischer, Duncan Campbell's daughter, was a special delight, and I greatly enjoyed our several conversations, and the fond stories she shared about her father.

A great big thank you to Richard Powell for his typesetting skills and various other forms of assistance on the manuscript. Last but not least, thanks to my Lewis friend (the Rev) Brian Macleod for his encouragement and friendship over the years.

Dedication

I dedicate *Island Aflame* to the memory of all those whose lives were so beautifully transformed by the spiritual outpouring that graced the isle of Lewis and Harris between the years 1949 and 1952.

The Days of Outpouring on Barvas

In the years when revival was known in these parts,
The Spirit of God changed the hardest of hearts,
Unbelief and rebellion led to 'trust and obey,'
For such was the atmosphere back in these days.

A slumbering Church came awake at that hour,
By a mighty outpouring of heavenly power,
The ways of the world did no longer hold sway,
Conviction made many, from sin, turn away.

They found in the Saviour, their treasure on earth,
More precious than silver, of e'erlasting worth.
For such are the ways of the Spirit of God,
Who bringeth salvation through His gospel Word.

We yearn for such glory, again in our day,
Knowing prayer is the key to preparing the way,
Then just at the right time, heaven's doors open wide,
Poured out on His children, a spiritual tide.

Though the vision may tarry, t'will indeed come to pass,
Like the days of outpouring that came to Barvas.
However, whenever, that day will arise,
On Christ who will do it, must we fix our eyes.

Duncan Macaskill

Foreword

I have been deeply influenced by the Hebrides Revival of 1949–52. First, the knowledge of it and stories that emerged from it helped shape my own desire to see God work powerfully in my day.

Second, the man who was powerfully used in my life by helping me understand my own call to the ministry was Dr. John Sutherland Logan, a Scotsman who told me stories of the revival and who knew a lot about the Rev. Duncan Campbell. His affirmation of what happened on the Isle of Lewis in 1949–52 created a hunger for more of God in my life and ministry.

Third, to my surprise and great honor, I was invited to preach alongside the Rev. Kenny Borthwick in Stornoway in 2019 when the 70th anniversary of the Hebrides Revival was observed. There I met some of the people who were converts of the revival and also visited places about which extraordinary stories were told. It was also at that Revival conference that my wife and I met the author of this book; he shared with us a little background information on the revival, and spoke of Duncan Campbell's consistent belief in the sovereignty of God; something that resonated strongly with me.

Island Aflame by Tom Lennie is needed and abundantly helpful for those who have an interest in historic revivals in church history. As for these extraordinary and interesting stories that have emerged from the Hebrides Revival, they continue to inspire and increase one's faith in the knowledge that God is alive and on His throne and could, if He is pleased, do it again. These accounts remind one of the sovereign power of

God and possibilities that one might not have imagined, such as the conviction of the Holy Spirit suddenly coming upon merry-makers at a late-night community dance, the singing of biblical Psalms replacing Scottish folk melodies, and partiers quietly leaving the hall in the wee hours of the morning in solemnity and deep thought.

As Tom Lennie says, 'Everyone loves a good story'. And all of us are prone to believe what seems so exciting – and hate it if told that what we heard and were excited by may not be true after all. If I might be forgiven for going from the sublime to the ridiculous, I always hoped to see the Loch Ness monster one day! I hate the thought that it does not exist. The question is, do I really want the truth?

Many readers may well be initially disappointed to discover that some of the stories that came out of the Hebrides Revival were either exaggerated or simply not true at all! And yet the more I read of this book the more I was reminded of the German theologian Rudolf Bultmann (1884–1976). He came up with the theory of demythologizing. He believed the accounts of the miracles of Jesus in the New Testament were myths. But he applied them by demythologizing them. The problem was, by the time Bultmann finished explaining them and attempting to apply them, there was nothing left to believe! According to Bultmann, the supernatural was never to be taken literally.

Not so with this book. The author wholeheartedly embraces the fact that God worked powerfully in the Hebrides during those days. He is driven by a scholar's caution but with the fervent hope that God will do it again! The beautiful thing that comes from Tom Lennie's book is that, although some of the well-known stories may not have been entirely factual, MANY OF THEM WERE TRUE INDEED! I was left being greatly edified and encouraged. We are reminded again and again of the raw power of the Holy Spirit and the supreme knowledge that He – like Jesus – is "the same yesterday, today and forever"

(Heb. 13:8). Furthermore, what ultimately matters is not merely the supernatural manifestations of the Hebrides Revival but that so many people were genuinely converted in those days. They not only persevered but some went into the ministry.

This book is to be highly recommended.

R. T. Kendall
Minister of Westminster Chapel (1977–2002)

Introduction

The Lewis Revival

Scotland has played host to a vast array of religious revivals over the course of five remarkable centuries. A number of them have become particularly famed in Scottish revival history. Notably, the dramatic Kirk o' Shotts awakening of 1630, centring around the soul-searching season of a Presbyterian communion; the Cambuslang Revival of 1742, featuring English evangelist George Whitefield; the remarkable spiritual movement that overtook Kilsyth and Dundee in 1839 before fanning out across the country; and the potent bursts of intense revival that shook Charlotte Baptist Chapel in central Edinburgh at the turn of the twentieth century.

By far the best-known Scottish revival of the twentieth century is the Lewis revival of 1949 to '52 (better-known in America as the Hebrides revival). In a wider context, this spiritual awakening has been viewed as part of an international movement of post-World War II revivalist enthusiasm. Similar spiritual optimism and evangelical growth followed in the wake of World War I – notably by way of the Fishermen's Revival of 1921–22. The late forties and early-mid fifties witnessed the most extensive attempt at outreach by the Protestant Churches in Scotland in the twentieth century (the Tell Scotland Movement); along with the remarkable All Scotland Crusade led by Billy Graham. In America, as well as the flourishing of mass crusade evangelism, occurred a widespread burst in college revivals across the country, along with the more controversial 'Latter Rain' and 'Healing Revival' movements.

1

News of the Lewis revival spread quickly through its retelling by the evangelist most associated with it, the Rev. Duncan Campbell. Indeed, not only is this revival Scotland's most famous awakening, it has found its place as one of the most famed spiritual movements in world history. There is little in the way of general revival literature that doesn't include mention of its occurrence. This is a staggering achievement.

The 1949 Lewis revival differs in essence from some other highly prominent revival movements of the last century. Consider the Korean Pentecost of 1903; the East African revival of the 1930s and onwards; the Welsh revival of 1904–5; the great Chinese revival of recent decades. Truly remarkable movements, every one. What makes the Lewis revival stand out, however, is that while each of the above was national or international in scope, the Lewis revival of 1949–52 was highly localised – being confined to a number of sparsely populated communities on a west-Scotland island. Why a community revival in an obscure location gained such worldwide renown is a question that requires a considered response.

Reasons for the revival's popularity are in fact easy enough to find. Everyone loves a good story, and a great many stories associated with the Lewis revival quickly capture people's imaginations – the impactful account of the two elderly sisters who prayed the awakening into being; the ministry of the evangelist at the fore of the movement; the dramatic testimonies of many who came under its influence; exciting accounts of the supernatural; the revival's advance in the face of opposition; and its lasting impact on many island communities. All these elements, and more, have helped make the Lewis revival one of the most popular the world has known.

Revival Dissemination
News of the dramatic spiritual awakening spread quickly. As early as the summer of 1950, just six months after revival first broke

out, several Christian periodicals in America were issuing reports on it.[1] News spread especially fast on its retelling by the evangelist who fronted it. Even during the movement's progress, Campbell was invited to speak at churches and conventions all over Britain, where he keenly recounted recent events in the Western Isles. As a result, many church leaders and other interested parties travelled to Lewis to witness goings-on for themselves.

In 1954, Duncan Campbell produced a short account of the movement, under the title *The Lewis Awakening 1949–1953*.[2] This was followed by several other short publications in the sixties, by which time Campbell had become an increasingly popular conference speaker, preaching as far afield as South Africa, Switzerland, Canada and the United States. Invariably his topic was 'Revival,' and recordings of his messages can still be procured.[3]

So too can an official biography, *Channel of Revival* (now out-of-print), penned by former Faith Mission student Andrew Woolsey shortly after Campbell's death in 1972 – a well-researched and finely-presented account. One revival convert in particular helped spread the story of the awakening. Mary Morrison's personal story, *Hearken O Daughter*, was published in 1966; in subsequent years she appeared on numerous Gaelic TV and BBC Radio shows, and spoke on the revival at countless conferences, seminars and church meetings all over the world. A sixty minute video documentary, *Wind of the Spirit*, was produced by Ambassador International in 1990 and proved highly popular.

---

1. These include *Awakening* (July 1950), *Intelligence Digest* (Aug 1950), *The Pentecostal Evangel* (Oct 1950), and *Herald of His Coming* (Oct 1950). The secular press was not so quick to report on the revival; one of the first Scottish newspapers outwith Lewis to do so was *The Glasgow Herald* in December 1950.

2. Reprinted 2017, independently published.

3. e.g., on Sermonindex.net.

There arose a resurgence of published material on the Lewis revival from the beginning of the twenty-first century. This included a fresh biography of Duncan Campbell entitled *Catch the Wind*,[4] and the release of *Sounds from Heaven* in 2004,[5] by far the most authoritative account of the movement up to that point. The revival has featured on various television documentaries (such as Revelation TV's *Lewis Revival 60th Anniversary*, in 2009). A *Revival Conference* held in Stornoway in 2019 drew four hundred people to commemorate the seventieth anniversary of the start of the movement. Duncan Campbell's life story has even been created in cartoon format.[6] Aided by several further video productions and a host of self-publications,[7] a plethora of material has been made available on the Lewis revival.

Of much significance regarding the revival's popularity is the fact of its relatively recent occurrence. A great many of Campbell's converts survived him by several decades, and some are still alive at the time of writing. The Lewis revival is widely regarded as one of the last significant revivals in the British Isles, and even in the western world.

Revival Familiarity

'*The Lewis revival*' was the name accorded this movement from a very early date, and almost everyone knows it by that name, and no other. '*The Lewis and Harris revival of 1949–52*' is rather too wordy for common usage; '*The Duncan Campbell revival*' suggests

4. Brad Allen, *Catch the Wind: The Story of Spiritual Awakening on the Hebrides Islands,* Tarentum, 2001.

5. Colin and Mary Peckham, *Sounds from Heaven: The Revival on the Isle of Lewis, 1949–1952,* Fearn, 2004.

6. Alec Stevens, '*The Abundant Life Found in Christ,*' Calvary Comics, 2023.

7. e.g., Kathy Walters, *Bright and Shining Revival, An Account of the Hebrides Revival 1948–52,* 2000; Jessica Meldrum, *Floods On Dry Ground: Story of the Hebrides Awakening,* 2004; Alec Dunn, *The Hebrides Revival and Awakening 1949–1953: A Short History,* 2004; William K. Mackie, *Yesterday's Man: A Tribute to the Late Rev Duncan Campbell,* 2015.

the movement was dependent on one man and might be seen as giving undue focus to Campbell rather than to God.

But the title *'The Lewis revival'* is contentious, for believers on Lewis are well-aware that their island has played host to numerous moves of God's Spirit. Ask many a Christian in Lewis their thoughts on the Lewis revival and you may just receive the teasing response: 'What Lewis revival are you talking about?' (although, in truth they will have little doubt.) While, throughout this book, I often refer to this movement as *'The Lewis Revival of 1949–52'*; *'The 1949 Lewis Revival'*[8], or simply *'The '49 revival,'* I also cave in to common usage, and, like everyone else, regularly find myself employing the term, *'The Lewis revival.'*

Most of us are very familiar with some of the most salient features of the revival passed on to us – of an island in a sorry spiritual state, with hardly a young person attending church; the two housebound sisters who knew how to plead with, and hear from, God; the seven men who prayed twice-weekly through the night in a barn; the dramatic outbreak of revival on Campbell's first night in Barvas, when the church service continued till the early hours of the morning and hundreds came under deep agony of soul.

We hear of scores of people flocking to church late at night, on foot or by bus, not knowing why or even where they were going. We recall accounts of multiple converts from a single house-meeting going on to become ministers; of visions of a 'gospel ship' in a Barvas field. Then there is the overall impact of thousands from all over Lewis & Harris turning to Christ, of the island being brought out of spiritual darkness, and of dramatic societal transformation. This study seeks to uncover the truth behind these and many other popular stories.

---

8. However, neither of these titles takes Harris into account, which district was also privy to the awakening under discussion.

PART 1

Revival Island

CHAPTER 1

Revival Myths

In keeping with its popularity, there has probably been no spiritual awakening on earth that has proved more contentious and created more confusion than the Lewis revival of 1949–52. Deeply conflicting accounts have appeared in various publications, and particularly on a plethora of websites – making it well-nigh impossible to glean fact from fantasy. Much of the difficulty relates to the many exaggerations that have arisen in connection with the movement.

Few people deny that exaggerations and falsehoods have surfaced in the retelling of this popular revival. It has been claimed that many of the myriad of revival myths that have sprung up originate with an individual at the very centre of the movement; we will consider this claim shortly. First, we note a number of inadequately researched narratives that have cropped up through the decades.

Location Location
Consider a portrayal of the movement which alleges that the New Hebrides islands was the location of the awakening, where, near 'Barvis,' close to the 'town of Lewis,' two women were 'the human instruments responsible for revival,' which came after Campbell, a grandfather, suddenly left the Keswick Bible Conference to come and minister.[1] There are a number of inaccuracies here, while others also crop up further on in this brief account.

---

1. Elmer Towns and Douglas Porter, *The Ten Greatest Revivals Ever: From Pentecost to the Present*, Ann Arbor, 2000, pp. 144–6.

The Lewis revival did not occur on the New Hebrides islands, which was the former name for a group of around eighty islands now formally known as Vanuatu, located in the South Pacific Ocean, some 10,000 miles distant from the Scottish Hebrides. Similarly, Lewis is not a town but an island, Duncan Campbell at this stage was not a grandfather, and it wasn't the Keswick Bible Conference that he left to come to the island; rather, his evangelistic work on the Isle of Skye.

Fixing the location of the revival as the New Hebrides islands is a mistake that many have made. A writer of whom Billy Graham claimed, 'no one is better qualified … to write on revival,' also speaks of 'the great New Hebrides Islands revival of 1949.' He goes on to state that 'within a few weeks the revival had moved across the island sweeping thousands of people into the kingdom.'[2] Here is another commonly-reported myth – that the revival led to many thousands of conversions in a short period of time. In fact, neither Duncan Campbell nor anyone else in Lewis made any claim to so large a number being saved during the entire course of the revival, let alone within a few weeks.

Tales From Across the Pond
Other reports are equally riddled with historical mis-statements. An 800-word summary of the Lewis revival on the website of a famous American Christian TV network includes well over twenty factual errors. Among these are that invitations to hear Campbell preach in Lewis were 'put in all the roads' and that on his arrival on Lewis he was explicitly requested to 'talk about God.'[3] In reality, the Lewis revival was never advertised in the

---

2. Robert E. Coleman, *The Coming World Revival*, Wheaton, 1995, pp. 43–4. Coleman states as his reference source 'Arthur Wallis.' Wallis, however, makes none of the errors found in Coleman's one-page account. Another writer speaks of the Hebrides revival occurring outwith Europe (Peter H. Lawrence, *The Spirit Who Heals*, Eastbourne, 2006, p. 330).

3. Ross Scott and Elmer Towns, *Flames of Revival: New Hebrides Awakening*, Christian Broadcasting Network (CBN), www.cbn.com/biblestudy/flames-

way specified, or in any way. The advice to speak about God would have been considered quite unnecessary; no Highland evangelist of his day ever preached on anything other than God and His gospel.

In a study of Nehemiah, in the context of spiritual renewal, an internationally popular author speaks of *Donald* Campbell and the Lewis revival. 'Whole shifts of below-the-ground miners would be too distressed to continue their work until they had resolved their relationship with God.'[4] The author is apparently confusing events of the Welsh revival of 1904 with those of the Lewis awakening; the former affected many hundreds of coal-miners, the latter affected none, for there were no underground pits in Lewis in the mid-1900s.

Another US author, in her very brief account of the Lewis revival, states, with no supporting evidence, 'More than 500 prayer groups, almost exclusively women, had been crying to God for an awakening.'[5] This statistic seems to have been pulled from thin air; it in no way corresponds to reality.

The blurb advertising one account of the Lewis revival refers to 'a powerful move of awakening to God that began with five men praying in a barn and expanded to over 20,000 conversions in three months … you will be able to duplicate this great outpouring in your own home, city or region, for truly God is no respecter of persons.'[6] Apart from the mythical conversion statistic quoted, how can any individual or group of people possibly 'duplicate' an outpouring of God's Spirit?

---

of-revival:-new-hebrides-awakening.

4. John While, *Excellence in Leadership: The Pattern of Nehemiah*, Leicester, 1986 p. 101, quoted in John Macleod, *Banner in the West,* Edinburgh, 2008, p. 262.

5. Mary Stewart Relfe, *Cure Of All Ills*, Montgommery, 1988, p. 151.

6. Rev. Owen Murphy, *When God Stepped Down from Heaven: Revival in the Hebrides*, self-published, 2017.

Home-spun Anecdotes

Lest anyone think I am deliberately picking on North American authors, I include some European examples. An English evangelist records that the Hebrides revival of 1950–1 was the third of only four 'historic genuine revivals' to have occurred in the British Isles in the twentieth century.[7] This 'heaven-sent Divine visitation' had as its theme, 'Your honour is at stake,' lasted ten months, and 'produced approximately 4,000 converts.'[8]

In a live discussion on a Christian TV channel, the leader of a national prayer movement re-iterated the universally held belief that the Lewis revival was initiated by the prayers of the two elderly Smith sisters, who, she said, were so desperate for God to move upon their island that they drew a circle around them and vowed that they would not move out of it, nor would they sleep or eat one bite, until God sent revival in answer to their persistent intercession. The immediate cause of the revival, continued the correspondent, was the power of God coming down upon a young girl standing on a chair![9]

Two young revival researchers noted, 'The first event which clearly showed that Mr Campbell was going to be powerfully used and anointed was when, prior to his arrival, a local man, who was either a dentist or a doctor, began to stir the people up against Campbell, in an attempt to hinder his influence. On doing so, the man instantly dropped dead.[10] There is no truth in this.

---

7. The first two, the author informs us, were the Welsh revival of 1904 and the Lowestoft revival of 1923. The most recent authentic revival in Britain, he records, was one which he personally co-led, occurring in Wigan, Lancashire in 1970. Apparently lasting six weeks and seeing 2,200 conversions, this movement remains unknown to most UK believers, and no revival historian I know has documented it.

8. Melvin Banks, *Nothing Is Impossible*, Chippenham, 2008, preface.

9. 'Pastor Kate' in discussion with Jonathan Oloyede on *Live @ Nine*, 07.12.2010.

10. Article on revival, The Australian Christian Assemblies International website, January 1991.

An Anglican minister wrote that the revival caused 'hundreds of very secular people to cry aloud for mercy … It was entirely God's work.' As a result of it, 'the ferries were discontinued on the Sabbath.'[11] The truth is that even prior to the revival, the people of Lewis could not be considered 'very secular' – the island being steeped in Christian teaching. Nor did the revival alter the running of ferries – these didn't operate on Sundays anyway.

One popular writer confuses George Macleod, ecumenical founder of the Iona Community, with Duncan Campbell as being the prominent evangelist in the awakening. He is also under the impression that Campbell was a contemporary of John Govan, founder of the Faith Mission. In fact, John Govan founded the Mission well before Campbell was born. He died in 1927, two full decades before Campbell set foot on Lewis.

A German researcher had it that the two Barvas spinsters 'had been praying to God for thirty years for a revival. First only young men were affected. They arduously prayed for their pastor until he confessed himself a sinner and devoted his life to Jesus. The spirit of repentance then came upon the elderly men and afterwards on the women and girls ….The Hebrides experienced two waves of revival; the first in 1949 and the second in 1953.'[12] None of these claims has any basis in fact.

Checking the Facts
The above statements are among the more outlandish mis-reporting of the Lewis revival. Sadly, the uninitiated reader is likely to take them as true. Many other accounts of this spiritual movement intermingle fact with error, thus creating overall distorted reports. That's not to suggest such narratives don't contain much in the way of valuable information. Most of

---

11. Michael Green, *When God Breaks In*, London, 2014, pp. 210–3.

12. Kurt Koch, *Die Erweckung auf den Hebriden*, on www.schriftenmission. de (accessed 12.10.2016).

them do. Nor is it to suggest that a reporter should never record anything unless he is 100 per cent certain of its veracity.

The author of this study, for example, can in no way guarantee that all the information he presents is error-free; I will have made numerous mistakes, albeit inadvertently. But the above accounts do highlight the need for historians to do their best to ensure accuracy by checking their facts where at all possible. Otherwise, the misinformation documented is likely to get further distorted by others over time, potentially leading to greatly aberrant revival accounts.

We close this section with a more relevant quote on the Lewis revival. In his classic book, *Why Revival Tarries* – one of the most pertinent studies ever written on the theme of revival – Leonard Ravenhill quotes a pastor who exclaimed:

"'We wish revival would come to us as it came to the Hebrides.' But fellow servant, revival did not come to the Hebrides by wishing! The heavens were opened and the mighty power of the Lord shook those islands because "frail children of dust ... sanctified a fast and called a solemn assembly," and waited tear-stained, tired, and travailing before the throne of the living God. That visitation came because He who sought for a virgin in which to conceive His beloved Son found a people of virgin purity in those souls of burning motive in their praying. No petitions were coloured with desire to serve the face of a failing denomination. Their eye was single to God's glory. They were not jealous of another group who was outgrowing them, but jealous for the Lord of Hosts, whose glory was in the dust, the "wall of whose house was broken down, and whose gates were burned with fire."'[13]

A Shocking Interruption

What may well come as a surprise to many is the charge that the greatest source of exaggerated information came from the

---

13. Leonard Ravenhill, *Why Revival Tarries*, Tonbridge, 1959, pp. 131–2.

very evangelist at the centre of the movement – especially in addresses given in the latter years of his life. The charge must be taken seriously, for this characteristic of Duncan Campbell has been belatedly accepted, not only by his opponents, but also by his closest friends. One revival convert stated, 'I was horrified at the exaggeration of details of this revival. Campbell often spoke about the revival and was accused of exaggerating. That accusation was justified.'[14]

Although he had his detractors, everyone I have spoken to who knew Duncan Campbell personally, or those I've read about who knew him, have spoken of him in the highest terms. He was universally regarded by all friends and colleagues as a warm-hearted, unassuming man of genuine godliness, who held a burning passion toward his Lord and Saviour. Testimonies abound as to his humility and life of holiness.

Reflecting on times spent with Campbell, writer Wesley Duewel noted, 'What a humble but fearless and anointed man of God he was.'[15] A student influenced by the evangelist said, 'If you didn't believe in God you could no longer be an atheist after meeting the man. You could see Jesus in his life and touch Jesus in his ministry.'[16] Close friend and Faith Mission colleague Andrew Woolsey said 'it was a rare privilege to know him. People meeting him were introduced to new spiritual dimensions, and could never be the same again.'[17]

All of these testimonies to the distinction of Campbell's character make his tendency to exaggerate or distort all the more baffling and disconcerting. Many who knew the man have been at a complete loss to account for it. It cannot have been

---

14. Mary Peckham, 'Revival Conference,' Evangelical and Theological College of Wales, 2002, audio tape.

15. Wesley Duewel, Heroes of The Holy Life, Grand Rapids, 2002, p. 36.

16. Quoted in Andrew A. Woolsey, Channel of Revival: A Biography of Duncan Campbell, Edinburgh, 1974, p.163.

17. ibid. p. 10.

for the purpose of personal aggrandisement (which, in any case, was contrary to his above-noted character). For, although his embellishments serve to aggrandise the Lewis revival's impact, in general they do not have the effect of making the evangelist look greater. On the contrary, Campbell often downplayed his own role in the movement.

I should state at this point my enormous personal respect for Duncan Campbell. Ever since I first heard of him over four decades ago, I have held him in great esteem. This is still the case, and I have not the slightest desire to cast aspersions on his character. I remember being shocked and confused on first discovering that he had misreported several stories of the Lewis revival. Given that Campbell was much more prone to making distorted statements about the revival in his later years – especially the late 1960s, I initially put it down to failing memory. I discuss the matter more fully in a later section of this book (see Chap 21).

In the pages that follow, I tread a narrow and often precarious path, ever seeking to be genuinely respectful of the sincerity and authenticity of Campbell's spiritual life and ministry, while at the same time acknowledging his tendency to inflate details of the revival for which he is so well known worldwide, which tendency has been overlooked for far too long. However sensitive and arduous the task may be, it is time to correct that massive oversight, for it has led to a very distorted picture of that revival being reported through a multitude of media.

As we have seen, Campbell has by no means been the only source of faulty information on the Lewis revival. Colin and Mary Peckham had long been aware that a lot of material available on the revival was either wrong, exaggerated or could not be verified. They decided to present a much more accurate representation of events, and in this they succeeded magnificently; *Sounds from Heaven* constitutes the most accurate and comprehensive record of the Lewis revival in print.

Intriguingly, and somewhat disconcertingly, the Peckhams' book has not succeeded in dispelling most of the myths of the revival. The resulting confusion has led to a great many diverging accounts – leaving big questions regarding even the most basic facts of the movement. In particular, existing sources significantly diverge in regard to answering the following questions:

1. What were the spiritual conditions on Lewis prior to revival breaking out?
2. Was the revival initiated by the prayers of two spinster siblings?
3. Was revival ongoing in Lewis prior to Campbell's arrival?
4. How and when did the movement begin?
5. What is the truth behind some of the revival's most popular stories?
6. Why did opposition arise against Campbell?
7. Did Campbell preach the baptism of the Holy Spirit?
8. Was revival universal throughout Lewis and Harris and across the Hebrides?
9. Was this the last revival to occur in the British Isles?

Among other things, this book seeks to provide as clear an answer as possible to each of these questions.

In the process we will have to deconstruct a number of popular stories of the Lewis revival, stories that turn out to be mythical, either in part or in whole. It's only in stripping back the *untruths* that the glorious *truths* of this famed movement become prominent – truths that are every bit as inspiring and faith-building as the myths they replace. For while such stories have endeared and inspired countless thousands of believers across the globe for the past seven decades, they form part of the Lewis revival that never was.

CHAPTER 2

Revival Heritage

Lewis Revival in Context

Lewis has been privileged enough to experience innumerable religious revivals since evangelicalism took root on the island in the early nineteenth century. How sad it is that only one of these is virtually ever referred to in revival literature.

The spiritual outpouring that suddenly descended on Barvas in 1949 did not occur in a vacuum. It occurred within the context of a rich, longstanding heritage of Reformed evangelical spirituality. Evangelicalism in Lewis was birthed in religious revival. Yet, in retelling the story of the 1949–52 revival, some writers have completely ignored this background. One wrote that between 1949 and '53 on Lewis, 'the majority of the population surrendered their lives to Christ ... and the entire fabric of Hebridean society was transformed by the gospel. All in just four years.'[1]

Such remarks have led many uninitiated readers to believe, as John Macleod puts it, 'that Campbell brought the Gospel to souls hitherto benighted in heathen darkness. Today many persist in believing that the present, relative strength of the Gospel in Lewis is his abiding legacy, and that he is the father of its Evangelical religion.'[2]

---

1. Pete Greig, *Dirty Glory: Go Where Your Best Prayers Take You,* London, 2016, p. 61.

2. Macleod, *Banner in the West,* p. 262.

Revival Heritage

Duncan Campbell is far from being the father of Lewis evangelicalism. Partly through the influence of Gaelic schools, started in 1811, and the translation and circulation of the Gaelic Bible, Lewis slowly began to emerge from deep spiritual darkness. The island's first evangelical revival began in a township in Barvas in 1822, spreading from hamlet to hamlet, and also to other parishes. A number of lay preachers held impromptu open-air meetings in different areas, drawing great crowds.

Rev Alexander Macleod

Around this time, in 1824, Alexander Macleod was inducted to the parish of Uig, where, through his powerful evangelistic ministry, a mighty revival soon emerged in the district. The movement intensified and seemed to be at its strongest between 1828 and 1830. In the former year an estimated 9,000 people from all over the island assembled for a communion at this remote location.

The movement spread to other parts of Lewis (notably Lochs, under Robert Finlayson) and also to Harris, where the preaching of converted local blacksmith and poet John Morrison carried great influence. These Outer Hebrides were never to be the same again, retaining ever since an evangelical identity stronger than virtually anywhere else in Scotland.

There were stirrings of revival in several Lewis localities, particularly Uig, around the time of the Disruption in 1843. Meanwhile, the 1859–61 revival, which had potent effect in nearly all Scottish counties, did not fail also to spread throughout Lewis and Harris, being perhaps strongest felt in Ness, Lochs and Stornoway. An equally little-known movement is one which sprang up in Ness in 1874, during the time of the widespread 'Moody revival' on the Scottish mainland.

Potent localised revival movements were not uncommon in different parts of Lewis and Harris during the 1880s and '90s. Notable among these was one that burst forth in the newly built Martin's Memorial Church, Stornoway in 1880, led by the Rev. Donald John Martin. Notable tokens of deep spiritual awakening coursed through both denominations affected by the union of the Free Church and the United Presbyterian Church in 1900, not least in Carloway, where a stirring revival commenced in 1903.

The early 1920s saw revival grip the parish of Ness through the effectual ministry of Roderick Macleod (*Roddie's revival*), while later that decade, a stirring spiritual movement broke out in north-west Harris, before spreading across that mountainous region.

One of the most significant revivals to have occurred in twentieth century Scotland, and one of the most extensive and influential ever experienced in Lewis, sprang up in various parts of the island between 1934 and '39. Beginning in Carloway, where its reach was especially pervasive and deep through the ministry of the Rev. John Maciver, it took something of an anti-clockwise direction over the course of six years, extending first to South and North Lochs, then to Point, across to Barvas, and back to Carloway. Subsequently noted for the unusual manifestations experienced at house-meetings, the movement was later termed '*The Laymen's revival*' owing to the absence of direct ministerial leading.

The 1949 revival constituted another notable awakening in the remarkable spiritual history of the Outer Hebrides, albeit differing in the sense that it was one of the very few occasions where a spiritual revival sprang up in a Lewis district as a consequence of a mission held by a visiting evangelist, and the very first time revival spread across the island owing to such.

Barvas Church

It's interesting to note that the congregation of what eventually became Barvas Church of Scotland actually began during a time of revival. The old building of Barvas United Free Church was taken from that congregation in December 1904, at a time of division within Scottish Presbyterianism in the early 1900s. Worshippers were forced to hold services outdoors in mid-winter, sustained by the conviction that they were obeying the will of Christ, whatever the cost.

Barvas Church of Scotland

At the first communion, held in the open-air in the middle of March 1905, a spiritual movement began which continued for some years. During this time, many, young and old, came to a saving knowledge of Christ. This manifestation of the work of the Spirit gave the people strength and encouragement, and made the loss of their church property appear very small. As it transpired, the commodious building they subsequently gained proved much more comfortable.

In 1929, the United Free Church of Scotland merged with the Church of Scotland, and so Barvas United Free Church became Barvas Church of Scotland, which it remains almost a century later. The early 1900s saw further spiritual stirrings in Barvas – there being a mini revival in the early 1920s, and another bursting forth a few years later. Then again, as alluded to above, widespread revival coursed through the parish in 1939, as it did in various other parishes around that time.[3]

---

3. For detailed information about all these revival movements, see Tom Lennie, *Glory in the Glen*, Fearn, 2009.

CHAPTER 3

Revival Preconditions

Spiritual State Post-war

To say that there has been considerable contention regarding the spiritual state of the island immediately prior to the 1949–52 revival is to make an understatement. Indeed, of all the accusations of 'unscrupulous distortions and absolute falsehood'[1] that have been directed at Duncan Campbell in his reporting of the Lewis revival, perhaps none have led to more concern and outrage than his remarks on this matter.

Low State of *'Vital Religion'*

In a report of the Lewis awakening presented to the Keswick Convention in 1952, Campbell made the assertion that, in the years prior to the revival, 'the stream of vital Christianity appeared to be running low' on the island, to the extent that 'the Free Church Presbytery, in October 1949, found it necessary to call a special meeting in Stornoway,' to discuss, among other things, this matter. This led to the issuing of a resolution calling Free Church congregations on the island to personal repentance and reform.[2]

The Rev. Kenneth MacRae of Stornoway was one who was greatly irked by Campbell's claim. MacRae emphasised that the

---

1. Kenneth MacRae, *The Resurgence of Arminianism*, Stornoway, 1954, p. 29.

2. Campbell went as far as believing that it was the prayers of the Smith sisters that 'moved the (Free Church) Presbytery of Lewis to do something' (Duncan Campbell, *Revival in the Hebrides*, [Ed. Wayne Kraus], 2016, p.32).

resolution came initially from the General Assembly of the Free
Church in Edinburgh and referred to Scotland *as a whole*. It
requested that each presbytery give special attention to the matter
within its own bounds. In line with this proposal, MacRae said
that the Lewis presbytery 'drew out a resolution bearing upon
the low state of religion in the *land* (MacRae's emphasis), which
was to be read from all the pulpits within the Presbytery.'[3]

This is inaccurate. The declaration from the Lewis presbytery,
as printed in *The Stornoway Gazette* on 9th December, 1949,
refers to 'the low state of vital religion *within their own bounds*,
and throughout the land generally' (emphasis mine).[4] In
misrepresenting the facts of the matter, the Stornoway minister
himself is culpable of the very wrongdoing for which he is so
outraged at Campbell.

In later years, Campbell commented further on the bleak
spiritual state of Lewis prior to the revival. He claimed that at that
time, 'not a single young person attended public worship.'[5] One
could argue that such claim is open to interpretation, because the
author doesn't make clear if he is referring to the island as a whole,
to one particular denomination, or to a specific congregation.[6] In
context, he appears to be referring to the situation within Barvas
Church of Scotland. But either way, there is no truth in his brash
claim, as many Barvas Christians have testified.

One might argue, in Campbell's defence, that he couldn't
be blamed for not knowing the spiritual conditions on Lewis
prior to the revival, given that he didn't belong to the island,

---

3. MacRae, *The Resurgence of Arminianism*, pp. 27–8. J.M. makes the same
misrepresentation over fifty years later (Macleod, *'Banner in the West,'* p. 265).

4. *The Stornoway Gazette*, 09.12.1949.

5. Transcript of message delivered in Viroqua, Wisconsin in 1968, quoted
in Campbell, *Revival in the Hebrides*, p. 32.

6. One writer insisted, 'My parents, their sisters, their brothers and many
classmates and nineteen-somethings regularly attended church then'
(Macleod, *Banner in the West*, p. 264).

and had never visited it prior to 1949. He was simply relying on information received from others. Such defence, of course, is inadmissible. He should have sought to verify his information before sharing it in written form and on public platforms across the country. There would clearly have been a lot less confusion and backlash had he done so.

A relevant anecdote here relates to the late Ernest Lloyd, the well-known Jewish missionary who served with Christian Witness to Israel. A frequent visitor to Lewis both before and after the war, Ernest told how once, while waiting in Glasgow between train journeys, he went to a meeting where Duncan Campbell had been invited to speak. Campbell commenced his address by a description of the 'godless' state of Lewis society when he went there in 1949 and what a change had come over it by 1952, largely through the revival that swept through the island. According to Ernest, this was so exaggerated and inaccurate that, uncharacteristically, he rose, repudiated Campbell's allegations, and left the meeting.[7]

It is perhaps such remarks, repeated many times by Campbell, that led to a British author stating: 'In 1949 the spiritual condition of the Hebrides was dreadful … people had simply let go of the concept of a living God.'[8] A plethora of booklets and Christian websites give a similar impression regarding the spiritual state of Lewis and Harris in the post-war period. Such remarks have grieved believers in the Western Isles, who are well aware of their falsehood.

Continuation of the '30s Revival

Many people in Lewis believe that the 1949–52 awakening was not a fresh outpouring of the Holy Spirit. Rather, it was in effect a continuation of the glorious revival that graced the island in the

---

7. Personal communication with Rev. Dr John S. Ross, 13.04.19.

8. Bruce Atkinson, *Land of Hope and Glory: British Revival Through the Ages*, London, 2003, pp. 287–8.

1930s. That earlier movement, they claim, was somewhat rudely interrupted by the outbreak of war, prematurely dampening the flames of revival that had burned so brightly. Its embers were never quite extinguished but remained as a quiet glow throughout the 1940s, before fanning back into flame in a sweeping blaze of revival fire towards the close of the decade.

The reflections of several revival converts appear to endorse such viewpoint. Margaret Macleod's father was converted during the 1930s revival in Barvas, and growing up in that parish, she fondly remembers many neighbours and family friends who had been similarly revived by that movement.

She recalls of the later 1940s: 'The Lord's people were alive! They met often and would pray and sing in the homes. That is my abiding memory of that time; in fact I do not remember the children of the Lord behaving in any other way. All that time as a young person and into adulthood, I knew the Christians to have been in this wonderful, revived manner of living. There was great expectancy and much prayer – always! A visit to a Christian home, where the conversation would invariably be on the things of God, ended in prayer. God was at work everywhere and the longing of the people for the Spirit to break through in the community was intense.'[9]

Catherine Campbell expresses similar sentiment in stating that the spirit of prayer in which the 1930s revival was birthed continued during the war years and afterwards, 'eventually increasing until the 1949 revival broke out.'[10] Norman Murray from Ness was in the Forces during the war. When he returned to Lewis, he felt the atmosphere was 'still heaven on earth.'[11] Records show a good number of additions to Church membership in the

---

9. Peckham, *Sounds from Heaven*, pp. 203–4.

10. ibid., p. 223. Donald John Smith of Upper Shader was also strongly of this opinion (personal communication, 22.09.2006).

11. Personal communication with Norman Murray, 14.11.2008.

early years of the war, though most of these were of people saved during the pre-war revival.

Arnol and Bernera

But the controversy over the spiritual state of Lewis prior to the revival doesn't stop there. Campbell makes a more specific claim in regard to Arnol. In this village, he asserted in 1952, 'not a single young person darkened the doors of the church; the Sabbath was given over to the drinking house and poaching.'[12] Kenneth MacRae said he had preached to the Free Church congregation in Arnol occasionally during the sixteen years prior to the revival, mostly on weeknights. He testified to seeing 'scores of young people at all these services.' He was therefore completely unable to accept Campbell's description of the village in 1949.[13]

In the same address referred to above, there is yet another apparent instance of Campbell mis-representing the spiritual condition of a Lewis community. The 1952 Keswick Yearbook found its way into the hands of Bernera resident K. J. Smith. Smith, in turn, wrote a letter to the island's weekly newspaper, *The Stornoway Gazette*,[14] in which he stated, 'with pain, grief, and the utmost regret,' that he found it necessary to challenge Campbell's account of religious life in Bernera prior to his arrival. Campbell had testified to, 'Firstly, no weekly prayer meetings

---

12. *Keswick Week*, 1952, p. 146. Or, as the Rev. Gordon I. Thomas put it, the youth 'spent much of Sunday in their beds or drinking away their time' (Duncan Campbell, *The Lewis Awakening 1949–1953*, Edinburgh, 1955, p. 6).

13. MacRae's annoyance at comments pertaining to the transformation of Arnol was probably exacerbated by the fact that it was 'an old elder of the Free Church' that later drew Campbell's attention to the closure of the village's drinking house within two days of Campbell conducting a highly memorable meeting there, also informing him that numerous of the young men who frequented it were now praying in the (Free Church) prayer meeting (*Keswick Week*, 1952, p. 146).

14. Most surprisingly, one of the very few references in *The Stornoway Gazette* to any aspect of the revival – each of which is confined to the correspondence section.

on the island. Secondly, when he arrived there the spiritual atmosphere of the island was "as hard as rock." These statements alone we wish to challenge as they are most misleading and utterly untrue,' insisted Smith.[15]

The letter was brought to the attention of Campbell, who responded by staunchly rebutting the allegations made against him, insisting that any error in his account was due not to himself, but to his reporter (a Keswick transcriber). 'What I did say,' Campbell continued, 'and here I quote from my manuscript, was: "I found the island spiritually dead, public worship at a low ebb, and interest in the prayer meeting practically nil."'[16] In actual fact, there is little difference between this and the published Keswick account, which states, 'In Bernera things were difficult; the stream of Christianity was running low, the churches empty, there were no prayer meetings.'[17]

Some of the discrepancies in these various accounts begin to subside when one accepts that, broadly speaking, Campbell is referring to conditions within the Church of Scotland (from accounts which were told to him by others within that denomination). MacRae and possibly Smith, on the other hand, are giving information from their own knowledge of the situation within Free Church congregations at the time in question. Certainly, townships like Arnol were traditionally Free Church strongholds, so Free Church attendance was significantly higher than for the Church of Scotland. But in truth, no one has shown that *spiritual* conditions between the two church groups on the island differed significantly prior to the revival.

---

15. *The Stornoway Gazette*, 27.01.1953

16. ibid.

17. *Keswick Week*, 1952, p. 146.

Religious or Lively?

The spiritual condition of the Outer Hebrides in the latter half of the 1940s was multi-faceted. The Western Isles suffered considerable loss of life during the war, especially at sea, and there was much mourning. Servicemen who returned were often bewildered and disillusioned, and there was a readiness among many of the young to turn aside from the teachings of their childhood. The religious fervour and faith that had distinguished Lewis for a long time seemed to have largely lost hold upon a new generation. As one old sea-captain said, 'There's been a rough edge on our young people since the war.'[18]

That there were yet many godly men and women on the island, no one has doubted. Even Campbell conceded, 'In every congregation, both the Free Church and the Church of Scotland, God had His watchmen on the walls of Zion,' and in Barvas in particular, 'there were men and women who were deeply burdened.'[19] One believer from Ness remembered many 'saints of God' in her community.

MacRae goes much further, insisting that Lewis in the late 1940s was 'one of the brightest spots in Scotland as far as vital godliness was concerned.' The Free Church in Stornoway could always count upon an 'attendance of 200–250' at the central weekly prayer meeting, while on the Saturday evening prayer meeting of the communion 'one could, and can, always look for an attendance of 800–1,000.'[20] This is a powerful testimony,

---

18. I. R. Govan, *Spirit of Revival: The Biography of J. G. Govan*, London, 1938, p. 205.

19. *Keswick Week,* 1952, p. 144.

20. MacRae, *Resurgence of Arminianism*, p. 25. One Free Church member irked by Campbell's suggestion that Lewis was, as he put it, 'virtually pagan' just prior to the revival, claimed, 'In fact a great many churches were almost full, and four had congregations of over 1,000.' He also felt the revival came as a 'hijack' to an island already swathed in Christianity (personal communication with A.M., 20.03.2007).

although it needs to be said that numbers alone are not always an accurate gauge for vital spirituality. Many felt the spiritual temperature on the island before the revival was far more religious than it was lively.

We must also remember our earlier observation that the embers of the 1930s revival were never quite extinguished by the sudden arrival of war, but remained as a quiet glow throughout the following decade. We note, too, the lively spirit of prayer that prevailed in some communities during these years, particularly Barvas, the observation that 'the people were alive,' and the felt sense of expectancy among believers that the Spirit of God was brooding over the district.

Certainly, there existed a generational variation. While many young people did have an active faith, the spiritual indifference shown by a great many youth in the post-war years was a source of significant concern to older believers. Yet, while noting also that to a degree, conditions would have varied from parish to parish, we have good evidence that the general spiritual health of Lewis prior to the revival was a far cry from the picture painted by Campbell, of an evangelical Church that was virtually in terminal decline.

CHAPTER 4

Revival in Point

On the east side of the island, there had been a spirit of expectancy and awakening in the parish of Point for several months prior to the November communion of 1949. The Rev. William Campbell of Knock Free Church so strongly sensed an imminent moving of the Spirit that on November 13th he publicly declared that the Lord was about to do a great work in their midst.

Spirit of Unity

In preparation for this, the minister said he was going to conduct services every night for a week in each part of the parish. Boldly he exhorted his people, 'Come out and seek Christ as your Saviour. I am acting on the authority of the Word of God and I am sure that the Lord will honour His Word.' The text impressed upon him was 2 Samuel 5:24, *And let it be, when thou hearest the sound of a going in the tops of the mulberry trees, that then thou shalt bestir thyself; for then shall the Lord go out before thee, to smite the hosts of the Philistines.'*

This marked the beginning of a revival among the Knock congregation. Campbell preached virtually every night for five weeks, and there was barely a service without someone new coming out for the Lord. Though some parts of the Point peninsula were not affected, the villages of Garrabost, Knock and Shader were especially moved, as people from the Free Church, the Church of Scotland and the Free Presbyterian Church came together as one under the Spirit's anointing. The Free Church was at times packed to capacity, with even the window ledges being

33

lined with people eager to hear the Word. Some who had no history of church attendance came to the meetings, and not a few were converted, sometimes after enduring a period of deep conviction.

The Rev. William Campbell

A young convert from Barvas remembered 'going in a special bus in November '49 to the Aird Free Church where Rev. William Campbell was holding evangelistic services in his own congregation. Many came to the Lord there at that time. Our own minister, Rev. James Mackay, a man noted for being zealous for the Lord's cause and very enthusiastic, was the one who organised that trip, and he was with us.

In Point there was a very good relationship between the ministers of both churches and among the people (certainly since the revival of 1939 and perhaps even earlier). The village of Shader in Point was the one I knew best as my uncle was missionary in the Free Church there. There existed complete harmony between members of both congregations and we had many, many times of fellowship together.'[1]

---

1. Personal communication with Margaret Macleod, 27.05.2020.

Cottage Meetings

One night the church was so full that a considerable number couldn't get in. The minister requested that the local missionary lead them to '*Tigh Mhurchaidh a Bhac,*' a believer's house situated nearby. Some went but, as it was a beautiful evening, others remained in the open-air. The Spirit moved among them and quite a number turned to the Lord for salvation.

William Campbell was not in good health at this time, which may have been partly induced by his tireless endeavours. He would preach each evening till around 9 pm, pause at the manse for some tea, then proceed to a cottage meeting, where he'd teach, pray and fellowship until twelve or one in the morning. On Sunday nights he would hold a prayer meeting in the manse, led by one of the elders.

Believers marvelled at a particular row of four homes in the parish where, in each one, souls were saved. A man and his wife in one; next door, a man, his wife and his sister; a man and his wife in the third, and, in the last home, a mother and her son – making a total of nine altogether. The special sense of the Lord's presence continued well after the initial burst of conversions.

One local Christian, Alexander Macleod, (*Sandy Mòhr*–'*Big Sandy*'), recalled an occasion when he, the minister, his wife, and an elder named Donald (*Domhull an Thangaidh*), visited the first of these houses and conducted a time of worship. From there they proceeded to the next house where they noticed a lantern hanging at the gate. Taking this as an obvious invitation to enter, they went in, and after greeting the household, conducted worship there also. This same pattern was followed in all four houses where salvation had recently come, the occupants of each being keen to fellowship with and learn from these more mature believers.

The group had unusual liberty in worship in the last home, and fellowship continued till after 1 am. By that time, the minister's wife was anxious to get home to attend to the milking of a cow, which had just calved that morning. It should have been milked hours before, and she was concerned it might have fallen in the stall. 'Oh, woman,' replied the minister, 'the Lord created the cow and gave her to have milk. Surely He can look after her until we get back.' Sure enough, when they finally reached home at 2 am, they found both cow and calf in fine health.

Potent Preaching

It was William Campbell's preaching in particular that brought souls alive; he especially loved to delve into the Song of Solomon. (Remarkably, fifty years on, some people I spoke with were still able to recall his favourite texts from this book.) It was said that one never knew who was converted through the services because even the unconverted would show signs of being moved. It was only on attending the prayer meeting that one could discover who had 'come out.'

Knock Free Church, Garrabost

Campbell conducted special services in the homes of the house-bound. Often, neighbours and people from other villages would pack into these meetings, eager to hear God's Word expounded. Thursday was the night of the main prayer meeting; even unconverted people who didn't attend, and who were labouring on their croft or in the peats, would cease from working and return home as a sign of respect.

During the week-long evangelistic services held in various parishes during the winter, a busload packed with people would head off in search of teaching and fellowship, sometimes as far away as Bernera or Ness. Nothing but thick snow or ice would hinder them, and psalms and hymns would ring out from their lips as they travelled.

The Point revival was far from the first move of God's Spirit in the parish during the ministry of the Rev. Campbell; nor was it to be the last.[2] Indirectly, it also acted as a form of precursor to a more widespread movement of spiritual awakening that was soon to be initiated on the other side of the island. It is to this movement that we now turn our attention.

---

2. See Lennie, *Glory in the Glen,* pp. 349–51, 364–71.

PART 2

Barvas Breakout[1]

---

1. This section covers all the districts of Barvas other than Arnol, Bragar and Shawbost. Because these latter communities are adjacently located on the southern edge of the parish, and because Arnol, in particular, experienced a distinct expression of revival to Barvas/Shader, these townships are considered separately (see Chap 10).

CHAPTER 5

Revival Beckons

The Smith Sisters

It is largely due to Campbell's later acquaintance with siblings Peggy and Christine Smith, then aged 84 and 82 respectively, that their names were to become synonymous with the beginnings of revival in Barvas. The Smith sisters have become famed in revival folklore, their hidden ministry as infirm intercessors endearing them to successive generations of believers.

Peggy and Christine Smith with Duncan Campbell

Such popularity has been gained despite only the barest of information being known about these siblings. There was in fact a third sister, Ishbel, who had lived with the other two; she had been bed-ridden for some time and died shortly before the revival began. In addition, Peggy and Christine had lost three sisters and two brothers many years earlier. All of the family were unmarried.

Duncan Campbell visited Peggy and Christine frequently, owing to both their depth of spirituality and to their physical frailty: Christine was badly affected with arthritis; Peggy was totally blind.[2] Most accounts have it that Christine (known locally as Chirsty) was also confined to the house. In fact, although feeble, she was still mobile. She would walk to church, to the Post Office, to the shop and to visit close neighbours. The Smith sisters had been brought up in a croft on Loch Street, a long, narrow, well-populated road in Lower Barvas. They moved to Stornoway for a time, before settling back in Barvas, in a small cottage by the main road, one of the first houses to greet visitors arriving from Stornoway.

Barvas Connections

It is of little surprise that the Smith sisters bonded so well with Duncan Campbell, for all three had strong links to the Faith Mission.[3] Peggy and Christine had been converted through the

---

2. Catherine Macleod from Brue remembers visiting the Smith sisters with her mother in 1944 at the age of four. Peggy was the first blind person she had ever met. The elderly siblings fussed over the little girl, offering her some biscuits. Mrs Macleod (nee Smith) was converted in 1921 at the age of seventeen, during a local revival. She became a member of the Free Church in Barvas (her husband was a deacon and precentor). Catherine was nine when the '49 revival broke out, and volunteered to babysit her one-year-old sister while her mother attended at least one or two revival meetings (personal communication with Catherine Tysinger, 22.03.22).

3. For an earlier powerful connection between Campbell and a female intercessory duo, see *Glory in the Glen* pp. 188–9. The Rev. W. H. Millard recalled the experiences of his father-in-law, J. K. Grant, who was a Baptist pastor before becoming a newspaper editor. In his small congregation in Eyemouth, there were two women who prayed regularly for revival in Scotland. On one occasion, he was asked to come to the church immediately. When he arrived, it was crowded, and that was the beginning of a great spiritual blessing, which became known as 'the '59 revival' (*Montrose Review*, Nov 1954).

Mission around forty-five years previously, when evangelist D. M. Miller held a mission in the neighbourhood.[4] Peggy, especially, had a cheery, kind, outgoing personality and a quaint turn of phrase – referring quite naturally to the Lord as her 'husband,' for example. The siblings enjoyed being visited. Their humble cottage became a sanctuary where they met with God.

Smith sisters' cottage

It was only following their own conversions that many of the young people in the parish began to appreciate the spiritual depth of these and other mature believers. Campbell said the Smith siblings enjoyed an intimacy with Christ and a power in prayer that was phenomenal. When they received a promise from God in their spirits, they leaned all their weight upon what He said, believing it absolutely. Campbell saw in this a genuine faith and dimension of spiritual life of which he had no previous knowledge.

---

4. D. M. Miller had been engaged with the Faith Mission in Rothesay, in N. Ireland and various other places before joining the Africa Inland Mission in 1913. He served wholeheartedly in North Central Africa (where he also got married) for many years. Miller, recently returned from Africa, was one of the speakers at the Bangor Convention of 1952. One can only wonder if Campbell, also a speaker at that conference, got a chance to chat with him, and to tell of the influence that two of his early converts played in the already famed Hebrides revival.

Donald John Smith[5] left Lewis to join the army in 1951, during which time he was stationed in Germany. He remembers arriving home on leave at one point when the revival was still in progress, only to find that some of his civilian clothes, which the army had supposedly sent back to Lewis, had got lost in transit. So keen was he to attend a prayer meeting in the Smiths home that he went along dressed in his full army uniform!

Donald Smith of Shader used to pray and read the Bible with Christine and Peggy whenever he called at their home. What he said of them could equally have been said of other elderly Christians in the parish: 'The fragrance of heaven was in that humble home. They just lived from day to day depending on the Lord. They were seeking first the Kingdom of God and His righteousness – trusting that all other things would be provided for them. They were concerned with the souls of men and where they would spend eternity. It grieved them when Christian people filled most of their conversation with everyday secular events instead of being centred around the Lord.'[6]

Revival Inspiration

To a great many people, Peggy and Christine Smith are the real heroes of the Lewis revival. Housebound due to infirmity and therefore of little further 'use' to society, they knew full well how to be useful in the spiritual realm, spending much of their

---

5. Two Donald John Smiths are referred to throughout this book. To help distinguish between them, I refer to Donald John Smith of Ballantrushal by using his full name; the other Donald John I denote by his district of residence, i.e., 'Donald John Smith of Upper Shader'.

6. Personal communication with Donald John Smith of Upper Shader, 20.09.2001; letter from Donald John dated August 2000, on www. notjustnotes.ws. Scottish hymn-writer John Moore made a point of going to chat with the Smith sisters during his visit to Lewis shortly after the revival there. He told how Peggy insisted that God be magnified in all aspects of life. 'If we do not give God the glory, He may never come back to our island again,' she said (Dr Johnny Pope, Houston at www.christchurchbaptist.org, accessed 06.04.2020).

time bowed in intercession before the Lord, engaging in spiritual warfare and pleading with Him to rend the heavens and visit their district once again with showers of divine blessing.[7]

Such a beautiful, endearing story has acted over the decades as a powerful lesson that no one is worthless in the kingdom of God; everyone has a significant role to play. No matter how weak or worthless we may feel, by surrendering our lives to God, we will be powerful instruments in His hands. *'My grace is sufficient for you, for my power is made perfect in weakness … For when I am weak, then I am strong'* (2 Cor. 12:9–10).

Virtually everyone who knows anything at all about the Lewis revival knows about the two praying sisters. These two, above all others, except perhaps Duncan Campbell himself, have been regarded as 'the human instruments responsible for the revival.' It has even been repeatedly claimed that if it weren't for the prayers of these two siblings, there would have been no Lewis revival at all.

Few, if any, revival converts, however, have viewed things in quite this light. On the contrary, they have been appalled to read that the revival was the result of the prayers of this person or that group. 'How can anybody possibly ascertain that?,' they ask. Rather, they have always been careful to ascribe all the glory to God and to the work of the Holy Spirit.

Nevertheless, given the pathos of the story with which they are connected, the Smith sisters have become greatly venerated in revival folklore. Peggy and Christine (rather than, for example, Duncan Campbell) are even accorded a short chapter in a book documenting the lives of *Those who Turned the World Upside Down;* appearing alongside evangelical worthies such as John

---

7. Somewhat ironically, given the subsequent worldwide fame of these intercessors, the prayers of Christine and Peggy, and all the other godly women of the parish, were never heard in their own church. The Church of Scotland, like the Free Church, prohibited women from praying aloud at the weekly prayer meeting.

Wesley, George Muller and Charles Spurgeon.[8] Efforts have even
been made to link the siblings to a former President of the United
States, to which story we now turn.

The Myth of Donald's Bible

A five-minute video-clip, *Donald's Bible,* went viral in April
2020, creating great excitement, especially among Republican
Christians in the United States. It began as a popular story
in 2017, centred on the remarkable discovery that the Smith
sisters were in fact the great-aunts of the 45th President of the
United States of America. The story goes that these two sisters
donated their '*Hebrides Revival Bible*' to their niece, who in turn
bequeathed it to her son, a young Donald Trump. Additional
details soon got added to the narrative – paving the way for
the video.

It's an intriguing story for sure. And at first glance it seems
quite possible. It's no secret that Trump's mother, Mary Anne
Smith Macleod, hailed from Lewis. Her own mother's maiden
name was indeed Smith – she lived from 1867 to 1963. This
would have been roughly contemporaneous with the lives of
Peggy and Christine Smith.

But sadly, the story's not true. In fact it's riddled with problems.
There are hundreds of Smiths in the Western Isles, and the names
Peggy and Christine Smith do not match with Trump's relatives.
Further, Lewis is a relatively small, well-connected island where
people know genealogy well, and we are dealing with just two
generations. People on Lewis who knew Peggy and Christine
Smith insist that they were not directly related to Mary Anne.
Also, Mary Anne Macleod came from the east Lewis village of
Tong, just north of Stornoway; the Smith sisters, on the other
hand, lived in Barvas, on the west side of the island.

---

8. Frank J. J. Di Pietro, *The Fire That Once Was: Those Who Turned the World Upside Down*, self-published, 2017.

The teenage boy that the video claims Duncan Campbell became dependent upon during the revival was Donald MacPhail from Arnol. He is incorrectly referred to in the video as Donald Smith. There is no evidence to suggest that Donald MacPhail was a cousin of Mary Anne, as the video claims. In any case, MacPhail's life of faith and intercession could not have inspired Trump's mother to name her son after him; the Lewis revival began in 1949 and MacPhail became a Christian the following spring, in May 1950. Donald Trump, however, was born in 1946. Did he live without a forename for the first four years of his life?

Further, Trump's own uncle was called Donald; so was his maternal great grandfather. There was no need for Mary Anne to look to some religious revival on the other side of the world for someone to name her son after.[9] In fact, Mary Anne left Lewis in 1930 (not 1936 as the video claims), before Donald MacPhail was even born. That means she also emigrated long before the 1949–52 revival ever broke out on the island. Although she visited her native Lewis in later years, it is quite possible she never knew of the spiritual revival of Duncan Campbell fame.

Even if Peggy and Christine Smith were Mary Anne's aunts, no one has provided a reason for them choosing to donate their Gaelic Bible to Mary Anne rather than one of their many other nieces and nephews (Mary was one of ten children). Besides, their Bible would probably have been the last thing the godly sisters would have parted with. Well-worn after a lifetime of use, and full of hand-written notes and markings as it probably was, it would almost certainly have been their most prized possession. Rather than post a heavy Bible to their niece in the States in any

9. There are, however, stories of couples naming their babies after Duncan Campbell in the hope that they would grow up to become faith-filled revivalists (e.g., see Eileen Vincent, *Faith Works: A True Story of Radical Obedience*, Bloomington 2013, p. 83).

case (the siblings were not wealthy), it would have been far more convenient to send a postal order so she could buy a new one.[10]

And that leads to another problem. Mary Anne *did* give her son a Bible when he was young. Rather than being in Gaelic (a language quite unfamiliar to Donald), it was an English translation; and it was a Revised Standard Version. The RSV was first published only in 1952, by which time the Lewis revival had virtually drawn to a close. Trump's Bible was presented to him at First Presbyterian Church in the Queens district of New York in 1955, when nine-year-old Donald graduated from Sunday school there. (Indeed, he swore in on this Bible when inaugurated as President in 2017.) Trump proudly refers to this as the Bible his mother gave him – he has made mention of no other.

Everybody loves a good story, and *'Donald's Bible'* is one that many have found inspiring. But it seems clear that the 45th President of the United States of America kept no *'Hebrides Revival Bible'* in the Oval Office. On the contrary, as with his mother, it's doubtful Donald Trump has even heard of the Lewis revival, let alone of his would-be great aunts. The entire story, sadly, is a mammoth fabrication.

Simultaneous Prayer

It has been suggested that a significant reason for several hundred people meeting outside Barvas police station in the middle of the night near the start of the revival was because it was considered a hallowed spot owing to the saintliness of the Smith sisters who lived immediately next door. This, of course, is hagiographic nonsense. Christine and Peggy weren't regarded with anything like the veneration they have been accorded over recent decades; this explanation, rather – like many others in regard to the Lewis revival – has been written back into the storyline.

---

10. The Smith sisters would never have regarded their Bible as a *'Revival Bible'* in any case; nor would they have seen it as in any way special simply because they owned and read it during a time of spiritual awakening.

Peggy and Christine Smith (c/o Alec Stevens)

Duncan Campbell said that the Smith sisters decided to spend two nights a week in prayer for revival to come, and that they called on the minister to request that the church elders meet at the same time for the same purpose. This, however, is also problematic. It is significant to note that this claim, like virtually everything we know of these elderly siblings' godly sayings during the revival, came directly from Campbell – especially from his later addresses. No one else attested to these simultaneous all-night prayer sessions.[11]

Further, we have good reason to believe that the elders did not gather to pray as often as two or three nights a week (see p. 57). Campbell also repeatedly states that Peggy and Chirsty would pray 'on their faces' (at other times 'on their knees') before God. It seems an unlikely posture, given that they were both in their

11. Could this narrative have been to some extent influenced by events that occurred when Campbell ministered in Skye as a FM pilgrim in the 1920s? In one area where he faced opposition, two or three local women, after issuing a prophecy that revival blessing was guaranteed, agreed to pray through the night for the desired breakthrough, while, simultaneously, Campbell prayed through the night in a barn (see Lennie, *Glory in the Glen,* p. 188).

eighties, and that Chirsty was described by Campbell as being almost bent double with arthritis.

No one doubts that Peggy and Christine were faithful, persevering prayer warriors. Just how frequently they spent interceding in their own humble dwelling for revival to come, and for what duration, we will never know. We only have Campbell's word – with no supporting evidence – that they prayed till three in the morning twice a week – and we've shown that his testimony on this matter, sadly, cannot be fully relied upon.

Spiritual Discernment

Campbell related several appealing stories that highlight the Smiths' depth of spiritual discernment. It is generally accepted that Peggy Smith received a revelation from God that revival was coming to Barvas and the church of her fathers would again be crowded with young people. In some of Campbell's accounts, it was also revealed to Peggy the very evangelist who would be the channel of that revival.[12]

Other reports from Campbell, however, suggest Peggy did not know the name or even identity of the evangelist, for he quotes her as foretelling: 'I cannot give a name, but God must have someone in His mind, for I saw a strange man in the pulpit.'[13] No revival convert has testified that the Smith sisters were given the identity of the channel of revival blessing that was to come to their parish.

Then there was Peggy's prediction that God was about to 'save seven communists who will become pillars in the church of my fathers.' As we note elsewhere (p.*), the number 'seven' and the term 'communist' were peculiar favourites of Campbell's and are likely to have come from him rather than from Peggy. In any case, there is no record of any communist, nor of seven men

---

12. Colin N. Peckham, *Heritage of Revival: A Century of Rural Evangelism*, Edinburgh 1986, p.167.

13. Campbell, *Revival in the Hebrides*, p.34

from the district in question, getting converted on the occasion in question.

Indeed, it may come as a remarkable observation to many that the most authoritative published account of the Lewis revival – *Sounds from Heaven* – only mentions the Smith sisters a couple of times in the entire book, nor does it place any emphasis on their prophetic gifting. Perhaps even more striking is the fact that none of the twenty-four individual testimonies recorded in that volume makes any reference to the influence of the siblings.

Curiously, no one from within Barvas has shared specific stories of the depth of the Smiths' spiritual perception. Campbell's own accounts in this regard perhaps need to be treated with a touch of caution. Nevertheless, revival converts have been of one accord in acknowledging that the Smith sisters enjoyed a deep, healthy relationship with the Lord, and that they had a keen and uncommon sense of spiritual discernment. But such gifting was not unique to the Smiths, being shared, for example, by several other believers in the community.[14]

Pastor's Testimony

Note, for example, the following testimony, shared by one who was minister of Barvas Church of Scotland some years after the revival occurred. 'One Saturday evening, early in my ministry in Barvas, I was preaching through the Seven Churches in Revelation Chapters 2 and 3; and as I prepared the sermon, I felt the material was very challenging and hard-hitting. I left the study, went into the kitchen and told my wife, Millie, that I couldn't preach the material I had prepared. "It is too difficult," I said, "I can't do it. I'm going to abandon this series and preach an old sermon – a one-off." My wife was quiet but troubled and

---

14. It is also curious, given Campbell's preoccupation with these siblings, that no specific mention is made of their active participation in the revival in their Barvas parish a decade-and-a-half previously.

just said, "Are you sure?" "Yes, I'm sure," I replied; "that's it decided."

'I went back to the study to look out old sermon notes. It was late, about 11 pm and as I started reading, I heard someone come in through the back door and talking to my wife. I went to see what was going on. It was Kate MacDougall from across the road; a prayer veteran of several revivals, and a contemporary of Peggy and Christine Smith. She looked at us both and asked, "What's wrong in here tonight?" We tried to assure her all was well, but she was not having it: "There is something going far wrong," she affirmed.

'I spoke up like a little boy confessing a misdemeanour, "Well, I have decided to abandon tomorrow's sermon from Revelation and preach something else." She responded, "Ah, that's the issue! You will not abandon your sermon, however hard hitting it is! It is God's Word and He has given you that to preach. Whatever it costs you, you have to preach it. Remember what it cost the Saviour!"

'I listened, and felt thoroughly rebuked. God had spoken straight to my heart through a neighbour who knew nothing of the situation. The following morning, I did indeed preach through the Revelation messages, with a fresh unction given me by the Lord. But the more remarkable part of the story relates to the outcome of my sermon. For in the course of this message, and shortly thereafter, at least three men of middle years (Colin, Donald and Johnny – all now in glory), along with some five younger people, all committed their lives to Christ.'[15]

A Community at Prayer
The above beautiful story reveals that Peggy and Christine Smith were far from the only believers in Barvas who enjoyed unusual spiritual discernment and whose lives centred on prayer. Prayer was woven into the very fabric of the church. As one convert

---

15. Personal communication with the Rev. Aonghas Macdonald, 10.07.2020.

testified, 'The Christian church was a community at prayer.'[16] Christine and Peggy Smith were simply two, sincere, godly and well respected members of that praying community.

William Macleod remembers around twenty elderly women in the district as well as many younger folk of both sexes who were faithful in prayer during this era. Encouraged by the spiritual stirring within the parish in the early part of 1949, 'a great volume of prayer ascended from Christian folk all over the Barvas area for revival. The place was soaked in prayer. It became a way of life – to seek the Lord for His mercy.'[17]

The memory that most Barvas believers hold of the Smith sisters is clearly as part of a wider group of praying people. One convert ably sets the context, 'When I was a little girl, our cousin, Mary McDougall, lived right beside us in a small house. She was a really godly Christian and her very close friend was Peggy Smith. Both were well and active then. They had two other close friends who made up their group of four. These four met at Mary's house every Thursday after the weekly prayer meeting, which was held at twelve noon, both then and for many years afterwards. Mary and Peggy were unmarried and Catherine Mackay and Annie Smith were widows.

'As a child I called them "Mary's Ladies." I also visited Mary on Sunday evening after the service. This continued all the time they were able to attend church. It was in the mid-to-late forties that Mary was struck with arthritis and Peggy's sight deteriorated. I remember going to fetch Peggy one day so she could come up to spend time with Mary, who was lame and walked with a stick. Peggy's mobility was OK but she needed help to walk on the road because of failing sight. She had been in the habit of taking a stroll up to visit Mary at any time, and both of them missed

---

16. Personal communication with Margaret Macleod, 18.09.2016.

17. Peckham, *Sounds from Heaven*, p. 111.

that. Catherine and Annie were still well and were regular church worshippers at the time of revival and indeed later.

We had lots of meetings in our house and the house was always full of visitors, so Mary was very much part of everything that was happening. Then, and for the rest of her life, she always asked the same question when we returned from the Prayer Meeting; "Was there anyone new in meeting?" She was always expecting new converts. She would ask the insurance collector and any other visitor if he was a man of prayer. She loved having people pray and read Scripture with her. By this time she was living with us.

'These four and about six other older women sat in the front seat in church. All were faithful professing Christians but these were the ones I knew best and I would say were the leading lights. There were others who were younger but were also bright Christians throughout the congregation.'[18]

Seven Men in a Barn

Then we come to another feature of the lead-up to the outbreak of revival – the seven men who prayed in a barn (assumed to have been the Rev. Mackay along with six elders and deacons). It is recorded that these men committed themselves to coming together two nights a week with their minister in an old barn to share their hearts' yearnings with the Lord.

One evening a young deacon read a verse from Psalm 24: *'Who shall ascend the hill of the Lord? …'* and, as he read, he felt deeply convicted, knowing it was hypocritical to be praying for others in the parish when his own life was full of unrighteousness. Consecrating himself more fully to God, the man was filled afresh with the Spirit and fell to the straw-covered floor in a trance. All present came into a new awareness of God's glory that night, believing also implicitly in the promise of revival.

---

18. Personal communication with Margaret Macleod, 02.05.2020.

*Thatched blackhouse inhabited by intercessory deacon
Kenneth Macdonald & his elderly parents*

The story is deeply impactful and has inspired many a praying believer over the years. However, a number of questions are raised by the above series of events. It is unclear how many men actually met together. Duncan Campbell's earliest accounts speak of a number of 'men, led by the minister,' and of 'the minister and his faithful few.' It is only his later accounts that refer to specifically seven men. It's highly probable that this figure came from Campbell's later enthrallment with that number (see p. 107). Donald Saunders and John Smith were certainly among the number; it is possible that Ruiridh Alex Macleod was too, while the Rev. Mackay may also have sometimes attended.

The men didn't meet in a barn as almost universally reported, but in an existing home.[19] This consisted of an old-fashioned, low, thick-walled thatched cottage known as a 'blackhouse,' and it was inhabited by Donald Saunders and his wife and family (Campbell was one who regularly visited the Saunders' home). The 'young deacon' who read Psalm 24 was Kenneth Macdonald,

---

19. Oddly, one of the Barvas elders who met to pray was also present at Keswick when Campbell testified to them having met in a barn. It would appear that elder never corrected Campbell on this matter (or, indeed, other errors in his Keswick address), for the evangelist continued to repeat the same mistake in his many talks over subsequent years.

a middle-aged man, colloquially known as *Coinneach Beag* (small Kenny). One or two of the men who met here to pray (including Donald) were converted during the 1939 revival in the area, and they were well familiar with the power of prayer.

Ballantrushal home of Donald Saunders. The garage to the right was the site of the old thatched cottage where some church officers met to pray

John Smith was converted during an earlier revival still – a localised movement occurring in the mid-1920s. Nicknamed *'an gobha'* (the blacksmith) John became an elder in Barvas church, and was much respected for his godly life and spiritual leadership. A leader of the 1930s revival in Barvas, he was also a noted precentor and Sunday school teacher (for an impressive 42 years). A powerful intercessor who knew his Bible well and who quoted it frequently, John taught his family that whenever seeking God for something, to always support the request with a suitable Scripture.

John ('Gobha') Smith

His son, Donald John Smith, along with Donald Saunders Jr. – whose father was also an elder in Barvas Church of Scotland during the '49 revival – has testified that the men did not gather to pray two or three nights a week, nor did they pray through the night. Rather, they met together irregularly, not more than once a week, in the early evening, to pray for an hour or so. Donald John well recalled his father going out to these informal prayer meetings.

Campbell places great emphasis on the significance of this praying group, stating in one address that as they were interceding intently one night in the barn, that was the very moment when 'the power of God swept also into the parish … an awareness of God gripped the community such as hadn't been known for over one hundred years. And on the following day, the looms were silent, little work was done on the farms as men and women gave themselves to thinking on eternal things gripped by eternal realities.'[20]

This is an ill-judged claim. Campbell wasn't on the island at the time, so could hardly have known that the spiritual awareness

20. Campbell, *Revival in the Hebrides*, p. 34.

that gripped the parish was stronger than occurred, for example, during the 1859 or the 1930s revivals. More significantly, no one else gives testimony to the entire community suddenly coming under deep spiritual conviction on a particular day directly following a night of prayer in the 'barn.' Not even those who attended the 'barn' meetings ever testified to such. Such oft-repeated claims are made only by Campbell, and only in one of his later addresses.

What is also rather astonishing, given the emphasis that Campbell places on these meetings, is that most believers in Barvas knew nothing of them at the time. Certainly, it would have constituted just one of a number of cottage prayer meetings held across the parish at that time, as the people of God earnestly sought His face. But that no church member seemed to be aware of such twice-weekly half-night prayer meeting attended by their minister and office-bearers does further call into question the reality of these gatherings as described by Campbell.

Indications of Coming Revival

Many in Lewis were hoping and praying for another revival on the island. 'As far back as I can remember,' noted John Murdo Smith, 'the word "revival" was a very familiar word in our household. My mother and father were constantly praying and longing to see a revival. They had lived through several before, and were longing to see the next one. The words that came from the lips of my mother constantly were,

"Oh, for the floods on a thirsty land,
Oh, for a mighty revival!
Oh, for a sanctified, fearless band
Ready to hail its arrival!"[21]

---

21. John Murdo Smith, on *Wind of the Spirit: The Story of the Lewis Revival,* video recording, Belfast 1990.

'The revival started with the people of God in the first place,' observed Mary Morrison. 'They were hungering for God to come. And they were praying for God to come.'[22] It was amidst such expectancy that the minister of one church in the area received a promise from the Lord that his parish would see a significant spiritual ingathering. Meanwhile, his wife, in a dream, could see a church filled with people in anxiety of soul, and a strange minister in the pulpit.

Another unusual 'premonition' of the revival occurred in the home of the Morrison family of Shader. The older family members were engaged in family worship[23] one evening when suddenly they heard a terrible screech. Mrs Morrison rushed upstairs to check on the rest of the family, but they were still asleep. Her husband said at the time he believed it was the devil. He was affirmed in this belief when revival later broke out, and claimed, 'The devil knew that something good was afoot and the screech was one of anger.'[24]

Indications of desired spiritual blessing occurred in March 1949, when during a period of vacancy in Barvas Church of Scotland, divinity student John MacNaughton became the locum minister for a few weeks. His ministry had a potent impact on several young folk in the parish, not least Margaret MacDougall, in whose home MacNaughton was staying. His prayers during family worship, personal conversations with her, and preaching on Sunday evenings all provoked an inward struggle in Margaret's soul.

'Finally, I cast myself on His mercy and, come what may, I resolved to be in the prayer meeting at noon next day', related Margaret. 'What a welcome I received from the Lord's people,

---

22. Mary Peckham, on ibid.

23. A longstanding tradition in Lewis, usually conducted morning and evening, a time when some or all family members come together to engage in Bible reading and prayer, and sometimes the singing of psalms and hymns.

24. Peckham, *Sounds from Heaven*, p. 174.

what love and support'. Her cousin and friend Peggy MacIver came to Christ the following week, both joining the church (along with three others) at the September communion. Following this, another cousin and friend, Maggie Mary, was also converted. And 'so the three little girls who had played together as toddlers now rejoiced together as sixteen-year-olds in their Christian faith. ... Thus, we became part of the Christian fellowship in Barvas that prayed for revival and were completely caught up in it and blessed by it when it came'.[25]

Margaret MacDougall

When the Rev. James Murray Mackay did a locum in Barvas Church of Scotland during April 1949, he felt a strong sense of spiritual expectancy in the community. Indeed, on returning to the mainland, he said to his wife on a number of occasions, 'It only needs a spark!' In succeeding months, prayer intensified and anticipation increased that God would visit Lewis again in revival power.

Mary Morrison believed Campbell was 'a prepared man coming to the island. The interesting thing is that some people who had never met him before recognised him as the one God

---

25. ibid., p. 203. MacNaughton later served as the Barvas minister from 1953 till 1962.

had sent. I think of someone from our congregation – a retired teacher. She dreamt beforehand of Duncan Campbell, whom she had never met. When she sat in the pew in Barvas and looked in the pulpit, she said, "This is the man that I saw."'[26]

A Barvas elder was another who predicted a coming revival. Christina Smith records, 'When I was converted, I was very much alone. Older Christians used to visit the house quite a lot. This godly man used to tell me that there was a big revival coming, and I would soon have plenty of friends. I didn't know what to make of this. These godly people used to come and we used to sing a lot. However, the following year the revival did come. Duncan Campbell came, just as Donald Saunders said he would.'[27]

In another district Angus MacDonald, an ex-sergeant of the Seaforth Highlanders, was frequently the only one to attend the weekly prayer meeting in the small church near his home. But he would go through the normal pattern of worship as if the hall was full. Much was his joy to find his prayers being answered when at last converts from the revival began to flock to the meetings.

There were many burdened souls in Barvas who were giving themselves to intercession and constant pleading with God for an outpouring of His Spirit. A number of these received promises from God regarding the coming of revival. The revelation given to Peggy Smith and her sister Chirsty was that revival was on its way and that the church of her fathers would again soon be crowded with young people. Along with it, a verse from Scripture was given, *'I will pour water on him that is thirsty, and floods upon the dry ground'* (Is. 44:3).

---

26. Mary Peckham, on *Wind of the Spirit*.

27. Christina Smith, ibid.

CHAPTER 6

Revival Begins

An evangelistic mission – *'orduighean beag'* ('little communion') was held in most Lewis parishes each winter. Preparations were made for the 1949 occasion in Barvas. The Rev. Mackay's first choice of speaker stated his inability to come, but suggested that Duncan Campbell, a popular evangelist with the Faith Mission, be invited instead. An invitation was sent to Campbell, who was evangelising in Skye at the time, where he was experiencing real blessing.

Not only so, but Campbell had arranged for a conference to be held on the island the following year. Faith Mission Headquarters therefore advised him to decline the Barvas invitation. Campbell did so, even though, he felt such decision 'goes against my own leading and judgement.' Being told of his inability to come, the praying believers in Barvas were not put off, and insisted he be contacted again. 'Hadn't God spoken?,' they asked rhetorically. As it turned out, the proposed Skye convention had to be unexpectedly cancelled. Within two weeks, Duncan Campbell arrived on the island of Lewis.

All of Campbell's innumerable chronicles of the Lewis awakening begin with a dramatic account of how revival first broke out in Barvas. The problem is that there is considerable disparity among his accounts in regard to what form this took – and when. Thus, highly significant variations have cropped up in booklets and scores of websites over the years, resulting in considerable confusion.

Popular Version

The gist of most popular versions can be summarised by the following. On his arrival by ferry one December evening, Duncan Campbell was met at the Stornoway pier by the Barvas minister and an office bearer. Following a greeting, the hosts remarked that Campbell would be ready for his evening meal after a long day travelling by train from Edinburgh and then by boat.

Nevertheless, he was asked if he would address a short meeting in the Barvas church before heading to the manse for dinner. Campbell never got his evening meal, for he was quickly whisked to church, where, remarkably, around three hundred people had gathered, despite no meeting having been scheduled that night. 'Nothing really happens during the meeting,' Campbell modestly avowed. It finished around 11 pm.

After the benediction was pronounced, a young deacon approached Campbell as he stepped down from the pulpit. 'Don't be discouraged,' he said. 'God is hovering over us. I can already hear the rumbling of heaven's chariot wheels.' The congregation began to leave for home. The deacon lifted his two hands and started to pray. He called on God for around forty-five minutes, before falling on the floor in a trance. Then the back door of the church opened, and the local blacksmith appeared. He urged Campbell to come and observe the scene outside. Campbell went and looked out, and to his astonishment, saw around six hundred people gathered expectantly outside. Having had no previous knowledge of the service, they had all been drawn by some invisible force to the Barvas church in the late evening.

Among their number were men and women who had gone to bed, arisen again, got dressed, and made for the church. Among them, too, were over one hundred young people who had been at a dance in the parish hall. 'They weren't thinking of God or eternity,' Campbell claimed. 'God was not in all of their thoughts. They were there to have a good night when suddenly the power of God fell upon the dance. The music ceased and in a matter of minutes, the hall was empty. They fled as a man fleeing from a plague. And they made for the church.'[1]

Standing at the door of the Barvas church, the elder suggested they might sing a psalm. The crowd outside lustily sang Psalm 126. 'They sang, and they sang, and in the midst of it,' noted Campbell, 'I could hear the cry of the penitent, I could hear men crying to God for mercy.'[2] The people poured back into the church, which was now packed to capacity with some eight or nine hundred souls. Convicted sinners were crying aloud all over the sanctuary. A local grammar school teacher was lying prostrate on the floor of the pulpit, weeping her way to the Cross. A further service commenced, during which numbers were converted. This meeting continued till four in the morning.

As Campbell finally began to head back to the manse, it was requested he instead make his way to the police station, where over four hundred people were now gathered. Certainly, the police sergeant was known to be a keen Christian. As he walked the mile or so from church to police station, Campbell saw people on their knees, crying out for mercy. One of these was a young lad in his late teens. 'That night God saved him and he is today the parish minister ... Converted in the revival with eleven of his office bearers,' Campbell reported.[3]

Among the number present at this impromptu open-air gathering was a coachload of people who had come from over ten miles away in the middle of the night, without knowing why they were travelling or where they were even going. Campbell didn't preach, nor was there any singing; God Himself was dealing with anxious souls as they cried aloud to Him under the open sky.

---

1. Campbell, *Revival in the Hebrides,* p. 37.

2. Duncan Campbell, *When God Stepped Down,* audio tape.

3. A number of accounts have it, incredibly and with no basis in fact, that 122 young people over the age of seventeen came to Christ on that first night of the revival.

Eventually, as a new day began to dawn, Campbell made his weary way home, utterly exhausted and quite famished, but overwhelmed and overjoyed at the remarkable events he had witnessed since his arrival on the island just nine hours previously. Revival had broken out in dramatic fashion in Barvas parish.

Barvas Police station

Details Challenged

Many of the details of the above story act as the opening scenes in almost every account of the Lewis revival – indeed for many it is the defining story of the awakening. The problem with them is that no one has ever confirmed such a dramatic course of events, even if one assumes they took place over the course of several nights rather than on one single evening.

Neither the authors of *Sounds from Heaven* nor any of the revival converts who contribute to it, nor indeed any other revival convert that I have spoken with, has made mention of anything like the above series of events taking place. Nor, significantly, did the then Barvas minister, Rev. Mackay, in his account of the beginnings of the movement.

Campbell had not travelled by train from Edinburgh the day he arrived in Lewis; he had crossed on the ferry from Skye. He did not address any meeting in Barvas church on the night of his arrival, which wasn't scheduled, and which no one turned up for. Campbell did get his supper that evening!

His first meeting in Barvas church was the evening following his arrival on the island. Many turned out to hear the visiting speaker, but the meeting was largely uneventful. It was several nights later before the big break occurred.

One who attended the service on that wonderful evening stated simply, 'I remember us singing outside the church as no one wanted to leave and then returning inside and continuing worship.' But as to the description of the anxious loudly crying out for mercy, he insisted, 'That is not accurate. That did not happen in church, though you were often aware of distressed souls sobbing.'[4]

Barvas Church of Scotland

The deacon who prayed was Kenneth Macdonald, and although he was known to sometimes get carried away when communing with his heavenly Father, no one I spoke to remembered him

---

4. Personal communication with M.C. 12.07.2017.

praying publicly for as long as forty-five minutes, or anything approaching it. While it has been testified that a group of people were gathered outside Barvas church at the close of the first service, no one has suggested it was as many as one hundred, far less the six hundred claimed by Campbell.

Revival convert, M.C. has no recollection of a grammar school teacher, or anyone else lying prostrate in the church. Indeed, he stated, 'there was no female graduate teacher at the time. Further, church meetings never continued till after midnight, and usually ended well before.'[5]

One other detail – the local police station, being the house where the local police sergeant lived – was located just a quarter of a mile from church. PC John Macleod had been converted in the 1939 revival, while his wife was a bright church member of many years standing. Many house meetings were held in their home.[6] They also had the joy of seeing their daughter, Mary Ann, coming through to faith and joining the church in the early weeks of the revival.[7]

The Barvas Dance & Night of Prayer

Another problem that emerges from Campbell's accounts of the revival's beginnings in Barvas is his assertion that over one hundred people fled a local dance under conviction of sin. There was no community hall in Barvas at the time, though dances were sometimes held in a wooden hut located next to the game-

---

5. ibid.

6. Margaret Macleod noted that, also having been converted during the revival of 1939, her father was very friendly with PC Macleod, and their wives were also close friends. She noted of the meetings held in the policeman's home, 'I would almost certainly have been in all of them' (personal communication, 22.0.2020).

7. A native of Aultbea, Wester Ross, John Macleod was regarded as a very fine policeman and was universally liked. Married with a family of five, he had a famous nephew, the well-known accordion player, Bobby Macleod of Mull, who was popularly known as *'the Jimmy Shand of the Highlands.'*

keeper's house near the Barvas Free Church. However, dances, always held on a Friday night from around 9 pm, were not held in Barvas during the revival. Certainly, converts of the revival that I spoke to knew nothing about the dance that Campbell refers to, nor anything of the Spirit of God falling on a party of revellers. 'There was no dance,' noted one Barvas convert, simply.

Indeed, nobody over the years has publicly testified to having been at that dance, to having fled the hall in terror, or to seeing or speaking to any of the merry-makers at the police station in the early hours of the morning. Nor even of knowing anyone who claimed to experience any of these things. Notably, Colin and Mary Peckham, in their carefully documented account of the revival, make no mention of these events. Campbell later named one of the partiers – the young lad kneeling by the road – as young 'Willie' Macleod.[8] But William Macleod testified to being at no dance that evening, nor to getting converted on his knees outside the police station in the middle of the night.

Precisely the same is true, both of the supposed 'invisible force' that caused hundreds to get up from their beds and spontaneously congregate outside Barvas church that same late evening, and of the busload who mysteriously travelled from the other side of the island. No one has testified to these experiences, or to knowing anyone else who did. Despite constituting deeply inspiring stories of spontaneous Holy Spirit-leading, none of these accounts appears to bear witness to reality. While various details of the above version of revival beginnings in Barvas may be correct, the story as a whole forms part of the Lewis revival that never was.

There is one further apparent anomaly in Campbell's accounts of the revival's beginnings. In his earliest public account of the movement – Keswick 1952 – he said that after his first meeting in Barvas parish church – which had been a 'very ordinary' service,

---

8. Dunn, *The Hebrides Revival and Awakening*, p.17

he went with some thirty others to a nearby cottage, where they spent the night in prayer. 'We were on our faces before God. Three o'clock in the morning came, and God swept in …. I see about a dozen men and women prostrate on the floor, lying there speechless.' Campbell said that he made his way home in the middle of the night, to find men on their faces by the roadside, 'crying out to God for mercy. There was a light in every home, no one seemed to think of sleep.'

Oddly, no one else has referred to this Spirit-filled late-night prayer meeting, and on no other known occasion did Campbell speak of it. One might further suggest that if as many as thirty Barvas parishioners were keen to spend the night in prayer following a 'very ordinary' mid-week church meeting, then the spiritual condition, at least of many in the parish prior to the revival, was considerably stronger than Campbell elsewhere gives credit for.

Shader Breakout

For what is perhaps a fuller understanding of what occurred during those early days of Campbell's Lewis mission, we need to turn to what is by far the earliest account of the revival – the evangelist's hand-written reports, compiled on a weekly basis for inclusion in the Faith Mission's *Pilgrim News* letters. We need to add to these the testimonies of others present during those early days.

This latter element is highly significant, firstly because Campbell's accounts focus – naturally perhaps – almost entirely on events that he personally witnessed. Secondly, the common consensus among nearly all early revival converts, and supported by both the then parish minister, the Rev. James Murray Mackay as well as by Colin and Mary Peckham, is that 'the real breakthrough' in regard to revival in Barvas parish came on Sunday 11th December, four nights after Campbell's arrival on Lewis.

Campbell arrived in Stornoway on Wednesday 7th December 1949, was picked up at the Stornoway pier by the Barvas minister and one of his elders. He spoke in the Barvas parish church the following evening to a congregation of possibly two hundred people. The text of his message was Matthew 19:16, *'Good master, what good thing shall I do, that I may have eternal life?'*

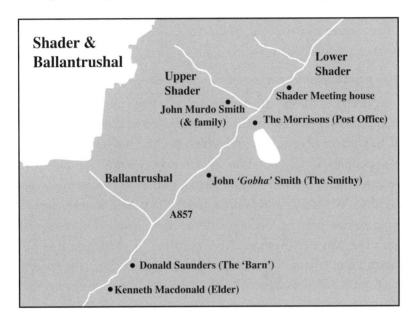

It was announced that a house meeting would follow in the MacDougall home across the road. Young Margaret MacDougall, recently converted, rushed home to tell her mother, who was looking after younger children, that a meeting was about to be held in their house!

While there was no big breakthrough in those first few days, many were deeply impressed with the pathos and depth of Campbell's addresses, and hearts were already being dealt with. Not least, that of an elder who felt so convicted that, instead of going home after the evening meeting, he walked across the moor and knelt by a peat-bank to pray that God would meet him afresh.

One early convert proposed that Campbell was so discouraged that no 'break' had been achieved in the first few days that he actually contemplated closing the mission and returning to Skye.[9] This is curious, because just two days after his arrival on the island, Campbell noted, 'God is already at work and the opportunity is great but the strain is very heavy. It seems to me that we are on the verge of something grand and glorious here. I just regret my time is so short ....'[10] Attendances increased further on subsequent nights.

The Big Day

On Sunday evening, 11th December, at 6 pm, Campbell preached in the smaller church in Shader, around three miles to the north of Barvas parish church, and which accommodated upwards of 200 people. Agnes Morrison, a fifteen-year-old girl in her third year at junior secondary school, had good cause to remember that evening. 'My father and mother and my two older sisters, they all went to the meeting in the Shader church. I stayed in the house with the two that were younger than me. An old lady had just died in the village. My mother said to me, "I don't think we'll have anybody in tonight after the meeting."' She felt they would all be at the wake that particular evening. But that turned out not to be the case.

'One of my sisters, Maggie Mary, had broken down in church – she was weeping profusely. And she surrendered her life to the Lord. Duncan Campbell spoke with her. She was the first convert of the Lewis revival. Campbell went back to the manse afterwards, along with Mr Mackay. Before I knew it, our sitting-room was full of people. They were being drawn to our home. When my sisters came in with my mother, along with Mrs Macdonald –

9. Personal communication with John Murdo Smith, 03.05.2008 ; Peckham, *Sounds from Heaven*, p. 271.

10. Duncan Campbell, FM Report, December 1949.

they had tears running down their faces. They were weeping with joy.

'I remember we ran out of chairs, and had to take some planks in from the back for folk to sit on. I ran to the kitchen, and also started to weep. I wept and wept but didn't know why at first.

Shader meeting hall

After a while my mother felt something. She came down to the kitchen and asked if I wanted to come up with the rest. I did, only to discover that others who had been at the meeting, and had gone home afterwards, had felt constrained to come out to our house. It was all of the Lord.

'And that's why I was weeping. Having said that, I had no conviction of sin. That only came later. I knew the gospel. And I knew that I was a sinner. But I felt I was just swept into the kingdom. I remember when I got up the next morning, I forgot completely about going to school. School just went out the window. Oh, the joy and the peace and the change that came into my life. My mother was just beaming – three sisters saved that night! At that point, I had never even seen Duncan Campbell. He came to our house the next night.'[11]

Agnes & Dolina Morrison

Another who attended that Shader meeting was John Murdo Smith, a young man recently demobbed from the RAF. Deeply unsettled at the lack of routine in civilian life, Smith went to the meeting partly to please his parents who enthused at the sermons of this 'great new preacher,' and partly out of curiosity. Campbell delivered a forceful message and Smith felt as if his life story was being revealed. He felt deeply challenged but resisted the Spirit's prompting. Another who was awakened that evening was John's sister, Catherine, who broke down outside the church after the service. She found peace in Christ exactly a week later.

John Murdo went home from church with no intention of going to the cottage meeting. But Chirsty Ann Macdonald, a

11. Agnes Morrison, *Revival Conference*, Stornoway, June 2019.

senior schoolgirl from Shader who lived next door to the Smiths, pleaded with him to accompany her to the after-meeting. Finally, he relented, but only because she had no one else to go with. The house filled up with folk. As the group began to pray together, the Holy Spirit swept in, resulting in deep conviction and much weeping.

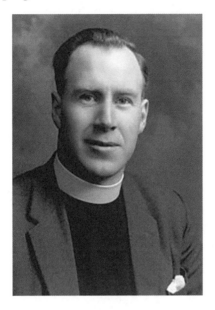

Rev John Murdo Smith

John Murdo's mind was in turmoil. Christmas and New Year parties were already arranged for the parish, and he was to provide the accordion music. On the one hand he felt it was his duty to attend these functions; on the other he knew that God was speaking to him, and that if he 'closed with the Lord,' he would have to abandon all such worldly entertainment. The battle was fierce, but despite a strong temptation to leave a commitment to God till later in life, John Murdo yielded to Christ that evening. He was the first man to be converted in the revival, and his heart sang with pure joy. Within twenty-four hours he had heard the call to preach.[12]

Apart from John Murdo and three of the Morrison sisters (Maggie Mary, Margaret and Agnes), two other young women were converted that night; these were a cousin of the Morrisons, Cathie Ann, who lived next door to the family, and Chirsty Ann Macdonald who lived next door to the Smiths.[13] For many in the parish, there is no question that the Barvas revival began in the community of Shader that eventful winter's evening.

---

12. He became a Church of Scotland minister and was still preaching in North Uist well over sixty years later.

13. A fourth sibling, Doileag (Dolina), was also converted shortly afterwards, as was a brother of Chirsty Ann.

CHAPTER 7

Revival Blossoms

Barvas Breakthrough

The real breakthrough in the Barvas church seems to have occurred on Monday, 12th December. Campbell noted in his diary that he preached in three different churches that day, each to packed audiences. At the last meeting, the text of his message was Matthew 11:23: *'And thou, Capernaum, which art exalted unto heaven, shalt be brought down to hell: for if the mighty works which have been done in thee had been done in Sodom, it would have remained until this day.'*

'The Lord manifested His power in a gracious way,' Campbell wrote in his notes, 'and the cry of the anxious was heard all over the church. I closed the service, but the people would not go away, so I gathered the anxious ones beneath the pulpit and, along with the minister, did what we could to lead them to Christ.'[1]

Margaret Macleod well remembers the occasion. 'For me that was just a down-pouring of the Spirit. The Lord dealing with me and with one of my close friends who had been following the Lord for a few months. It was just another wonderful, wonderful occasion of praise and blessing, as we saw the five new converts (from Shader) at the front of the church. From then on there were friends and older people and younger people, and the church was full every night.'[2]

---

1. Duncan Campbell, FM Report, 14.12.1949.

2. Margaret Macleod, on *Wind of the Spirit.*

A week later, Campbell could record, 'We are in the midst of a glorious revival. God in His great mercy has been pleased to visit us with showers of blessing, and the desert is rejoicing and blossoming as the rose. Some of us will live to praise God for what our ears are hearing and our eyes are seeing these days in Lewis. Meetings are crowded, right up to the pulpit steps. On several nights the meetings continued until three and four o'clock in the morning in the homes ... we are dealing with anxious souls in every meeting.'[3] Remarkably, within around ten days of commencing his mission, Campbell could report around seventy adults having professed conversion – by far the greatest number within a similar time period of the entire revival.

It is at this point that Campbell reports on the meeting that features so prominently in his later addresses. 'Last night at our fifth service (of the day), just as the people were leaving, a young man began to cry for mercy at the gate leading from the church. Just then, an elder began to sing the 102nd psalm and the whole congregation took it up, singing verses 13–16. The congregation then came back into the church and before we dispersed twelve men and women sought the Saviour.'[4]

The Barvas church seated 600 people comfortably. During the revival, benches were often placed in both aisles and folk sometimes sat on pulpit steps. There was no church hall as such, but a door led from the church to the vestry. (Here the weekly prayer meeting was held, as well as the Sunday evening service if the minister was not present and it was conducted by the elders.) At the height of the revival when the church was packed, this door was sometimes opened to seat around sixty more people.

_____

3. Duncan Campbell, FM Report, 21.12.1949.

4. ibid.

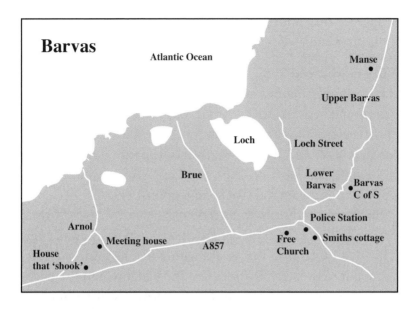

The Lady Missionary

One person overlooked in virtually all accounts of the revival was the lady missionary serving in Barvas. Cathie Maclennan hailed from Balallan, Lochs, and had been a fellow student with the Rev. James Murray Mackay at the Glasgow Bible Training Institute. She certainly shared his zeal. Cathie had been appointed to Barvas Church of Scotland in the summer of 1949.

Although small and slight, she was diligent in visiting and caring, and most days saw her on the road, walking from place to place. She was a godly woman of prayer, who poured heart and soul into the revival. She made a point of visiting and encouraging new converts, both in Barvas and the surrounding villages. Her home in Loch Street was open for meetings and for young believers to have fellowship.

One convert recalled: 'I started teaching with her in Sunday school in Barvas very shortly after she arrived in the parish. Together we arranged Christmas parties, gifts and summer outings for the children of the congregation. She was very much my mentor and a close family friend.'[5]

William Macleod

Many other testimonies spring up from around this time. Annie Murray and her close friend Annie McDougall had been faithful Christians from the age of twelve or thirteen while still pupils at Barvas school. As natives of that westside parish, both had lived through several local revivals, and both became wholehearted supporters of the revival that sprang up in 1949.

Prior to its outbreak, Annie said to her son, 'William, I think there's an awakening in the congregation – a spiritual awakening.' William recalled that 'this awoke within me the spirit of revival. I went out to the services for two or three nights, and listened to the glorious gospel of the Lord Jesus Christ. Nothing was hid, because the Lord was present. It was so obvious that the Lord Jesus Christ was moving in our midst.

'At the close of a wonderful meeting in the church hall in Barvas, I went back in for prayer and counselling, with at least four others from our village who were also seeking the Saviour. I came home that night, 18th December 1949, and I knew that the Lord was speaking to me. I found myself praying between one and two in the morning. I used to say a wee prayer prior to that, but that was just what I learned from my mum. Now I was really praying. Praying that God would accept me as I was.

'I slept well that night, and I woke up the following day a new man in Christ. The world had changed; people had changed, because a change had come over me. I found myself pouring out my heart to God. I lost my appetite for food for three or four days, but I found an appetite for spiritual food; the Word of God, and for prayer. Not so much with words, but with groanings of the spirit. My life was completely

---

5. Personal communication with Margaret Macleod, 22.04.2020.

transformed. The future opened at my feet. A new world was ahead of me.'[6]

'I felt that the whole village was transformed,' William noted. 'There was a change in the very rugged beauty of the village. I went to Stornoway that day. I knew that something had happened, for all the time I was in town, I was yearning to get back to the meetings.'[7] It transpired that at a meeting in Shader earlier the same night as William was converted, and attended by Campbell and the Rev. Mackay, another group of young people found the Lord. All went on to become faithful witnesses to Christ.

William Macleod

In was also in the early days of the revival that Margaret MacDougall (who later became William Macleod's wife) invited two of her school-friends – Katie Mary and Joey, both in fifth year at school in Stornoway – to come and spend the weekend with her in Barvas. That first night, they were both converted in

6. William Macleod, *Revival Conference*, Stornoway, June 2019.

7. William Macleod, on *Revival in our Times*.

Barvas church. Later the same evening, they attended a blessed cottage meeting in the policeman's house, just along the road.

Both Margaret's friends went on to become effective and fragrant intercessors, and both also became teachers. Katie Mary spent most of her life serving the Lord with the Free Presbyterian Church in Rhodesia; later returning to Lewis, where she taught English at the Nicolson Institute. Joey became a lively witness in the Free Church, and an Infant Mistress in Stornoway Primary School. Quite a number of senior pupils were also converted in other parishes in the island.

Typical Revival Service

A visitor reporting on the revival in 1950 noted that the meetings consisted of 'Bible reading, prayer, Psalm-singing and the sermon. The first hour of the service was usually devoted to prayer and singing. The singing, without accompaniment, and led by a precentor,[8] was like nothing I have ever heard. He sang a line of the Psalms by himself, then led the congregation in that line, sang another line by himself, and so on. It required ten to fifteen minutes to sing one Psalm. The most impressive thing in all the gatherings was the presence of God. Sometimes there would be periods of silence in which the presence of God was so real that no one dared to speak.

'The sermon was delivered in a forceful manner. Some of the audience wept as Duncan Campbell preached. At the conclusion no invitation was given. The people quietly filed out as the messenger descended the stairs of the vestry. Revival breezes had not yet blown through this community, but they were on their way. I found Duncan Campbell, whom God is using, to be a humble man who had discovered the secret of spiritual power –

---

8. i.e., leader of congregational singing of psalms, without instrumental accompaniment, common in Gaelic Presbyterian church services.

death to self, that the life of Jesus might be released to do mighty exploits through him.'[9]

The Lewis Film Society took a travelling picture-house to various outlying villages in the post-war period, as the only cinema on the island was located in Stornoway. They stopped their visits to Barvas as a result of the revival, owing to a sudden lack of interest.

Some accounts have it that the local drinking house closed its doors to the public in the midst of the revival, the proprietor's entire family having been converted during the movement. This is untrue. No public houses were located in any of the rural parishes; the only pubs on the island were to be found in the town of Stornoway, and even here, none closed because of the revival.

The various *bothans* (*bo'ans* – drinking huts) that existed on various parts of the Westside were not run like public houses and were not owned or run by a proprietor. They were just social gathering places for the men and youths of the local area, who chose to club together to buy alcohol to consume there. There were two *bothans* in Ness, one in each of Borve, Shawbost and Arnol, but none in Barvas or Brue. Of the five, only the Arnol *bothan* was permanently closed as a result of the revival.

During his mission in Barvas, and during return visits to the parish, Duncan Campbell was transported to meetings by the Rev. Mackay in his car, one of relatively few motor vehicles owned by anyone in the parish at that time. The Barvas minister accompanied Campbell to nearly all services and cottage meetings. Occasionally, the evangelist was offered Mackay's car so he could travel to meetings on his own.

At a later point, Campbell procured a motorcycle, which he rode all the way from Edinburgh to Lewis, and which took

9. Dwight Wadsworth, *The Pentecostal Evangel,* 01.04.1951. Wadsworth served in the US Army in Europe during WW2, after which he founded the Klostermuehle Bible School and conference centre in Germany, where he served for 25 years.

him to meetings all over the island. Following a couple of spills, however, he lost his nerve and abandoned his bike, and again depended on volunteers to take him around.

On Revival Leave

Duncan Campbell came to Lewis for a single two-week mission in Barvas, unaware that a dramatic revival was about to break out in the parish during that time. Sure enough, when his fortnight was up, the evangelist left the island and returned to Edinburgh for a fortnight's rest. Apparently, he left with very mixed feelings, rejoicing that revival had broken loose in such power; at the same time sorrowful to be leaving the scene of such glory.

Of course, it was Christmas time, and it's understandable that the hard-working evangelist should want to be with his wife and family at home on the mainland.[10] He certainly deserved a break, not least because he had gone to Lewis directly from Skye, where he had been labouring since early November, following a short interval in Edinburgh. He had written shortly after his arrival in Lewis on the 7th of December, 'I am very tired after a heavy time in Skye, but I shall get a good rest when I get home.'[11]

He certainly got no rest in Lewis. For the first six months of the revival, Campbell testified that he did not get to bed before 4 am, and that for many weeks he had only three or four hours sleep a night. During this period in particular, he had a variable but intense routine of going from church to mission hall to

---

10. Christmas had never been a major celebration in Scotland, and that was still the case in the 1940s. People still worked on that day, post still got delivered, etc. Only in 1958 did Christmas become a public holiday north of the border. For his part, Campbell was sometimes known to be away from home at Christmas time, e.g., in 1955, when he spoke at a Christmas Conference at Derriaghy Mission Hall, Belfast. The celebration of Hogmanay and New Year was a bigger event in Scotland, though that, too, was nothing like the major thing it is today. For example, a Faith Mission convention was often held in Duns on New Year's Day in the 1950s, to which Duncan Campbell occasionally went to speak.

11. Woolsey, *Channel of Revival*, p. 116.

cottage meeting, often into the wee hours of the morning, and sometimes right through the night.

Nevertheless, Campbell's sudden departure from the throes of revival is surprising, even astonishing. It meant that during the first dramatic month of revival in Barvas, Campbell played no direct part in the movement for half of that time. Such action is certainly a rarity; indeed I can barely think of a comparable scenario in revival literature. Rather, again and again in revival accounts you find ministers and evangelists being forced to markedly alter their schedules following the sudden outbreak of a revival, so that they can remain in its midst.

On one hand it would appear an irresponsible decision on Campbell's part to leave the scene of a remarkable outpouring of the Spirit. With God moving in such demonstrable power, one might expect him to make the most of every moment, especially given that his mission in Barvas had by no means concluded – he went on to hold many more meetings in the district in the early new year. One might have expected him, rather, to stay on the island, enjoying two or three days rest over Christmas, and continuing to lodge with the Murrays in their commodious Barvas manse, but taking full use of every opportunity to preach the gospel, not just in Barvas, but in other parts of the island, from which people were already flocking to hear him preach.

On the other hand, the action Campbell took appears to show that he was able to trust God to lead the movement in his absence in whatever way He wished. He didn't see the revival's progress as being dependent on him; rather, he was quite content to leave the situation in the human hands of the parish minister and to the spiritual guidance and care of the Holy Spirit. This shows his lack of personal desire to control or guide the movement.

Naive and irresponsible, or a bold act of faith, the revival *did* continue, still being in full flow on his return to Lewis in early January.[12]

Conversion of Fay Macleod

It was also in the early days of the revival that a youthful Fay Macleod gave her life to the Lord. Months before, conviction had begun to grip her, and worldly pleasures were losing their appeal. With the outbreak of revival in Barvas, a close friend, Chirsty Ann was converted. Fay was thunderstruck by the news, not having a clue what had actually happened to her. 'I went to see her; I took one look at her, and her face was transformed – there's no other word for it – she was simply glowing. I said, "You've got it!" She replied, "Oh, Fay, we were so blind. It's not 'it' at all, it's Him! The Lord Jesus Christ." I threw my arms around her, and wept and wept on her shoulders.'[13]

Fay Macleod

Chirsty Ann invited Fay to a meeting. Instead, Fay went to the local Christmas concert, at which she was playing a leading

12. Indeed, meetings continued in Campbell's absence, even between Christmas and New Year. Converts said they don't remember them stopping at all.

13. Fay Macleod, on *Revival in our Times: The Story of the 1949–52 Hebridean Revival as told by the Islanders,* audio tape, Ambassador Productions, 1983.

role in a play. As soon as the show was over, Fay felt utterly condemned for attending the concert at all. Demoralised and confused, she went to visit her newly converted friend in Shader. The love this Christian family showered on her overwhelmed her and she broke down.

She went with them to hear Campbell preach. Fay recalled, 'It just seemed like every word we were singing was the very cry of my heart put into words. I sat between Chirsty Ann and her father – and I sobbed and sobbed, dripping tears onto the floor. Chirsty's dad passed me his big handkerchief – and I continued weeping into that.

'Duncan Campbell preached beautifully, on The Song of Solomon – *"The voice of my beloved"* – and being behind the lattice. He talked about the various walls that separate us from God. He mentioned one "wall" after another – and they were all very real to me. He said, "You're sitting there saying, 'I do pray.'" And that's exactly what I was thinking at that moment. And he said, "But what do you pray for?" And I thought, "Well I'm asking God to make me good." And Campbell said, "You're asking God to make you good? My dear friend, if God could make you good, why did the Lord Jesus Christ have to come into the world? It's a prayer God cannot answer." I thought, "Oh, no! I'm undone." The only prayer I had, and he's saying it's a blasphemy! My prayers had been a prop, which Duncan Campbell had just demolished. And for that moment, I truly believed that I was without hope.

'Campbell said that Jesus Christ came to demolish this terrible darkness, to bridge this terrible gulf. To bring us back to God. And it was just as Song of Solomon went on to say – the singing of birds, and the heart freed from this awful, awful darkness, and the Lord Jesus Christ actually setting you free. And you wondered how you had never grasped this before, when you knew it all so well. But now it was really actually happening! And you were from that moment a child of God, through the Lord Jesus

Christ, delivered, set free; with the singing of birds; and the whole hall just seemed to be full of song!'[14]

Along with Fay, five or six others were also converted that night. Her life utterly transformed, Fay later went on to serve with her husband as missionaries in Thailand.

Stuck on the Moors

In one talk given in 1968, Campbell adds on some fascinating details to Fay's testimony. He says that when her friend, along with other school chums, first went to Barvas to hear Campbell speak, the bus on which they were travelling suddenly pulled into the side of the road on the moors. The driver, overwhelmed with conviction, said he could take them no further, and slumped over the steering wheel, crying out for mercy. God's presence filled the bus, and everyone began to pray.

After three full hours at the roadside, the bus resumed its journey to Barvas, arriving at the church at one o'clock in the morning. The service was still in progress, and, remarkably, everyone who had been on the bus was converted that night, including the four girls from the hostel. Their friend Fay was converted through their personal witness when she came to Barvas the following evening.[15]

Nowhere else in his extant recorded messages does Campbell relate the dramatic episode of the three-hour conviction on the stationary bus. Nor, for that matter, has anyone else. No one has ever been named as having been on the bus when these events occurred. You'd think that if true, the story would have become one of the most popular of the entire Lewis revival. It appears to have been a sensational embellishment to an otherwise genuine and beautiful testimony.

---

14. ibid.

15. Allen, *Catch the Fire,* p. 76. Did this story emerge from the fact that among the many people finding salvation were thought to have been at least two bus drivers hired to transport passengers to the meetings?

'Remote Village' Revival

Campbell delighted to share the story of Peggy Smith having a vision in which she saw seven men from a remote village being converted and 'becoming pillars of the church of our fathers.' She sent for Campbell and told him what God had revealed to her.[16] Campbell replied, 'Peggy, I have no leadings to go that village ... there is no church there, and the schoolmaster is one of those men who would never dream of giving me the schoolhouse for the meetings.' Peggy retorted, 'Mr Campbell, if you were living as near to God as you ought to be, He would reveal His secrets to you, also.' Campbell took it as a rebuke from the Lord.

The evangelist suggested that he call on the parish minister to come and spend the rest of the morning together with them on their knees in prayer for the village in question. As they bowed before Him, Peggy prayed, 'Lord, do You remember what you told me this morning when we had that conversation together? I'm just after telling Mr Campbell about it but he's not prepared to take it. You give him wisdom because the man badly needs it!' It was agreed that Campbell should go to the village the following evening at 7 pm. Asked where he was to hold the meeting, Peggy replied, 'You just go, and He will do it.'

Campbell went to the village and found a huge crowd (amounting to several hundred people) gathered outside a seven-room bungalow. They hardly knew why they were there – they just felt led to come. The house was so crowded that Campbell couldn't get near it. So he stood on a hillock in front of the main door, and gave out his text from Acts 17:30–31.

---

16. The notion of the Smith sisters 'sending for' Campbell, or for the Rev. Murray Mackay is one that crops up a number of times in Campbell's accounts. But it is one that is alien to Barvas residents, as if these men were at the sisters' beckon call and they had a butler to run and do their bidding. Most likely, they simply waited till the next time they met Campbell or Mackay, and shared their views with them then.

He preached for about ten minutes when one of the five ministers present came to him and reminded him of a message Campbell gave at five o'clock that same morning in a field, when he spoke from John 10:27–8: *'My sheep hear my voice, I know them and they follow me. I give unto them eternal life and they shall never perish.'* The minister requested that Campbell go to the end of the house to share that verse with some men who 'we are afraid will go mental, they are in such a state.' The men were said to be communists, three of whom had turned to that ideology while living in America for a time.

Campbell followed the minister and found the seven men that Peggy had seen. They were crying to God for mercy. All seven were saved within a matter of days. 'And if you go to that parish today,' claimed Campbell, 'you would see a church with a stone wall built around it, heated by electricity and all done by the seven men who became pillars of the church of Peggy's fathers.'[17]

New Life in Loch Street

The facts of the story as related above differ considerably from those gleaned from other corroborated sources. It transpires that it wasn't a remote village that Campbell went to; rather, the community of *Sraid Na Loch* (Loch Street), situated in Lower Barvas, less than a mile from Barvas Church of Scotland. It seems that, formerly, the further reach of this road was called – on translation to English – the *'far-in village,'* which might help explain why Campbell referred to it as being 'remote.'

Campbell did not visit the community by chance, whereupon a meeting spontaneously arose, as the story suggests. Rather, the meeting was planned, with both the venue and time of meeting known well in advance. Early in the revival, the Smith sisters had asked the Rev. Mackay, who organised most of the meetings in Barvas, if there was any word of a house meeting being held in

---

17. Campbell, *Revival in the Hebrides,* p. 51.

Loch Street, a row of houses very much on their hearts, because it was here that they had grown up.

No meeting had yet been arranged for this community, but Mackay asked the lady missionary, Cathie Maclennan, and, with the permission of the owner of the house which she rented, a meeting took place in her home – 13 Loch Street – after an evening church service (these were still being held on a daily basis). There was no schoolhouse in the district, as referred to by Campbell. Nor was the house a seven-room bungalow – a most unusual structure in Lewis at the time – but a fairly small two-room cottage, which modest edifice still stands, albeit now derelict.[18]

13 Loch Street (home of Ms Maclennan)

18. One revival researcher, trusting Campbell's version, identified the 'remote village' in question as Bragar. There was no present-day church in this location, he discovered, but there could be found the ruins of an ancient sanctuary (which he took to be the 'church of our fathers' as referenced by Peggy Smith). With the help of a local resident, the researcher also located a 'seven-room bungalow.' This house and no other, he was convinced, was the very place where hundreds spontaneously gathered to hear Campbell preach following Peggy's night-time vision.

I have spoken to several people who clearly recall attending the very house-meeting in question. While they point to a good attendance, they say the idea that hundreds were forced to stand outside while Campbell preached to them from a nearby hillock is fanciful (besides, there was no nearby hillock). There would probably have been no more than thirty people present. No one stood outside for the meeting, not least Campbell, who gave his address to a seated audience indoors.

There weren't seven people under deep conviction (nor were they gathered outdoors at one end of the house); rather, three or four, at least one of whom was female. None of them were in such a mental state that they caused particular concern to church leaders present, who numbered, not five as claimed by Campbell, but two (the Revs. Mackay of Barvas and Maclennan of Carloway).

Recalled one revival convert, 'We remember the night well. It was a wonderful meeting with several people seeking the Lord, including two local pipers. One of these was the man who was booked to play the pipes at a concert in neighbouring Carloway that same night.'[19]

This was Willie Smith, brother of John Murdo Smith. Willie had come under conviction a couple of nights earlier, after going to hear Campbell following his mother's pleading. He knew God was speaking to him, but he strongly resisted, determined to go to the Carloway dance. But he was under such conviction that he found himself attending a cottage meeting the very evening of the dance. Unable to resist any longer, Willie yielded to Christ. Life transformed, the young musician

---

19. Personal communication with Margaret Macleod, 22.04.2021. Many accounts mistakenly have it that both the Shader pipers were due to be playing at the Carloway concert and dance. In fact, only Willie Smith was due to play there.

no longer had the slightest desire to attend any concert, dance or other social function.[20]

Donald John Smith (of Ballantrushal) and Willie Smith – the two Barvas pipers

Campbell curiously referred to the seven men who came under deep conviction as hard-line, educated 'communists,' who 'formerly would spit in your face.' In actual fact, none of those who came under conviction that night were known to be of that political persuasion, nor did they have any particular left-wing leanings. Donald John Smith, one of that night's converts, said he couldn't begin to fathom why Campbell should refer to him, or the others, as communists.

On various occasions the evangelist related several other stories of Lewis socialists who surrendered their lives to Christ during the revival. One of these addresses, curiously, dates to as early as January 1953.[21] Two of the stories carry no

---

20. The incident must have brought back powerful memories to Duncan Campbell, who had also enjoyed playing the bagpipes as a young man, being a formidable step-dancer, too. Both of these endeavours he completely abandoned on his conversion.

21. Portion of a message shared by Duncan Campbell at the Portadown Youth for Christ Fellowship in Edenderry Presbyterian Lecture Hall, published in *Portadown News,* 24.01.1953.

geographical or social context, and various particulars of the storyline fail to carry the ring of truth. I was unable to find trace of a communist society on Lewis in the 1950s, and no known communists were converted during the revival (although the Labour party was strong in the islands at this time). The 'communist-to-Christ' testimony appears to have been a favoured innovation of Campbell's, one which he delighted to express in various guises).

CHAPTER 8

Revival Broadens

Revival in Full Flow

Fully aware he was in the midst of a remarkable and ever-expanding work of grace, Campbell felt compelled to cancel all future engagements outwith the island. By this time the whole community appeared to be in the grip of a powerful awakening. News of the movement had spread throughout the island faster, as one man put it, than the speed of gossip, and busloads of people continued to stream from many parts of Lewis to the near nightly services in Barvas.

The revival and its converts were the main topic of conversation everywhere – even at secular gatherings. One revival convert recalled that at the Nicolson Institute in Stornoway, unconverted pupils in her own class 'were very interested and respectful of the revival. A good proportion of them lived in the school hostels, and they would regularly ask me if I had been at meetings in their home areas and if there had been conversions.'[1]

Even well before his conversion, Willie Smith had shown great interest in goings-on at the meetings. 'Every night when my mother and father would come home, I would ask, "Was there any converted tonight?" "Yes" they would say, "There were some of your friends, some older people, some middle-aged people, somebody from Ness, somebody from Carloway" and so on.

---

1. Personal communication with Margaret Macleod, 22.03.23.

I was rejoicing. I can't understand that to this very day. Why I was rejoicing and I wasn't even converted.'[2]

Calls began to pour in from other Church of Scotland parishes for Campbell to preach there. He rarely declined an invitation, but he sometimes irritated ministers by refusing to provide definite dates, feeling led to remain in an area where he was so obviously being used as an instrument of salvation for as long as the Spirit moved him. Campbell was not, of course, the only preacher in Barvas during the awakening.

Local minister, the Rev. Mackay threw himself into the revival work in his large parish. Noted as a fine Gaelic preacher, Mackay had a pastoral heart, and quickly won the hearts and minds of his Barvas parishioners, being described as 'exceptionally helpful to young converts.'[3] It was of enormous delight to him when his own daughter Isabella (one of two children from his first marriage), was converted during the early days of the Barvas revival.[4]

Agnes Morrison observed, 'When the revival was underway, my parents took turns at going to the meetings, for one of them had to stay home to look after the children – remember, there were six of us. Mum would go one evening, and my father the next. She would return home after a meeting in church, even though she was longing to go with the rest to the after-meeting in someone's home. My father would go out in her place. But she

---

2. Willie Smith, in *Wind of the Spirit.* That all changed for Willie one memorable night soon after, when he was gloriously converted.

3. A fifty-year-old native of Uig, Mackay, along with his two brothers, had been converted as a young man during a time of spiritual quickening in that parish in the 1920s. All three went on to become ministers. Inducted to Melness Church of Scotland in 1933, Mackay moved to Strathconon in 1938, where he remained for ten years before accepting the call to Barvas (personal communication with James Mackay – the Rev. Mackay's son – 19.03.2020).

4. From his second marriage, Rev. Mackay had two boys. Mrs Mackay was a good singer and taught the young folk in the Barvas congregation a number of Psalm tunes, notably 'St David.'

was greatly comforted by hearing the Lord saying to her, "Even if you have to go home, I'm still with you."[5]

Rev. James Murray Mackay

William Macleod remembers one old man in his eighties who was called upon by the Rev's. Campbell and Mackay in the course of their visitation. The man agreed to attend some meetings. His neighbours noticed him coming and going from his house more often than usual and wondered if God was working in his life. This turned out to be the case; he was attending the revival meetings and was converted soon after. Another Barvas man, much younger, and home on leave from the Merchant Navy, was converted the night before he returned to the ship.

Another elderly local, Mary, was crippled with rheumatism and was no longer able to attend church. However, as a committed believer, she loved attending the many house meetings held in a neighbour's house, and was a fervent prayer supporter. At one point during the third week of the revival, she pleaded to be taken to hear Duncan Campbell preach in the Barvas church, very close to where she lived. Her neighbours decided to take her to a 9 pm service, knowing it would be

---

5. Personal communication with Agnes Morrison, 19.09.2016.

less packed than the meeting held earlier in the evening. Mary loved every minute of the service, but despite waiting for the later meeting, her neighbours were still afraid she might get knocked down and hurt in the crowd, and the outing was never repeated.

Jack Macarthur vividly recalled 'a lovely, saintly and very quiet Christian lady getting up out of her seat in a packed church, and gliding – that's the only way I can describe it – gracefully down the aisle, and standing on the pulpit steps as Mr Campbell preached – her face just glowing with God, without any distraction either to Mr Campbell or to the congregation.'[6]

Some of the older believers said that the revival rejuvenated them, and they felt like they had been converted all over again. 'What a wonderful experience the older Christians had, to go through all of that,' noted one convert. 'I would love to go through the same again!'[7] Many converts spoke of the profound sense of joy that welled up within them. 'The joy of it all was beyond explanation,' said one. 'This was one of the unspeakable gifts which we as the Lord's people had at that time. This indescribable and overwhelming joy.'[8]

Catherine Campbell testified, 'I was naturally shy and timid, and would never be to the fore in company. But God loosened my tongue and made me bold for Him.' William Macleod also testified to converts being given a boldness during the revival; 'a boldness to witness, a boldness to rejoice, and with it the freedom to tell whoever was listening that we had surrendered our lives to Christ. We were so full of it, we simply couldn't help but share our faith with others.'[9]

---

6. Jack Macarthur, *Revival in our Times.*

7. Margaret Macleod, ibid.

8. William Macleod, ibid.

9. Catriona Campbell, William Macleod, ibid.

Free Church Attitudes

Although a significant number were converted from within the Free Church, there was no general movement within that denomination in the large Barvas district where revival flourished so powerfully. Any opposition voiced to the revival usually came from the Free Church minister or some of his office bearers. The minister at the time of the revival was the Rev. John Macleod, a native of Leurbost, who served in Barvas from 1922 to his retirement in 1956. Like Kenneth MacRae, Macleod appeared to be opposed to both the revival and in particular, to Duncan Campbell. And there were some who agreed with him. Most ordinary church members, on the other hand, tended to be much more open, both to the revival and its main evangelist.

Barvas converts fondly remembered Bella Smith, who never missed a meeting. Blessed with a retentive memory, she could repeat the sermons of Duncan Campbell in a very good imitation of his voice and accent – to the great delight of many. Along with her husband, Donald, a Free Church elder, she was a great support to the young folk, and their home was always open for fellowship. Donald felt unable to attend the church meetings owing to the dissension it might cause in his own church – in any case, they had two young boys so one parent needed to be at home.

One convert shared, 'How we enjoyed his singing of the Gaelic hymns and his precenting of Gaelic Psalms. A particular favourite was on the theme of the Prodigal Son. Donald also taught in the Free Church Sunday school for many years. My brother and I used to attend it in addition to our own Church of Scotland Sunday school, as they were at different times. As we were growing up the Sunday school was in church immediately after the morning service and the teachers were the minister and his wife, the Rev. Donald and Mrs MacDonald.

'The Free Church Sunday school was initially in a member's home at 3 pm but then moved to the Barvas school. We also followed the syllabus in their youth magazine, *The Instructor*, and did the tests and gained certificates. After the MacDonalds emigrated to Canada and following the arrival of a lady missionary, the Church of Scotland Sunday school was moved to 3 pm.'[10]

People who engaged in common activities, such as croft-work, peat-cutting, etc., had very close bonds irrespective of denomination. The same was true of neighbours and former classmates. During the winter months (both before 1949 and afterwards), both churches would have cottage meetings; most folk went to both if they were within walking distance.

Occasionally, relations between the two denominations in the parish were less than warm-hearted. Owing largely to the Free Church minister's vocal opposition to the revival, one revival convert recalled that Christians of the two churches would at times walk past each other on their way to their respective churches on Sunday mornings. 'Even if one party said hello as they passed, there was often no response from the other, no acknowledgement whatsoever.'[11]

'A great many of my Free Church friends came to Duncan Campbell's meetings,' recalled Agnes Morrison, 'and of these, many got converted. I was fifteen and still at secondary school. I invited two Free Church friends, Chirsty-Anne and Annetta, to come to the meetings. But before that, the two of them were saying, "Will we have Agnes out with us again?" They both came to the meetings and were gloriously saved! Mary came, as did Chirsty-Anne. Then there was Donald Smith, who married my own sister – he later became an elder in the Free Church. And Duncan Mackay, who owned an engineering business in Barvas, was another one. There were more than that – and all from the Shader–Ballantrushal area alone.

---

10. Personal communication with Margaret Macleod, 24.03.2022; 23.01.23.

11. Personal communication with Donald John Smith, 19.09.2016.

'These people weren't accepted as members of the Free Church at first', continued Agnes. 'I'll tell you about these four or five. After attending the meetings, they all went to their own church the following Sunday. The minister got up – I don't know all that he said – but he said in effect, "You're not allowed to join the Free Church of Scotland, nor to hear Duncan Campbell." So they got up and left.

'They came to our church, to the evening service. The Rev. Mackay said to them, "You go back to your own church. You'll become pillars of that church yet." And so they were – the men were. Mr Mackay was very wise. "You go back, no matter what happens. You stay there – that's your place." And so, their departure from the Free Church proved temporary. For although others left that church altogether, this group stuck it out, remaining within the denomination of their youth.

'I went to the Lionel Secondary School for three years, instead of going to the Nicholson Institute. I knew them all. Even after their conversion, a few of them were not allowed to come to the meetings. They used to throw their shoes out of the window. They would wear their gym shoes and pretend they were going to the badminton! They couldn't stay away from the meetings. They were drawn.

'For example, there was Peggy Mackenzie. But she was by no means the only one. In the end the youngsters were accepted by their parents, because they saw the change in their lives. Initially, Catherine's mother was wild at her daughter, who replied to her mother, "I'm going to the meeting. You can't keep me from going." They were constrained – the Holy Spirit was at work.

'After she left, her mother was wondering, "What on earth can I do with her?" She felt a hand on her shoulder – a very heavy hand – though there was nobody in the house but herself. The Lord spoke to her, "Excuse me, do not touch mine anointed." She knew that this was a reference to Duncan Campbell. We used to go to that house, and were always invited in. Mrs Mackenzie was a bright Christian. She instantly changed her ways, for she knew she had received a rebuke from the Lord.'[12]

Duncan Mackay

One of the five mentioned above went on to become an elder. This was Duncan Mackay of Ballantrushal. Duncan publicly professed faith in Christ in March 1952, at the age of twenty-five. Already an adherent of the Free Church, Mackay remained a member for the following sixty-six years, being ordained as an elder in 1982. Duncan married a fellow convert of the revival in 1964 (Jessie Jane from Bernera). With a strong lifelong work ethic, what Duncan began as a small agricultural contracting business developed over time to become a major civil engineering business on the island – *Duncan Mackay & Sons, Ltd*. It was said that it wasn't unusual for Duncan to wear his church suit under his boiler suit on prayer meeting night, just to save a few minutes and ensure he got to church on time![13]

The MacDougalls
One of the most oft-visited homes during the revival was that of the MacDougalls, who lived just opposite Barvas Church of

12. Personal communication with Agnes Morrison, 19.09.2016.
13. Free Church *Monthly Record*, May 2019, p.21.

Scotland. 'My parents were very well known to Christians from all over the island,' Margaret Macleod reminisced. 'My mother had been a committed Christian from her teens, converted in an awakening. My father was a convert of the 1939 revival. Both were from Christian homes.

'As a member of Royal Naval Reserve, my dad was away for the whole of World War 2. My mother had to attend to the house and the croft, which she did in her usual capable manner with a smile on her face and her strong faith in Christ. As my father had been the Church Officer for years, we also attended to opening the church and, when necessary, lighting the Tilley lamps and heaters. As soon as I was able to turn the key in the vestry door, my brother and I attended to these duties.

Home of the MacDougall family

'For many believers, my parents' home was their first port of call when they visited Barvas for communion services or meetings during the revival and was very much missed when the Lord called my parents home in 1980 and 1982, respectively. We went to church and the church came to us. It was as if the two merged into one.

'We always had visitors popping in; whether it was neighbours or relatives, or on Sunday morning the folk who came by bus

from Shader about half an hour before the morning service. My
parents were always happy to welcome them and give them a
cup of tea. At communion times we had visitors from both our
own church and the Free Church. I accepted the dishwashing as
part of normal life! As children we also enjoyed the company.'[14]

The Saunders

In his younger days, Donald Saunders was a 'Sabbath heathen,'
refusing even to go to church. He was converted during the 1939
revival in Barvas. His wife was a deeply committed believer,
having been converted in the Fisherman's revival of the 1920s
on mainland Scotland. One day she persuaded him to attend
a meeting with her. He was gloriously converted and became a
man of power in prayer.

Donald's son's memories of him are of a man of deep and
constant intercession – so caught up with the Lord as he sweated
in prayer in the barn that even the children playing around him
could not distract him. Family worship was held in the home,
morning and evening without fail. Donald's wife, Mary, read a
Bible passage, after which her husband prayed.

Donald junior recalls one occasion, as a young boy, when he
entered the family home and his mother beckoned him silently to
a stool. His father was on his knees at the fireside, his arms raised
to heaven and his body trembling under the power of the Spirit.
Two other men, local believers, were sitting on a nearby bench,
and they, too, were transfixed, their hands raised heavenward.
The sense of the power of God in the room had a profound effect
on young Donald, and he could never forget it. His father could
be found in such a position for up to an hour at a time.

Being one of the Barvas prayer warriors prior to the '49
revival, Donald was not surprised when the Lord poured out
His Spirit once again. In the blacksmith's home where he often
fellowshipped there were meetings every night during both the

14. Personal communication with Margaret Macleod, 07.09.2020.

'39 and '49 revivals. Once, Donald senior could not be found. He was discovered in the barn, pleading with God on behalf of the community. This happened regularly during the '49 revival. Some days, prior to the prayer meeting, he would spend much of the day in prayer. Campbell was a regular visitor in the Saunders' home.

Mary Saunders was also a fine singer. Quite often at nights, when the kids were settled down in bed, she would pull a chair in by the fire, pick up the large family hymn-book, and start singing some well-known hymns. Two of her favourites were:

There is a fountain filled with blood
Drawn from Immanuel's veins;
And sinners, plunged beneath that flood,
Lose all their guilty stains ....[15]

And:
I do believe, I will believe,
That Jesus died for me,
That on the cross He shed His blood,
From sin to set me free.[16]

Revival Fires Never Die

During his years of highly eventful missions the length and breadth of Lewis and Harris, Duncan Campbell returned often to the parish where it all started – Barvas. It is evident that revival did not blaze across Barvas for the entirety of three whole years. Rather, after the first burst of revival in the winter of 1949– 50, there occurred several lesser waves of spiritual blessing at various times.

Nevertheless, a full year after revival first commenced on the Westside, the evangelist recorded that in Barvas, 'The revival spirit and blessing is as deep as ever .... The crowds attending the

---

15. William Cowper, 1772.

16. Public domain, nd.

services are as large as ever, with the same deep conviction. I am
addressing two and sometimes three meetings each night, with
a final meeting in some home to help the anxious.'

Holding a third mission in the parish church in September
1951, after 'a few days of hard going,' the Spirit of God broke
through again. Campbell saw crowded meetings in three
churches and many anxious cases. Things 'hardened up' again
the following week, however, when there was 'no-one seeking
the Lord for salvation.'[17] But then, as late as January 1953,
a weeknight meeting in one of the smaller churches in Barvas,
'fully sixty were turned away, the church was so packed.'[18]

On their Faces

As well as innumerable references to people praying 'on their
knees,' Campbell makes multiple mentions of both saints and
sinners 'on their faces' before God, crying out to Him. In a
Barvas home, where many believers gather for a night of prayer;
seven elders praying in a barn 'on their faces' before God; seven
weavers, in their respective homes, 'lying prostrate on their faces
behind their looms'; men on their faces by the roadside, 'crying
out to God for mercy'; people 'on their faces' in the pews in
Bernera church after the Spirit suddenly fell, etc.

Such is not a testimony reported by any other witnesses of
the revival. One early convert testified to never having seen, or
even heard of, except indirectly from Campbell, any person being
prostrate on the floor or ground at any point during the revival.
'Occasionally bent over the pew "prostrate in the spirit,"' she
said, 'but never stretched out on the floor.' Note also the example
shared of the two elderly Smith sisters who, Campbell relates,
would get 'on their faces' before God in prayer, an unlikely
posture given their old age and physical disabilities.

---

17. Duncan Campbell, FM Report, 03.10.1951.

18. ibid., 04.02.1953.

Sevens Abounding

One cannot listen to many of Campbell's later revival addresses without noting the frequency of his use of the number 'seven' (the most important symbolic number in the Bible). Almost everything seems to happen in sevens – or sometimes multiples of that figure, notably fourteen.

Thus, it was *seven* Barvas office-bearers that met in a barn two evenings a week to pray for an outpouring of God's Spirit on the parish. On the second night after Campbell's arrival on Lewis, *fourteen* buses diverged on Barvas Church of Scotland, bringing hungry souls from all over the island. That same night, *seven* men were being driven to the meeting in a butcher's truck when suddenly the Spirit of God fell on them in convicting power, and all *seven* were saved before they even got to the church.[19]

Campbell went to a certain village at *seven* o'clock one evening to find a large number gathered round a *seven*-room bungalow. After preaching to the crowd, he was taken to the end of the house, where he found *seven* men crying to God for mercy. All *seven* were saved within days.[20] That's three separate sevens – and no other number – in one story.

Campbell gives details of the Spirit of God moving supernaturally upon the Bernera township of Croir, 'a village *seven* miles away from the church.' This is somewhat improbable, given that the island is only five miles long and the church is located near the centre. Prior to revival breaking out in Arnol, 'only *seven* came near the meetings in the Parish church.'[21] Following revival there, *fourteen* young men who frequented the local *bothan* (drinking den) were to be found on their knees in the prayer meeting.

---

19. Walters, *Bright and Shining Revival*, p. 9.

20. Campbell, *Revival in the Hebrides*, pp. 49–51.

21. ibid., p. 70.

In the parish of Lochs, *fourteen* young men were lingering outside the community hall, preparing to buy booze for the weekend dance. All *fourteen* gave their lives to the Lord within an hour. Still in Lochs, a lorry conveying folk to a meeting *fourteen* miles away broke down *seven* miles from the church.[22]

The evangelist occasionally even reads the figure seven back into incidents from his early life. On service in France in World War I, *seven* Scottish soldiers requested that Campbell lead them in prayer prior to their unit making a charge towards German lines the following morning.[23] After preaching to fellow cavalrymen in the casualty clearing station following injury, 'within an hour *seven* Canadians were saved.'[24]

Such captivation with the number seven is clearly a later habit of Campbell's. I can find no reference to this figure in any of his weekly reports during the entire duration of the revival, and only occasionally in his 1952 Keswick address or his written account of the awakening, published in 1955.

Mysterious Multiplication of Ministers
A tendency of Campbell's in his later years was to relate an exciting story from the revival that led to numerous conversions, and then inform his listeners that several of these converts went on to become ministers. For example, at his very first meeting in Barvas Church, among those converted were, Campbell claimed to be 'sure and certain ... at least *five* young men who ... are today ministers in the Church of Scotland, having gone through university and college.'[25] In a different address, Campbell claimed that, 'From the group

22. Peckham, *Heritage of Revival*, p.171.
23. Allen, *Catch the Wind*, p.32.
24. Woolsey, *Channel of Revival*, p. 52; Allen, *Catch the Wind*, p. 34.
25. Campbell, *Revival in the Hebrides*, p. 38.

of young men who sought the Lord that night, there are *nine* in the ministry.'[26]

Elsewhere, Campbell tells the story of four drunk men getting on a bus to go for a night out, and being witnessed to by the conductress, who had recently become a Christian. The men were convicted by her words and instead made their way to a church, where all four were saved before two o'clock in the morning. Campbell concludes by noting that *three* of these four men later became ministers.[27]

In another address, Campbell talks of an elder in Barvas who had recently experienced a dramatic conversion following deep conviction of sin, and now called for a prayer meeting in his farmhouse. The Spirit moved powerfully at what became known as 'Donald Macleod's prayer meeting,' and 'out of that prayer meeting there are *four* ministers in the church today.'[28]

Still in Barvas, Campbell preached outside a packed house, where a number of men fell prostrate on their faces, crying to God for mercy. 'Today those men are pillars in the church; *five* of them became ministers.'[29]

The problem is that no one I've spoken to can identify *any* of the above-mentioned ministers and office-bearers – and there are a number of other similar stories. None of the above testimonies correspond to those of known converts like William Macleod, Kenneth Macdonald, Jack Macarthur, John Murdo Smith and Alistair Macdonald, all of whom went on to become popular ministers, and whose conversion stories are well known in the revival folklore of Lewis. It's believed that no more than a dozen or so converts from the entire Lewis revival went on to become ministers. Yet, if you add up the numbers claimed by Campbell,

26. *The Revival Hymn,* compilation audio tape.

27. Allen, *Catch the Wind,* p. 76.

28. Duncan Campbell, *The Lewis Revival,* Faith Mission audio tape.

29. Dunn, *The Hebrides Revival and Awakening,* p. 22.

and from the parish of Barvas alone,[30] you come to a significantly higher number.

Channel of Barvas Revival

Campbell claimed that 'God was moving and moving mightily before ever I thought of going to Lewis.'[31] Indeed, the evangelist emphasised at the very start of virtually every address he made that he did not bring revival to the island. Note the typical opening comments of one of his best-known addresses, given in 1968. 'It has grieved me beyond words to hear people talk and write about the man who brought revival to the Hebrides. My dear people, I didn't do that. Revival was there before I ever set foot on the island.'[32]

Typical Barvas scene (Ballantrushal)

---

30. One report – this time not from Campbell – has it that no fewer than twenty-two ministers and eleven foreign missionaries came out of the revival in Barvas and Shader alone (quoted in Allen, *Catch the Wind*, p. 169).

31. Duncan Campbell, *The Price and Power of Revival: Lessons from the Hebrides Awakening*, Edinburgh, 1966, p. 59.

32. This is certainly not the expression of someone who either 'belatedly conceded' or inadvertently 'let slip' that revival on the island preceded his arrival, as J.M. avows (Macleod, *Banner in the West*, p. 262).

But what must also be noted here is the modesty of Campbell's avowal. It is difficult to find evidence that revival was in progress in Barvas before Campbell arrived. Certainly, there were noticeable stirrings on the Westside – a mood of spiritual inquiry spreading through Ness and Barvas from the winter of 1948 and well into the following year, with several conversions occurring within both the Free Church and the Church of Scotland. William Macleod called it a 'stirring among the Lord's people.'[33] Beautiful as this movement was, it cannot be regarded as an outbreak of revival and no one at the time or since has referred to it as such.

Certainly also, just prior to Campbell's arrival on Lewis, there was some evidence of a quiet work of the Spirit in progress in the Free Church congregation in Point. But no one has ever suggested that this localised movement on the east of the island had a direct connection to a work of grace that broke out within a different denomination on the other side of Lewis, before sweeping across much of the island. It is evident that only after the arrival of Duncan Campbell in Barvas did a marked revival movement arise and spread through that community. The same is true of other localities (see Chap 17).

The modesty of Campbell's assertion is further seen in the fact that neither the Rev. MacKay of Barvas nor any of the early revival converts in that parish have suggested that revival was underway in Barvas prior to Campbell's visit. Perhaps what Campbell really meant when he said that revival preceded his arrival is noted in his repeated claim that 'revival began in a prayer meeting,' e.g., with the elders praying in the thatched cottage, and the Smith sisters and others in the parish interceding in their homes. At other times, Campbell made it clear that, 'revival began in an awareness of God.'[34]

---

33. Personal communication, 18.09.2017.

34. Campbell, *Revival in the Hebrides*, p. 40.

But the evangelist's modest avowals have been assumed to mean something quite different – that revival was in full swing well before his stepping foot on Lewis soil. Of course, in a Reformed church culture where the sovereignty of God is emphasised, it is natural to downplay the role of any particular individual. Nobody wants the glory to go to man. That said, the testimonies are of one accord – revival began in earnest sometime *after* Campbell began his mission on the island in December 1949. Duncan Campbell was indeed the human channel of the early fires of the Lewis revival.

Revival Statistics: Barvas[35]

The membership roll of the Barvas Church of Scotland, which stood at 148 in early 1949, reveals the following additions in the years of the revival:

Professions of Faith: Barvas C of S[36]

Year	March	September	Total
1948	1	0	1
1949	1	5	6
1950	**24**	**15**	**39**
1951	**3**	**3**	**6**
1952	**1**	**1**	**2**
1953	1	1	2

The figures show the result of the spiritual stirring in Barvas during the spring of 1949, when five females joined the church (including Margaret Macleod and Peggie Maciver). More significantly, they show that 1950 was by far the most prominent

35. The parish of Barvas had a sizeable population of around 5,100 at the time of the revival. This compared with Uig's population of 2,700; Lochs' of 3,100 and Stornoway's of 5,700. The total population of Lewis at the time was around 23,700 while that of Harris was just under 4,000.

36. Barvas church records forwarded by Rev. Hector Morrison, 14.08.2020.

year of additions to membership, with thirty-nine added to the roll; and in particular the period October '49 to March '50, when twenty-four names were added. Further, of the fifteen additions in September '50, two-thirds (ten) were converts of the revival in Arnol (a further two joined in March '51, after which only one further Arnol convert joined the church – March '53).

Thus, although Campbell's Lewis campaign lasted nearly three years, with several missions and many meetings in Barvas during that period, the great majority of converts in the parish made professions within the first four months of the revival (December '49 – March '50) – perhaps even the first two months – and had already joined the church by the early spring of 1950. It was clearly this very early period that constituted the main burst of revival in Barvas. There were relatively few additions to the church roll after that, other than as a result of revival in Arnol.

Other details gleaned from the membership roll are equally interesting. Of the twenty-nine people who joined Barvas church in 1950 (excluding Arnol converts), twenty were female and nine were men. It is a significant feature of revival movements that more converts are female than male. Intriguingly, though, of the twelve Arnol converts who joined in September '50 and March '51, exactly two-thirds (eight) were male. Interestingly, those twelve converts came from just five households (No. 10, 21, 26, 28 and 30 Arnol); revival in this community was clearly a family affair. It is also interesting to note that there were no professions of faith from Arnol in the months prior to Campbell's mission there in May 1950.

Another surprising feature that stands out is that the vast majority of Barvas professions came from either Upper and Lower Barvas (including off-roads like Pairc and Loch Street), or Upper and Lower Shader and Ballantrushal, as well as, of course, Arnol. Despite Campbell conducting missions in the sizeable districts of Bragar and Shawbost and meetings being held in Borve and Brue, no converts came from any of these communities (other than one from Brue). This, presumably, was owing to the fact that all these four locations were largely Free Church territories.

The Rev. Hector Morrison, former minister of Barvas Church of Scotland, has helpfully transferred membership additions throughout the twentieth century into line-chart form:

Professions of Faith: Barvas Church of Scotland

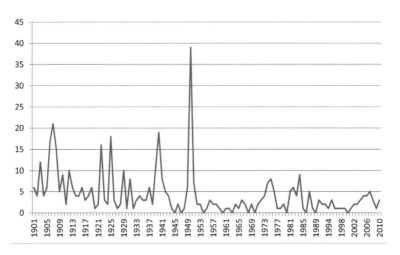

The chart shows the sudden spike in 1950, with the equally dramatic fall over the following year or two. It also shows previous lesser spikes in membership, signifying the revival of the late 1930s, two bursts of revival activity in the 1920s and the period of spiritual stirring coinciding with division within the Presbyterian Church in the first decade of the 1900s.

The total number of professions of faith for the three years 1950–2 was forty-seven. While clearly an impressive figure for a single parish in such a short period, it is less than half the figure quoted by both the Rev. James Mackay and Duncan Campbell, of over one hundred professions. Of course, we know that some revival converts were Free Church adherents, who sought to join Barvas Free Church. The church roll for that fellowship shows the following:

Professions of Faith: Barvas Free Church[37]

Year	March	September	Total
1949	0	3	3
1950	**3**	**1**	**4**
1951	**1**	**4**	**5**
1952	**3**	**5**	**8**
1953	4	3	7

Thus, there were a total of seventeen additions to Free Church membership during the years 1950, '51 and '52. However, it cannot be assumed that all, or even most, of this number relates to revival converts. Church roll additions in the years prior to the revival were generally between three and seven. Nevertheless, it would be reasonable to assume that some of the additions for 1950–52 – perhaps around half the total of seventeen – related to converts of the revival.

Unlike Barvas Church of Scotland, professions of faith in the Free Church were relatively low in 1950 and higher in succeeding years. This may have been a consequence of the church session taking a cautious approach to revival converts; testing their fruit over a period of time before accepting them as members.

Taking Church of Scotland and Free Church professions together, this still accounts for just over half of the oft-quoted 100 professions of faith pertaining to Barvas. Others were young people who moved to the Scottish mainland shortly after the revival to study or to work. Taking all these factors into consideration, it is still difficult to account for the 100+ conversions claimed by the Rev. Mackay over the three-year period in question, unless one assumes that some converts never joined a church – though such cases are thought to have been few in number.

---

37. Statistics forwarded by Rev. Murdo Campbell, Barvas Free Church of Scotland, 23.06.2022.

We make a similar observation in regard to Arnol, of which community it was said there were twenty-four conversions as a result of the revival. Yet official records show that only twelve people from Arnol joined Barvas Church of Scotland during the revival period (with one further addition in 1953).

PART 3

Revival Extended

CHAPTER 9

Revival Advance: North

Ness

Revival Beginnings

At about the same time as Duncan Campbell had begun to hold meetings in Barvas – December 1949 – the Church of Scotland in the neighbouring parish of Ness was holding its own *'orduighean beaga'* ('little communion') services. Here, the Rev. Murdo Macsween, Church of Scotland minister from Broadford, Skye, was the guest preacher.[1]

Night after night the building was crammed to capacity, with extra seats having to be brought into the aisles and some people being forced to sit on the stairs leading up to the gallery. Sensing the heightened spiritual atmosphere, Macsween shared with the local minister his belief that there would soon be a breakthrough in the parish, and when it happened to let him know at once! Increased attendance at meetings continued.

Then another visiting speaker – by coincidence, Murdo Macsween's brother – came to preach later in the month, leading to more packed services and several conversions. Already, before the arrival of Campbell to the area, Ness was witnessing a foretaste of spiritual blessing.

It was towards the end of the following month that Campbell moved north to the district, after having spent around five weeks

---

1. A native of Scalpay, Rev. Macsween had served as minister in Kinloch from 1933 to 1944.

in Barvas, where the work of God continued in his absence. Indeed, he had a period of overlap between the two parishes – addressing meetings each night in two different districts ten miles apart.

Ness Church of Scotland

In no time a gracious movement was underway in Ness, and Campbell noted in his diary, 'I am now at it night and day, and just getting sleep when I can.' Even at the start of the movement here, when buses came to collect people one night for a concert in the town, they had to return empty, for not one person went. Soon, two ministers from other areas came to assist with preaching, especially at the cottage meetings. It was with some relief that Campbell could note that at last he 'was able to rest a good deal.'[2]

Galson

Events were greatly encouraged by stirrings within the Macarthur family in South Galson, on the southern edge of the parish. The Macarthurs were one of the most non-churched families in Ness. Now, following dramatic events at a dance in Carloway (see Chap 10), things took a different turn. 'Although I wasn't

---

2. Duncan Campbell, FM Report, 01.02.1950.

converted,' recalled Annie Macarthur, 'I don't think I ever felt drawn to my knees so much as I did that night after we came home from Carloway, hoping that it was the Spirit of God working.'[3]

The Macarthurs' son Jack instantly knew there had been a change. 'I woke up the morning after the Carloway dance to a deadly quiet – and wondered if someone was ill or had died. Only to be told to keep quiet as something had happened the previous night. This aroused my curiosity immensely.'[4]

Donald Macarthur now felt that his home was to be given over to God. He had purchased a family Bible some years before for times of emergency, but it had remained unused in its box. This he now located and proceeded to conduct a short time of family worship. This included a recitation of the Lord's Prayer, for, being an unconverted man, Macarthur knew no prayers of his own.

Within a few months, both Donald and his wife became Christians, as did their son Jack sometime later, at the tender age of twelve (see Chap 14), as well as their eldest daughter. The Macarthur home, which had previously known nothing of God, now became a dwelling place of the Holy Spirit. House meetings became popular and visiting speakers were welcomed. The first was Duncan Campbell, who stayed there for several weeks while conducting a mission in the old school hall located next door to the Macarthur home.

The Galson meetings commenced at the end of March 1950, just three weeks after Campbell's first Ness mission. Remarkably, this community was, at that early date, according to the evangelist, the only district in the expansive parish of Ness 'that the revival has not touched.' That was soon to change.

Just a week later, as the Galson meetings closed, the situation looked entirely different. Accompanied by Willie Black of the

---

3. Annie Macarthur, on *Revival in our Times.*

4. ibid.

Faith Mission, Campbell reported being 'in the midst of the greatest move yet. The Spirit of God is mightily at work, and many have come to the Saviour. I am writing this report in the early hours of the morning, having dealt with the last lot of anxious ones at 1.30 am. The night meetings have been crowded and people turned away.'[5]

Tales of the Unconverted
Over ensuing months, Campbell made frequent visits to this northerly parish. One of the first converts from Ness was Roddy Murray from Port of Ness, while his cousin Donald (Dolly) Murray was another early convert. Roddy subsequently became a Church of Scotland minister in Kinloch and Bernera, while Dolly became a missionary in Point and Stornoway.

Meetings were held, not only in churches, halls and homes, but even in furniture and meal stores. One evening so many flocked to a particular house that not all could get in. Spilling out into the adjoining vacant lot, the joyous believers prayed and sang Psalms into the night sky. Campbell, who had been preaching inside, went out to exhort them. Soon, an elderly woman opposed to the revival threw open the window of her upstairs bedroom, demanding that they shut up and move away so she could get some sleep. One quick-witted young man shouted up to her, 'Ach, go away home yersell, *"cailleach"* (old woman/hag), you've been asleep long enough'!

---

5. Duncan Campbell, FM Report, 29.03.1950; 05.04.1950.

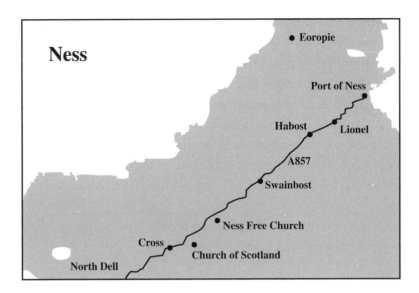

A butcher from the parish became a great helper in the revival, cleaning out his work-van each night and using it to convey folk to the meetings. Despite being unconverted, he became caught up in the movement and even temporarily overcame his drink problem so that he would always be sober enough to drive. In time he became convicted through the sermons he heard at meetings, and one evening when anxious folk were invited into another room for prayer, the butcher got up and walked to the door, hesitated, then turned away. It is unclear whether he ever 'came through' for Christ.

Another salutary story was told of a believer who called upon a family whose members were all Christians, except for one son. As they prayed, the lad went to his knees, and although going through the mechanics of conversion, his heart seemed dull and there was no sense of assurance. Tragically, this young man was killed in a car accident two weeks later.[6]

---

6. Bushby, *Adventures in Revival*, Tulsa, Oklahoma, nd, p. 32.

Catriona Macaulay

Catriona Macaulay (nee Macleod) shares her story. 'We began hearing about the revival in Barvas not long after it began. There was a great buzz among kids at Lionel School, which I attended; not least when it transpired that several of the pupils from Shader, who also came to school in Lionel, had been soundly converted. Everyone was talking about it in the playground. Some of the older Christians in the part of the parish that I lived in went up to Barvas, keen to sound out this evangelist that was creating such a commotion in that district. A great many of those who made the journey were Free Church people, though most of these stopped going after a night or two.[7]

Catriona Macaulay

'It became known that Duncan Campbell was going to be holding a meeting at the Macarthurs' home. I went along with some others from my village. I was unconverted at the time, and remember being scared of shaking Campbell's hand or getting too close to him in case he discerned sin in my life! My friends

---

7. Personal communication with Catriona Macaulay, 05.04.2020.

and I became quite determined that we weren't going to catch the *cúram*.[8] So we dodged him!'[9]

The three young girls had initially been wary, not just of shaking the hand of this unorthodox preacher that everyone was fussing over, but of going to hear him at all. They decided to go and ask a respected Free Church woman in their community, the grandmother of Mary Morrison, for her opinion. This woman had been confined to bed for the previous seven years with arthritis. Certain she would urge them not to go to hear Campbell, the girls were amazed to find the woman encouraging them to attend. Sure enough, the three girls went to the next meeting, and all three gave their lives to Christ.[10]

'I lived next-door to Mary,' noted Catriona. 'We were cousins, and very good friends. Mary and I were converted on the same night. I was just sixteen. On our way home from the after-meeting that night – it was particularly late, but such a beautiful mild evening – we all went for a walk along the beach, singing praises to God above the noise of the waves. And stopping to thank Him for His absolute goodness in saving sinners like us. It was such a joyous time. From that night on, we were hardly ever home – we were out every night at the meetings.

'Young converts of similar age met in groups and went everywhere together. There was Alistair Macdonald (who later became a Church of Scotland minister); and Donald (Dolly) Murray from South Dell. There was my friend Mary Morrison and Chirsty Maclean, and myself, and two others.

'Another thing we used to do when we were all walking home from a meeting together was to form a big circle by joining hands – right there in the middle of the road. Well, there were very few

---

8. A Gaelic term used derogatively to describe someone coming under conviction of sin.

9. Personal communication with Catriona Macaulay, 05.04.2020.

10. Personal communication with Mary Peckham, 16.08.2008.

cars on the road in those days. And we'd form this big circle, and we'd sing and we'd pray.

Mary Morrison

'We used to go to Cross (a village in Ness) for the mid-week meeting there on a Thursday night, which we attended in addition to our own mid-week service. After the meeting we went to a house in the village where there lived an elderly disabled man, bent over with a bad back. He was a lovely Christian and lived with his two sisters. We would always sing for this family – both hymns and psalms. They just loved hearing the singing of the young converts.'[11]

Revival Stories

The fascinating testimony of Mary Morrison coming to faith during the revival has been oft-told, and can be found in her book, *Hearken O' Daughter*.[12] Mary recalled that she and other converts were keen not to miss any meeting. 'One night we were returning in the back of a truck from a cottage meeting, expecting

---

11. Personal communication with Catriona Macaulay, 05.04.2020.

12. Also known as *I was Saved in Revival*, first published by Prairie Bible Institute, Three Hills, Alberta, 1966.

yet another meeting, but there was no further meeting that night. So we went to the Barvas manse and told the surprised, and now awakened, minister, the Rev. Mackay, that we were looking for a meeting. Mr Campbell was there and rose from his sleep to minister to these hungry, thrilled, but unwise, young people!'[13]

Catriona Macaulay remembers the boundless enthusiasm the young converts had for fellowship with God's people. 'There had been a meeting in Carloway to which a group of us from Ness had been driven by an unconverted man in his van.' Rather than accept the offer of a lift back to Ness, some thirty miles distant – this group of younger converts decided to stay for an after-meeting in the Carloway manse. 'We were young and keen and took no thought of the distance – we knew we'd enjoy the fellowship together on the long walk home!' As it turned out, they were indeed given a lift home after the manse meeting finished.[14]

When a meeting was held in someone's house, it was usually intimated in whose home the meeting would be held the following evening. One night no such announcement was made. In the northern Ness village of Eoropie, there existed a *bothan*, a small windowless building that local young men used to drink in. A young lad from the community, then aged around fourteen, decided to clean out the *bothan* and hold a prayer meeting in it. First, he had to get the agreement of the local lads who used to frequent it. Permission was readily given, and a meeting was indeed held in this unlikely venue!

At meetings held in Ness a year after revival first broke out, Campbell rejoiced to find that 'interest is as deep as ever. There was a mighty manifestation of the power of God last night. Wave after wave of Holy Ghost power swept over the meetings and strong men were broken down and crying for mercy.'[15]

---

13. Peckham, *Sounds from Heaven*, p. 149.

14. Personal communication with Catriona Macaulay, 05.04.2020.

15. Duncan Campbell, FM Report, 31.01.1951.

Ness bothan

Ina Graham

Ina Graham's family had cause to be deeply thankful for the Ness revival. Her father, three sisters and one brother all 'came out' during the movement. Ina was a young girl of twelve at the time, and a pupil at Stornoway's Nicolson Institute. She remembers Campbell holding house meetings in her parents' home – they were always full, including upstairs. Ina said, 'I was almost persuaded then, but somehow I resisted. I continued sowing wild oats, but eventually gave my life to Christ in my twenties.'

Ina's family was at that time affiliated to the Free Church. They were refused communion after applying for membership because it was known they had been converted through Duncan Campbell. 'Who were you converted through?' was the question posed to each of them. Ina believed that 'Ministers in the Free Church were jealous of the success Campbell was having. Some Free Churches were now virtually full of converts from Campbell's meetings. Their own ministers had been labouring for years to win souls, and this fellow from the mainland comes in, and a whole batch of rough diamonds gets swept into the kingdom!'

Ina was aware of another family, most members of which were converted through Campbell, and who also left the Free Church in Ness. Oddly enough, rather than joining the Church of Scotland, they applied for membership of the even stricter Free Presbyterian Church. 'I don't know how, but somehow they were accepted,' recalled Ina. 'A young woman in that family actually married a Free Presbyterian minister.'[16]

It was said that the Church of Scotland minister in Ness didn't openly resist the revival, but neither did he show any enthusiasm for it. He pretty much carried on as before. While he allowed revival meetings to be held in his church, he generally didn't attend them himself, and he did little to support the movement. Thankfully, this did nothing to dampen the outworking of revival in the parish or the enthusiasm of the many individuals converted there.

Allan Macarthur

Although confessing to having been spiritually awakened on the night of the famous Carloway dance (see Chap 10), Allan Macarthur felt he wasn't quite ready to surrender his life to Christ. He believed he had too much to live for. He had been given the amazing opportunity of going overseas to work as a meteorologist. In distinction, impressed with the effects the current revival was having on so many young folk in his parish, his own minister pressed Allan to go into the ministry.

This was the last thing Allan had in mind and he found the suggestion preposterous. Instead, in November 1950, he set off to serve with the Falklands Islands Dependencies Survey in the Antarctic. This was a fascinating, though at times intensely lonely, experience, which led to some men breaking down mentally under the strain. With hindsight, Allan felt that God's hand kept him during this testing period, even though he gave little thought towards his maker.

---

16. Personal communication with Ina Graham, 02.05.2001.

Allan MacArthur (in the Antarctic)

Allan returned to Lewis in June 1953, to find that things back home had altered radically. The revival that had broken out prior to his leaving had continued in various waves most of the time he was away. His own home had been especially transformed and his family seemed like new people. Many of his old friends had also been converted through Campbell's meetings; some of them were now even ministers! And the change for the better in their lives was unquestionable. All of this had a profound impact on the young man.

Now, for the first time in his life, Allan wanted to get right with God. Maybe his pastor had been on the right track all along. He was still the minister, so Allan decided to go and speak with him. To his absolute shock, it seemed like a totally different man that answered the door. In the years since they had last met, his minister had developed what Allan felt was a somewhat jealous attitude toward Campbell and all that had happened on the island as a result of his missions. For another thing, the minister said to Allan, 'Duncan Campbell takes these young converts and shows them off like some prime bulls at a cattle auction!'

In conclusion, the pastor's new advice to the young man was, 'Whatever you do, don't become a minister!'[17]

While shocked at the cleric's change of heart, Allan was unable to shake off his spiritual hunger. He felt he couldn't run away from God any longer. Campbell was still conducting the occasional mission on Lewis at this time. But it was primarily through the visit of a believer from Greenock in the late summer of 1953 that Allan said he 'finally came to my senses.' The visitor, like Allan's father, was a schoolteacher. This created a bond of friendship between them, and the visiting teacher stayed with the Macarthurs during his visit, holding meetings in their home.

It was at one of these that, during the course of sharing an address, Psalm 46:10 was quoted; *Be still and know that I am God.* Somehow the words spoke deeply to Allan's heart, which had already been considerably softened. Now at last, Allan surrendered his life completely to Christ, and all things became new.[18]

Village of Weavers
In one of the most remarkable stories from the revival – recorded in a number of later accounts – Campbell refers to 'a village of weavers.'[19] 'There was a row of cottages by the roadside. There were seven of them altogether. And in every cottage a loom and a weaver. One morning, just as the men were being called for

---

17. He also appeared to be peeved that many were now directing their largest offerings to the Faith Mission, through which ministry they personally had been so richly blessed.

18. Personal communication with Allan Macarthur, 20.08.2009. Soon after, Allan left the island again – this time to study at Glasgow University, before becoming a teacher of English, History and Geography. It wasn't until the late 1960s that he accepted a call into the ministry, being ordained to the charge of Lochcarron and Applecross in 1972, where he remained until his retirement in 1998.

19. Most written accounts mistakenly think Campbell is referring to 'the village of Weaver.'

breakfast, it was discovered that the seven of them were lying, and all of them in a trance … the seven men were saved that day. Now, I should say six of them were saved that day; one of them on the following day. But they came to understand that something supernatural had taken possession of them.'[20]

So, seven cottages, seven weavers, seven looms. It already sounds a little too perfect, and employing Campbell's favourite number – 'seven.' That all seven men were being called for breakfast by their wives at exactly the same time in the morning is somewhat comical. As for subsequent details – every man in his own home, completely unknown to each other, suddenly prostrated on his face by the Spirit of God, without human intervention or other influence; each man also going into a trance, and all but one instantly converted – the story hardly carries the ring of truth.

If it were true, it is difficult to see why Campbell wouldn't have chosen to share it almost everywhere he went. For so dramatic and otherworldly is it that it has to feature right up there among the foremost stories from the entire revival – or indeed any revival. But it's a story rarely shared by the evangelist, and one that nobody else has even begun to substantiate.

I came across a single sentence in an early report Campbell wrote to the Faith Mission that may possibly reveal the source of this tale. In April 1950, while labouring in Ness, Campbell noted, 'So great was the conviction of sin that strong men have even fainted behind their looms.'[21] Is this the grain of truth from which Campbell's tall tale grew?

---

20. Campbell, *Revival in the Hebrides*, pp. 41–2.

21. Duncan Campbell, FM Report, 05.04.1950. In a 1968 address, Campbell states that he visited these seven men on a 'recent' trip to Lewis and heard the amazing story again from their own lips. This may be a reference to one or two of the men who fainted behind their looms and who subsequently gave their lives to Christ.

Humbled Headmasters

As well as several teachers, reliable testimonies emerged of more than one parish headteacher on the island turning to Christ during the progress of revival in their area; such trophies were won in Uig and in Gravir, for example. Head-teacher testimonies seem to be a favourite of Campbell's, for he gives details of two further dramatic instances of schoolmaster conversions. The first relates to Bernera:

A schoolmaster was looking over his papers at home on the Lewis mainland, fifteen miles from the island, when he was suddenly gripped by the fear of God. He said to his wife, 'I don't know what's drawing me to Bernera[22], but I must go.' His wife replied, 'But John, it's nearly ten o'clock. I know what's on your mind – you're going out to drink! But you are not leaving this house tonight!' (He was a hard drinker). He said to his wife, 'I may be mistaken, but if I know anything at all about my own heart and mind, drink will never touch my lips again.'

And so, despite the late hour, the schoolmaster managed to get someone to drive him to the jetty, and, remarkably, even arranged for a small boat to ferry him across to Bernera. Arriving on the island, John somehow obtained information on where Campbell was holding a cottage meeting, and he made his way – presumably on foot – to that farmhouse. By this time, it was the early hours of the following morning. In a matter of minutes, the schoolmaster was praising God for his salvation.

There are several improbabilities with this likeable story – the most significant of which is that it has never been publicly told by anyone else, not even by the schoolmaster himself, whom no one has ever been able to identify.

The same problems emerge with the following story (thought to relate to Ness). It is five or six in the morning. Hundreds of people have been up all night, attending one revival meeting after

---

22. In the audio recording, Campbell says '*Barvas,*' but this doesn't fit the narrative; it is clearly Bernera the teacher was intent on going to.

another. Unable to gain entry to one late-night church service led by Campbell, a group lingers in a nearby field for several hours on end, many under deep conviction of sin. After the last meeting in church finally draws to a close, Campbell goes out to them.

He happens to come across the headmaster of the nearby secondary school, lying on his face on the ground, crying to God for mercy. On either side of him, two young girls around sixteen years of age, pupils of his school. They repeatedly urge their helpless headmaster, saying, 'Sir, the same Jesus that saved us last night in Barvas can save you tonight.' As Campbell watches on, incredulously, God sweeps into the man's heart, his life being instantly turned around.

Unfortunately, no one is aware of any secondary school headmaster on Lewis having been converted in the revival, let alone by the dramatic and unlikely means reported here. Much, if not all, of the story would appear to be the construct of a highly fertile imagination.

Nocturnal Assemblages

The earlier part of Campbell's narrative poses additional problems. Campbell had been preaching all evening, and right through the early hours of the morning, in churches and house-meetings in Barvas. Then, ' … after three o'clock in the morning, a messenger came to say' that the churches were crowded in another parish fifteen miles away (thought to be Ness) …. And we went to this parish … along with several other ministers. And I found myself preaching in a large church that would seat 1,000 – and the Spirit of God was moving in a mighty way! I could see them falling on their knees, crying to God for mercy. I could hear those outside praying. And that continued for, I'm sure, two hours. And then as we were leaving the church, someone came to me to tell me that a very large number of people had gathered on a field – for they could not get into the church, or any of the churches. Along with the other ministers I decided to go to the field. And here I saw this enormous crowd standing there as though gripped by a power that they could not explain. But the most interesting thing about that meeting was a sight that I saw' (Campbell goes on to tell of the schoolmaster lying face down on the ground ...).

I used to read this, and other similar narratives, and marvel at the thought of entire communities – consisting of many hundreds of people, along with their ministers – being fully alive to the Spirit, weaving their way from one impromptu meeting in a packed church to a crowded cottage meeting, and on to another service in a neighbouring parish church, and then to a field-meeting – all the way through the night.

Little did I know that this was not how things occurred. Services were never held in churches in Barvas or Ness late in the evening – and certainly not in the middle of the night (not least with over 1,000 in attendance, and as many gathered outside). And this was just one church. Apparently other churches in the parish were also packed to capacity at the same unearthly hour. All this despite the fact that denominations other than the Church of Scotland were quite against the revival, and held no revival services at any time during the spiritual awakening in question.

Revival Statistics: Ness

Professions of Faith: Ness C of S[23]

	March	September	Total
1948	0	1	1
1949	1	1	2
1950	**9**	**9**	**18**
1951	**10**	**1**	**11**
1952	**1**	**5**	**6**
1953	2	1	3

23. Ness church records forwarded by Rev. Hector Morrison, 14.08.2020.

We observe that in Ness, as in Barvas, 1950 was clearly the main year of revival, with eighteen additions to the church roll. In this parish, however, professions tend to be spread out more across the three years of the revival. This may be partly due to Campbell's several week-long missions across the parish during 1950 and '51; the first in January 1950, followed by a mission in Galson at the close of March '50 (the results of which might show in the September '50 figures above); and a further week-long mission at the close of January 1951 (which may have resulted in the ten additions in March 51).

Of the twenty-nine additions in 1950 and '51, twenty were female and nine male. The various townships of this northerly parish are represented in the statistics (including Cross, Galson, Europie, Habost, Lionel, Dell), with the surnames MacArthur, MacLean and Macleod featuring prominently. Mary Morrison (later Peckham) became a member in September '51, along with four other female residents of Port of Ness.

Once again, the fruit of the revival becomes clear when viewed on a line-chart (see below).[24] In this case, in distinction to Barvas, there is no corresponding peak in the late 1930s, as the revival of those years had no marked effect in Ness (though we can clearly observe the outworking of '*Roddie's revival*' of the 1920s).

Cliff House, Port of Ness, home of Mary Morrison & family

24. Courtesy of Rev. Hector Morrison, 14.08.2020.

Professions of Faith: Ness UFC/Church of Scotland

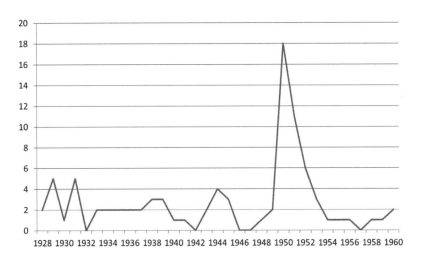

Barvas and Ness Line-Charts Combined

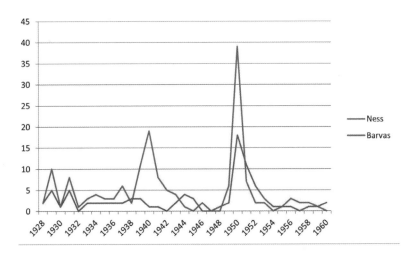

The earliest United Free Church record for Ness is 1910, when the church roll stood at 137. There was an upward trend over the next twenty years, up to the Union of the Church of Scotland with the United Free Church in 1929. In 1930, despite seven deaths, nine new communicants were added. Since then, the roll gradually fell to a low of 131 in 1948. The revival of 1949–52 led to a dramatic burst of additions, but membership, quite shockingly, fell by twenty-two to a new low of 126 within four years of the revival (1957). Such decline continued through the rest of the twentieth century.

CHAPTER 10

Revival Advance: West

Carloway

The Church of Scotland minister in Carloway was the Rev. Murdo MacLennan.[1] MacLennan had been helping with the services in both Barvas and Shader; now it was the turn of his parish to receive blessing. Early signs of revival came in January 1950, when an event that occurred became one of the most popular of the whole awakening. A concert and dance was to be held in Carloway, having been organised by Donald Macarthur, leader of the Galson Concert Party.

The Concert and Dance

This was the same evening that Willie Smith, who had been due to play the bagpipes at the Carloway event, was converted at a cottage meeting in Barvas, along with his piping colleague, Donald John Smith. The Rev. MacLennan and his wife had been present at that providential house gathering. With a deep longing for the youth of his own parish to come to Christ, the Carloway minister decided to call in along proceedings in the Carloway hall on his way home and tell of the wonderful salvation of the Shader pipers.

---

1. MacLennan was a native of Uig and served with the Royal Navy Marines during the First World War. He became minister of Carloway Church of Scotland in 1931.

This he did, arriving around 3.30 am, and entering via the back door of the hall. Allan Macarthur,[2] the headmaster's son, who was acting as emcee at the doo, was outraged at the sight of this dog-collared intruder. Never in living memory had anyone witnessed a minister attending a dance in Lewis! Demanding to see his ticket, the minister held up his Bible and declared that as the parish minister, this was the only ticket he required!

Carloway Hall

MacLennan had a brusque, fiery personality in keeping with his crop of red hair, but this evening he acted in a gentler, non-judgemental manner. He said he had heard a young lady sing in Gaelic as he neared the hall; could she now lead the audience in singing Psalm 139? An incensed Allan was by now almost hysterical with rage and his mother sought to calm him. It was agreed the Psalm would be sung and some of the audience joined in as it was rendered. Then the minister testified to the conversion of the pipers in Barvas, pointedly asking those present if they

---

2. Macarthur recalled that as he passed the Barvas church on his way to Carloway that night, Duncan Campbell was holding a meeting. 'I had my accordion with me, and I began playing it as hard as I could, thinking I was going to drown out whatever was going on there, little knowing what was going to happen to myself in a matter of five or six hours in Carloway!' (Allan Macarthur, on *'Revival in our Times'*).

would be as happy and fulfilled the following morning as these young men now were.

A sense of God's holiness pervaded the building and several young men and women began to weep for mercy. As the minister and his wife were about to leave for home, Allan approached him to apologise for his outburst, then ran out to the bus parked outside, where he wept profusely, broken by God. In particular, words sung from Psalm 139 had pierced Allan's heart. 'It was just as if something had hit me right between the eyes,' Allan later recalled. 'I know now what it was – the power of God in that place. I had met with God; it was a face-to-face experience with God.'[3]

All attempts to revive the dance failed; instead, the partiers quietly left the hall in solemnity and deep thought.[4] Many from Carloway had already attended Campbell's meetings in Barvas. This latest incident served to quicken the sense of spiritual awakening across the parish.[5]

Spiritual Blockage

Duncan Campbell came to hold a three-week mission in Carloway in the latter half of February 1950. MacLennan had prepared the way for it – calling his congregation to six weeks of dedicated prayer. 'To your knees, God's people – pray, pray, pray!' he implored them. If they complied, he promised, 'God

---

3. ibid.

4. Rev. Jack Macarthur, *Testimony of Revival*, Duncan Campbell Lectures, Faith Mission Bible College, Edinburgh, 18.02.2000, audio tape. MacLennan was later introduced at events, even on mainland Scotland, as 'the minister who went to the Carloway dance!'

5. An early American report of this incident incorrectly states, among other errors, that when the power of God came upon the dancers, '20 were saved' and the dancehall became 'a mission hall' (*The Pentecostal Evangel*, 19.11.1950).

will open the windows of heaven to pour out His blessing, and there shall be no room to contain it.'[6]

MacLennan became good friends with Campbell, who stayed with him in the manse during his visits. The Carloway cleric rejoiced greatly when his own daughter, Margaret, home on leave from nursing training in Edinburgh, became one of the first to turn to Christ during the movement in her father's parish.[7]

Rev Murdo MacLennan

At first there had been little sign of a breakthrough, but after a week Campbell could report, 'Revival has come to this parish.' Interest was intensified by it being communion season. Campbell said of his meetings, 'We simply cannot get the people away … practically every house in Carloway has visitors who have come to stay for the weekend.' The majority of people attending the meetings were Free Church people.

---

6. Murdo MacLennan, *'Intimations,'* quoted in Peckham, *Sounds from Heaven*, p. 82.

7. Margaret's sister, Johan, had given her life to Christ a year or two earlier, aged eighteen, and had already moved to Edinburgh before the revival in Carloway commenced.

Despite these most encouraging scenes, the going was tough, and Campbell strongly sensed that 'the enemy is at work.'[8] The full breakthrough he was seeking did not occur, and when he revisited Carloway a year later, he was disappointed to find the going 'stiff.' Despite the goodly number who had professed Christ the previous year and who were still 'very bright,' generally the parish was 'dead and indifferent to all that is happening.'[9]

The evangelist asked for prayer that revival might come once again. At a later date (early 1952), Campbell referred to the 'bitter opposition and misunderstanding' which hindered the work of revival since it first broke out in Carloway. For almost two years after that initial outbreak, he believed, 'little has been seen here' in the way of a deep movement of the Spirit of God.[10]

Arnol

Arnol, a community in the parish of Barvas and located three miles south of Barvas parish church, was a Free Church stronghold. Services held in the Free Church *tigh-coinneamh* (meeting house) attracted many, before, during and after the revival. Church of Scotland numbers were, comparatively, very low. Around five or six people walked the three miles or so to attend worship in Barvas Church of Scotland each Sunday morning.

In addition, a service was held each Sunday evening in the Arnol meeting house – as they were in Shader and Borve – there being no church building in the village. Conducted by the minister, lay missionary or elders, these attracted just a handful. The weekly prayer meeting in the same building had for years been led by a godly elder and deacon; at the time of the revival, few, other than these two faithfuls, attended.

---

8. Duncan Campbell, FM Report, 01.03.1950.

9. ibid., 26.04.1951.

10. ibid., 27.02.1952.

While awakening was flourishing throughout most of Barvas and Ness, Arnol remained aloof to the movement. With the news of Campbell's intended mission in the village, meetings in opposition to the revival were specially arranged to coincide with and counter it, many people coming from across the island to support them. These were held in the Free Church meeting house, located just two hundred yards from where Campbell was holding his.

Arnol meeting hall

Despite the vigorous opposition, within a few days of the mission opening at the end of April, the evangelist reported that his main difficulty was accommodating all those now coming to hear him, the great majority from outwith the community. 'We were crowded out last night,' Campbell noted, 'notwithstanding the fact that the island was swept with a snow storm.'[11]

Arnol's Outstanding Night
Yet still a spiritual breakthrough evaded them. It was suggested that an evening of waiting on God be held, and a local couple, God-fearing though not converted, offered their farmhouse

---

11. ibid., 26.04.1950.

for this purpose. Around thirty gathered one spring evening at 10a Arnol after a service in the local meeting house. The going was tough, and prayers seemed stiff and formal. Then, around midnight, Campbell turned to John Smith, the Barvas blacksmith, and asked him to pray.

Smith raised his hand high and prayed for quite some time, before raising the tempo and declaring, 'O God, You made a promise to pour water upon him that is thirsty and floods upon the dry ground, and Lord, it's not happening ... I stand before You as an empty vessel, thirsting for You and for a manifestation of Your power ....O God, Your honour is at stake. I now challenge You to fulfil your covenant engagement and do what You promised to do.'[12]

Some testified that at that very moment the granite house in which they were gathered shook; dishes on the sideboard rattled, and one person suggested there had been an earthquake tremor. 'Now it was nearing two o'clock in the morning,' Campbell noted. 'What happened? The house shook. A jug on a sideboard fell onto the floor and broke. A minister beside me said, "An earth tremor."'[13]

One young convert was sitting on the crowded stairs beside two unsaved neighbours, Christina Campbell and Donald MacLeod (both from Arnol). He recalled that both neighbours had been dozing off, but in a moment were wide awake and under deep conviction of sin. The two began to pray for mercy, Christina weeping and crying aloud for help. Both were converted that night.[14]

---

12. Woolsey, *Channel of Revival*, pp. 132–3.

13. Campbell, *Revival in the Hebrides*, p. 48.

14. Donald Macleod was a thirty-three-year-old weaver at the time of his conversion. When asked who had the biggest influence in leading him to Christ he replied with tears, 'No one! Only the Holy Spirit of God' (Allen, *Catch the Wind*, p. 166).

The house that 'shook'

Campbell recalled a biblical precedent for this unusual event (Acts 4), and, pronouncing the benediction around 2.20 am, went outside. Here he found others gathering around in distress of soul, some carrying chairs, concerned that there wouldn't be enough room for them in the hall. 'I saw the whole community alive,' Campbell testified. 'The Arnol revival broke out. And, oh, what a sweeping revival! I don't believe there was a single house in the village that wasn't shaken by God.'[15]

One witness spoke of 'Arnol's outstanding night' ending with a blessed cottage meeting which closed with the same Shader blacksmith singing (in Gaelic):

Praise God for He is good,
For still His mercies lasting be,
Let God's redeemed say so,
Who He from the enemy's hand did free.
And gather them out of the lands,
From north, south, east and west.[16]

---

15. Campbell, *Revival in the Hebrides*, p. 48.

16. Psalm 107: 1–3.

Stream of Blessing

A stream of divine blessing was poured out on the district, and during succeeding nights many professions of faith were made. In particular, meetings held one night in two neighbouring houses (26 and 27 Arnol) witnessed a surprising number of conversions and it was this that many regarded as the night of real spiritual breakthrough in the village.

By May 10th, Campbell could testify to being 'in the midst of a glorious revival here. Opposition has vanished, and the whole district is moved. People are being saved at work, and in the shops work is being suspended; churches are crowded, and crowds outside ....So deep was the distress of many that we had to remain helping them until the morning.'[17]

Campbell referred to his time in Arnol as 'the most fruitful of the revival' so far, one interesting feature being the number of middle-aged people who found the Saviour. It was reckoned that twenty-four people put their faith in Christ in Arnol – a remarkable number for such a small community – and the majority of conversions were said to have proved lasting. Another effect was that the '*bothan*' in the area became obsolete and a number of men who frequented it were instead to be found at the prayer meetings.

One who found the Lord at the time of Arnol's revival was Chirsty Maggie MacPhail. She came away from hearing Campbell preach, thinking, 'This has nothing to do with any man. This is something between God and me.' In her own room at home, a spiritual battle raged within her mind and soul for several hours. 'At a point of desperation something happened that I have never been able to explain. It seemed as if a cool breeze went through the room and I heard a clear voice say, "*Jesus of Nazareth passeth by*." It was so real that I put out my hand to touch Him and said earnestly, "Don't pass me," – and He didn't! I, as it were, touched

---

17. Duncan Campbell, FM Report, 10.05.1950.

Him and He saved me in that instant. The presence of God in that room was so real. Joy welled up within me and I knew that I was His.'[18]

It was said that where previously, two or three men constituted the prayer meeting on Thursday evenings and about five people attended the morning service on Sunday, there was now hardly a single family that did not engage in family worship both morning and night. In a majority of these homes, at least one person had got converted over recent months.

Donald MacPhail

The best-known of Arnol's converts was Donald MacPhail. As a schoolboy of fifteen, Donald came under deep conviction before he had heard of Duncan Campbell or knew that any revival was taking place. One day, walking on the moorland, questions arose in his mind as to the meaning of life. He sat down and sobbed, inwardly aware that he was lost. He turned to the sheep around him, envying the fact that they did not suffer from anxious thoughts!

Sometime afterwards, Donald heard of the minister who had arrived on Lewis, creating a commotion everywhere he went. He was apparently an unusual preacher, who didn't dress in black, and who once broke a pulpit ledge by banging his fist on it when preaching. This sounded like a spectacle worth seeing! Then Donald became aware of groups of children who were gathering together during school intervals, their lives somehow changed by the meetings they had been attending. Even unconverted pupils would enquire of recently 'saved' classmates as to what had happened at the meeting the previous night and who had been converted.

All this created in Donald a curiosity to go and hear Campbell for himself. When the evangelist came to Arnol, Donald was one of the first to occupy the back seat in the meeting hall. The

18. Peckham, *Sounds from Heaven*, p. 214.

meetings continued nightly, while two homes were opened up for after-meetings, beginning around 11 pm. Young Donald attended them all. Something about the atmosphere of the gatherings made him want to go back. He hardly slept at nights for turning over in his mind all that he had heard.

Donald MacPhail

At a house meeting in Arnol in the second week of the mission, people suddenly became aware of the presence of God. 'It was as if the power of God swept through the house,' Donald shared. Many came under deep conviction, leading to heavy sighs and groans. Donald, about to leave for home around midnight, noticed a man praying at the side of the wall outside. Expressing to him his own anxiety, the man immediately led the teenager back into the house.

'Kenneth Macdonald from Shader was praying and the presence of God overwhelmed me,' observed Donald. 'It was as though God came upon me and His presence went through me. I was suddenly released. I knew that I was forgiven and had peace with God.' At least five others found peace in believing that same evening.[19]

Largely as a result of Donald's witness, his dear mother was converted in church the very next night, and his father later the same week, their home becoming a centre of meetings. Such was

---

19. Peckham, *Sounds from Heaven*, p. 234.

the spiritual stirring in the Westside district at this time that Donald estimated that around thirty of the two hundred pupils at the junior secondary school at Shawbost turned to Christ in just a few months. One pupil in particular was known for his foul language. Converted during the revival, this boy later became a church elder.[20]

Donald's Witness

One visiting journalist was taken to meet Donald at his home in Arnol. He described him as 'a quiet, humble lad, with a shy manner. He is the typical schoolboy, tall and thin, with no outstanding characteristics, but a deep devotion to the Lord Jesus Christ, and a most unusual prayer life; he spends hours every day communing with God. He seems to walk in the very presence of God. I sensed this immediately when I met him.'[21]

Indeed, when MacPhail later transferred to the Nicolson Institute in Stornoway, a teacher testified that as the teenager walked into the classroom one day, she felt the presence of Christ so strongly that she had to leave the room to hide her tears. Meanwhile, the rector, Mr Addison, felt the need to summon him into his study to complain of his lack of homework and failure in exams due to attending so many revival meetings. At the same time, ironically, teachers were organising buses for pupils who wanted to attend these gatherings, also providing Scripture Union notes for follow-up work.

MacPhail became an outstanding witness in his community – having a significant influence on many family members, schoolfriends and neighbours, particularly in Arnol and Shawbost. He also quickly became a distinguished man of prayer in the wider Lewis revival. Campbell was particularly taken with the

20. The communion roll for Shawbost Free Church increased by fifteen in 1953. There was no Church of Scotland in the district (though there was a small meeting hall).

21. *The Pentecostal Evangel*, 19.11.1950.

spiritual precociousness of young Donald, who was often called to assist the evangelist with his bold, discerning intercession in various missions he conducted in Lewis.[22] Campbell said that once when visiting his home, he found the lad on his knees in prayer in the barn. Aware of his approach, Donald turned to the minister and said, 'Excuse me for a time, please, Mr Campbell, I'm having an audience with the King'![23]

Campbell said that Donald was known as '*The Evan Roberts of Lewis,*' though it transpires that nobody on the island knew him by that moniker. It's hardly a name MacPhail would have felt appropriate; a leading evangelist in the Welsh revival of 1904, Roberts might be better compared with Campbell himself, though the Scottish evangelist was far too modest to make that comparison. To further claim, as Campbell did, that 'more were saved through Donald MacPhail than through all Lewis ministers' is highly dubious.

The House that Shook

Few people have been left uninspired by the remarkable story of 'the house that shook,' and countless revival pilgrims visiting Lewis have requested to have the building pointed out.[24] Campbell generally put the number of people present at the meeting in

---

22. About a year after his conversion, MacPhail received a clear call into the ministry. After a severe battle within his soul, he yielded totally, and spent several years at Bible College before going on to serve as a missionary for many years in Yemen.

23. A young non-believer spoke of the profound influence an introductory meeting with Donald had on him, when Donald greeted him at a London church one Sunday morning while doing missionary training. 'There are some men and women you come across in life and you know you've met with Jesus,' wrote the young man, who gave his life to Christ as a result. Many years later, a man testified that at a house meeting in Lewis in 2001, when Donald entered the room, the whole atmosphere changed, such was the presence of God that he carried.

24. Photos of very different buildings have appeared in published accounts in attempts to identify the house in question.

Donald & Bella Smith's house (10a Arnol) at around thirty. In one or two reports, however, he sets the figure as high as seventy. As one researcher stated, 'With Campbell mixing up some of the information, it does bring a question to the authenticity of the event.'[25]

You'd think that the literal shaking of a large two-storey granite house would cause more than a few dishes to rattle, which is all the early accounts refer to. Only in the above-noted, much later account did Campbell claim that as much as a jug on the sideboard fell onto the floor and broke. No one has ever claimed that the floor shook beneath their feet, or any other typical response one might expect from such an 'earth-shattering' occurrence. And as they were to find out the next day, no other house in the area was shaken that night, nor did anyone else feel a tremor.

As to the public response to such a supernatural scenario, it's true that these were heady days, and so many exciting things were happening in people's lives as a result of the surprising visitation of God's Spirit. Nevertheless, one would think that with such a momentous occurrence as a house shaking, word would spread very fast, and the entire island would soon be talking about it. In fact, other young converts living in the very parish where the event occurred said they only heard about it a considerable time afterwards. The house-shaking story appears to have been popularised only on its retelling by Duncan Campbell well after the revival.

Strangely, Campbell makes no mention of the shaking house in his on-the-job weekly FM reports. Nor does he do so in his Keswick address in 1952, even though he does refer to the prayer meeting in question. Instead, the first recorded report comes a few years later, in Campbell's official account of the revival. One young man who was present that evening later testified that

---

25. Norman Afrin, *A Critical Analysis of the 1949–1953 Lewis Revival*, MRes thesis, Glasgow University 2018, p. 46.

'discussions were had' in the years after the revival as to whether the house really did shake: some questioned the reality of it. He personally had been sitting in a side-room just off the kitchen where Campbell was speaking. He attested to not feeling any tremor, and to wondering what the fuss was about.

Other testimonies raise similar concerns. The Rev. Mackay of Barvas mentions 'Arnol's big night' in his report on the revival in 1952 but makes no mention of a house shaking, even though he was present that very evening. Nor does Donald Macleod – a native of Arnol who was also in the house that night – when sharing his own testimony.[26] It has also been claimed on good authority that a convert of the Arnol revival (who was not present on the night in question but who knew everyone who was), later stated that he was never of the belief that the house literally shook.

Some have wondered whether in this crowded home, someone may inadvertently have knocked against the kitchen dresser, causing the dishes on it to rattle, which would have awoken anyone dozing off, and might have led one or two present to later suggest that perhaps there had been a small earth tremor. Then again, Campbell was known to be demonstrative in his preaching; often gesticulating with his hands and thumping on the lectern with his fist (on one occasion he broke a bone in his wrist when doing so!). It is quite likely that at a significant point in his address, Campbell might have banged his fist on the dresser or kitchen table, leading to reverberations elsewhere in the room.

Of course, it's impossible to either verify or disprove this intriguing story, especially seventy years after the event. Some would say that extraordinary claims require extraordinary evidence. Others will insist that it barely matters whether the house literally shook or not – what matters is that such was the spiritual intensity inside the building that it *seemed* to some as

---

26. Allen, *Catch the Wind*, p. 166.

if it did.[27] And perhaps that's all that counts. Either way, it is a story that is likely to capture the hearts and imaginations of a great many people for a long time to come.[28]

Bragar and Shawbost

At the start of 1951, a mission was held in Bragar, a village located in the south of Barvas parish. This was a predominantly Free Church community, and Campbell noted that the 'first few days were stiff.' The break came on the sixth night, after which the difficulty was to accommodate the people in the small meeting house. 'Windows and passages were crowded, and even then some had to stand outside.'[29] So many turned up in buses, vans and cars that word had to be sent to one district to stop them. 'Still,' Campbell noted, 'people gathered and stood outside the hall for three hours, till a second meeting commenced.'[30] Many of those apparently converted were men.

This may have been the spark that prompted Campbell to sense 'a remarkable change in the attitude of the Free Church,' during which period most converts were from that denomination.[31] Things appear to have become hardened again by the following year. For when Campbell conducted a ten-day mission in nearby Shawbost in March 1952, he noted that the meetings in the

27. My own mother claimed that one particularly stormy night when she was young and upstairs in bed, the large stone-built house in which she lived literally shook, terrifying her. No amount of reasoning in later years could change her mind (Tom Lennie, *'Rousay Remembered,'* self-published, 2017, p. 30). Both that Orkney structure and the house in Arnol (since renovated) are still standing strong many decades later.

28. Accounts of buildings being physically shaken by a supernatural power feature in other revival accounts too, not least on the very same island around fourteen years previously (see *Glory in the Glen*, pp. 360-1).

29. FM Report 17.01.1951. This update from Campbell was inadvertently missed out from the FM Reports as published in *Sounds from Heaven*.

30. Duncan Campbell, FM Report, 24.01.1951.

31. ibid., 20.12.1950.

small Church of Scotland sanctuary were 'bitterly attacked by (elements in) the Free Church, and this has caused a measure of unrest among the converts.' Nevertheless, as in Bragar, this didn't stop the Spirit moving. 'The crowds at our closing meeting exceeded anything we saw in Lewis,' Campbell observed. 'People who could not get in sat in the buses outside, while many had to return home.'[32]

There were one or two communities in the parish of Barvas in which Campbell did not hold a mission – such as the villages of Brue in the south and Borve to the north, neither of which had a church. There was, however, a missionary house in Borve; this was inhabited by the Barvas lay missionary James Macdonald, who acted as assistant to the Rev. Murray Mackay. Adjoined to the house was a small hall with pews, and here Campbell held a number of meetings. In addition, many from both Borve and Brue went to hear the evangelist preach in neighbouring districts, as a result of which not a few were converted.

Callanish

Campbell returned to Carloway for a third mission in February 1952, this one based in Callanish, to the south of the expansive parish. The campaign began with a 'very small meeting.' As attendance increased night by night, Campbell sensed things were 'beginning to move,' and he called out again for increased prayer, knowing that breakthrough would not come without his intercessors gaining victory first.

Thankfully, things were about to change for the better, at least in this one community – perhaps in direct answer to the very prayers the evangelist requested. At last, Campbell could report, 'The spirit of revival has gripped this parish ... and there is an air of expectancy in the whole district. We had a meeting on Saturday night in a house and it was crowded with unsaved young people. The four beds in the house were packed with them!

---

32. ibid., 02.04.1952.

All the rooms were full and beds were used for seating. We never witnessed anything like this in Carloway before.'[33] So determined was he to hold onto and extend the blessing that Campbell found it necessary to change his programme and remain in the district.

One Free Church member from Carloway went to hear Campbell speak in Callanish as a teenager, but found him 'rather extreme. His preaching was flowery, and he was unnecessarily loud.' P.M. said that at one point Campbell made a vivid description of the lost in hell, who he said now wished they had taken heed of gospel preaching while alive on the earth. 'This spoke close to many hearts,' P.M. recalled, 'and some folk actually cried out, and a few even fainted.' But she felt there was a danger that 'some were following Duncan Campbell rather than following God.' Another concern was that 'many started out through attending Campbell's meetings, but not all continued in their faith.'[34]

P.M. said that although not a Christian then, 'I knew my Bible, and I knew the Catechism, and I felt that Campbell went to the borders of Arminianism by suggesting that God can't do anything until you allow Him to.' She found Campbell's addresses 'very moving. I could quite easily be moved to tears, yet still not be spoken to in the heart. Others, though,' she added, 'were converted through folk testifying to them.' All in all, P.M., who came to personal faith in Christ some years later, felt the revival was 'a spiritually lively time, and, apart from one or two ministers, there was no bad feeling between Christians at that time.'[35]

In due course, Campbell was able to report from Callanish, 'The Spirit of God is working in the parish, and it is evident that a deep hunger for God has laid hold upon the people.... We had a

---

33. ibid., 05.03.1952.

34. Personal communication with P.M., Carloway, 23.09.2002.

35. ibid.

mighty meeting on Friday night. Several young men from Arnol came to our assistance, and as one of them prayed, God came down in mighty power, and before his prayer ended souls were rejoicing in deliverance. This meeting will stand out as one of the great meetings of the revival.'[36]

Meetings were being held in the afternoon, evening and on until the early hours of the following morning. People had been coming from other areas, including by boat from Crulivig in Uig. As the mission drew to a close, Campbell rejoiced that interest and blessing continued up to the end, but confessed, 'we did not witness the same move as in some other districts.'[37] Indeed, all three of his Carloway missions had been hard-going – and were among the toughest of all his campaigns in Lewis over the course of the revival.

---

36. Duncan Campbell, FM Report, 12.03.1952.

37. ibid., 19.03.1952.

CHAPTER 11

Revival Advance: East

Point

Duncan Campbell came to hold a series of meetings on the east Lewis peninsula of Point in November 1950. He jotted in his weekly report, 'We are having very large meetings. During the weekend we had as many as twenty seeking the Saviour at one meeting, and I addressed four (largely attended) meetings between Sunday and Monday morning.' Despite such favourable signs, Campbell was aware that 'the community is not yet stilled as in revival ... we have had a good week here, but not revival so far.'[1]

Divine Power in Point

Just a week later, Campbell could rejoice, 'We are in the midst of revival, and what scenes! The whole district is stirred. I counted eight buses taking the people to church today, not to mention cars and vans.' One farmer who had lived for a while in Canada was heard to say, 'I had to come home to my native island to find my Saviour!' Campbell remarked that men who never went to church, and who were regarded as 'hopeless, have been gloriously saved. In one community all the young men are saved or in deep distress of soul.'[2]

Another report claimed that at 3 am one mid-November morning, 'the roads were still full of people walking to and

1. Duncan Campbell, FM Report, 15.11.1950.

2. ibid., 22.11.1950

from the church, and practically every house in the village had lights burning. In three days, fifty people, most of them men, experienced life-transforming conversion.' Many of the converts were heads of families, multiplying the number of lives touched. Campbell called it the mightiest wave of divine power that he had yet seen on the island.[3] The mission in Point closed at the end of November, 'amidst scenes of revival, meetings continuing all through the night, with souls being saved at each meeting.'[4]

Campbell quickly developed a friendship with both the Rev. Harry Mackinnon of the Church of Scotland, and the Rev. William Campbell, minister of the Free Church in Knock, where revival had broken out some months prior to Campbell's arrival on the island. The evangelist often visited the Free Church minister, and while the latter disagreed with some aspects of Campbell's theology, he nevertheless saw clearly that God was ministering through him, and he supported him in his work. Somewhat unusual, though by no means unique between the two main denominations on Lewis at that time, William Campbell and Harry Mackinnon were also good friends and complemented each other's ministries.

Kenneth Macdonald

When Duncan Campbell came to Point, many in the area had already heard him preach in Barvas, to which location bus and van loads of people had often journeyed during the preceding year. Among them were the parents of Kenneth Macdonald. Kenneth remembers them returning home from meetings as late as four in the morning, and Kenny would invariably be woken up by the sound of his father singing psalms as he made his way to bed.

Kenny had thought of giving his life to Christ, but had invariably been put off by thinking of two elderly church-going

---

3. *The Pentecostal Evangel*, 01.04.1951.

4. Duncan Campbell, FM Report, 29.11.1950.

neighbours who always looked so stern and miserable. His most frequent prayer was, 'Lord, save me when I'm fifty or sixty!' With an increased longing for answers to life, he decided to attend a cottage meeting in his aunt's home in Garrabost.

Kenneth Macdonald

Following this, a further meeting was intimated in a room upstairs. Heart pounding and mind in turmoil, Kenny stood up to attend. As he did, he prayed, 'Lord, if you'll take me, I'll give you my all.' In that second, his life was changed; he was born again, and joy and love filled his heart. As he made his way up the stairs, an elder grabbed hold of him, hugging him with tears of delight. From that day on Kenny followed Campbell to every service and meeting he could get to, eager to soak in the Word of God.

When he went to appear before the kirk session at the following communion, Kenny was daunted by the questions he felt might get thrown at him by authoritative, censorious elders. Instead, the elders before him wept openly at the transformation they had already observed in the young man's life. He was accepted as a member at once. With a fine voice, he was also asked to 'precent' at meetings, before later moving to the mainland to study for the ministry.[5]

Norman Campbell

Norman Campbell had a remarkable testimony to share. One evening, Duncan Campbell and the Rev. MacLennan of Carloway were both preaching. The latter speaker was deeply stirred, and at one point said to the congregation, 'You are here tonight, but there was a time when you were in the stern of a ship, praying to the Lord and promising Him that if He would get you out of there alive, you would follow Him and serve Him. Have you kept your promise? What are you going to do tonight?'

Norman Campbell

Norman at once recalled an occasion when he and a number of other Lewis men were indeed put in the stern of a ship and some prayed. Feeling spoken to in his heart, Norman joined others in the church hall and was prayed for by Campbell. 'As I stood to pray, my chains were loosed and I was set free ….It happened in a moment. I was launched out on a sea of love. I felt that I was

---

5. Personal communication with Kenneth Macdonald, 20.08.2001.

no longer in the flesh. I left the hall feeling as if I were swimming in a sea of love.'[6]

Norman boarded a bus, which took him to a cottage meeting. Half the passengers went to one house; the other half to another. Norman walked in to find a table prepared and folk sitting down to eat supper. But Norman felt so caught up in the Spirit that he couldn't understand why anyone would want to eat! He was overwhelmed with a sense of the love of God.[7]

Margaret Macleod

Spiritual stirrings were still occurring in the Free Church in Knock around this time as well. As a young district nurse in Point, Margaret Macleod enjoyed the usual forms of worldly entertainment, such as dancing, music, and especially 'the pictures.' Every other night and on Saturdays she would go into Stornoway to see a film with friends.

Gradually, though, she became aware that a sense of personal fulfilment was evading her, and one Sunday in 1952 she made up her mind to go to church. A missionary from Barvas was preaching that morning on Ephesians 2: *'Christ and him crucified.'* Margaret realised she wanted to know Christ, but didn't know how to. Bowing her head for some time in conflict of mind, some in the congregation thought she had gone to sleep!

The following weekend an open-air 'road dance' was being held in her village and a friend urged Margaret to go with her. Normally keen to support such occasions, Margaret went along but found herself strangely removed from the merry-making taking place, and went alone to sit on a big stone overlooking the proceedings – the remains of a Nissen hut used during the war. Suddenly she took to leave, running the whole way home, yet at the same time aware that it was herself she was trying to run from, and that even at home she wouldn't be able to find the

---

6. Peckham, *Sounds from Heaven*, p. 186.

7. ibid., pp. 186–7.

peace she was desperately yearning for. All she knew was that she didn't know Christ.

That Sunday, Margaret was back in church, hearing the Rev. Campbell preach on Genesis 24:58, '*Wilt thou go with this man?*' Margaret was riveted, feeling the sermon was directed solely at her. She knew she wanted to close in with Christ, but 'self' loudly shouted 'No!' With the biblical question posed by Campbell confronting her again and again, '*Wilt thou go with this man?*' Margaret finally gave in: 'Yes,' she said, quietly but assuredly. 'Yes, I will go with this man!' Peace immediately flooded her soul and mind and she walked out of the meeting a new creature in Christ. Soon Margaret joined the church in Knock, where fifty years later, she was still a member.[8]

North Lochs

Kinloch

Well before his mission in Kinloch in February 1951, and before any indication that revival was going to break out there, Campbell visited this mid-Lochs area, and made clear his belief that 'reinforcements' were necessary – i.e., the prayer support of faithful intercessors.

His mission was due to begin on Sunday 11th February. Some from this congregation had been converted at meetings in Barvas. The Church of Scotland minister in Kinloch was the Rev. Angus MacKillop, a native of Berneray, who had been inducted to the charge in 1944.[9] Campbell arrived in the parish two days early, only to find that many had gathered for a service. So, his

---

8. Personal conversation with Margaret Macleod, 18.03.2012. Indeed, as she related the story of her conversion half a century previously, Margaret was moved to tears, fully aware of the never-failing grace of her Saviour who had remained wonderfully precious to her through those years.

9. MacKillop moved to Carloway following his ministry in Kinloch, but soon after retired due to ill-health.

mission began there and then. Early meetings were uneventful, but Campbell saw many hopeful signs.

His hopes were not disappointed. A movement began in the first meeting of the day, among believers; a meeting which Campbell felt sure, 'will not soon be forgotten in this parish.' Similar blessing at subsequent meetings led Campbell to be 'full of praise to God for what our eyes have seen and our ears heard ....The breath of revival has come to this side of the island, and there is great rejoicing among God's people ....Again last night men and women were in great distress. People are coming from all over the island, some a distance of twenty miles.'[10]

The movement continued to blossom. The following week Campbell described as 'a most glorious week, probably the best of the whole revival. Nowhere has there been such a sense of the presence of God or greater interest shown.'[11] Meetings were being held in churches, halls, the school, and even one night in a shooting lodge, where over 170 gathered and a deep spirit of spiritual anxiety was evidenced – the gathering continuing till three in the morning.

Leurbost

With such intense interest, Campbell felt led to cancel his next mission and continue his work in Lochs, now moving to Leurbost, further north in the parish. This was a smaller congregation than that of Kinloch. 'People are coming from all over, especially Free Church people,' Campbell noted in his week-to-week reports. 'God alone could have brought about the change in their attitude.'[12]

At the little Leurbost church, so many people from a neighbouring district gathered for the service long before the meeting was due to begin (11 pm) that the church was soon

10. Duncan Campbell, FM Report, 21.02.1951.

11. ibid.

12. ibid., 14.03.1951.

packed full and the regular congregation were content to sit in the vehicles that the visitors had vacated! A further (cottage) meeting was arranged which continued until three in the morning.

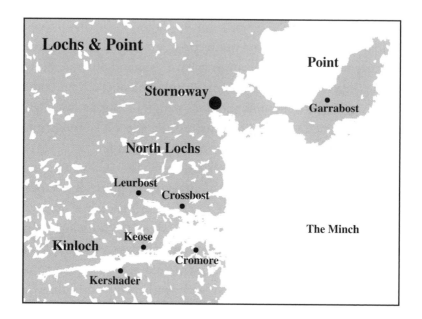

Looking back on his mission in Lochs, Campbell wrote, 'Interest was greater than in any other part of the island. On the last two nights, the church was crowded three times, between seven o'clock and two in the morning, and many sought the Saviour.'[13] Leurbost native Donald Maclean confirmed Campbell's report. 'A great many people from Leurbost went to Duncan Campbell's mission in the district, including a lot of Free Church folk. Many lives were transformed as a result.'[14]

Weekly FM Reports
A main source of information in this study is the weekly reports that Duncan Campbell wrote to the Faith Mission headquarters

---

13. ibid., 28.03.1951.

14. Personal communication with Donald (Dinnie) Maclean, 23.09.2002.

throughout his extended mission in Lewis. This may seem ironic given this author's insistence of the evangelist's unreliability at relating events. But such unreliability was mainly in regard to specific stories he told, usually years after the events in question. In distinction, his weekly reports, providing brief details about ongoing missions, are generally considered to be accurate, there being few evidences of definite inconsistencies.

Even here, though, one has to be wary of references to numbers of people 'seeking salvation,' meaning, showing evidence of having given their lives to Christ. For example, during his Lochs campaign, Campbell wrote of forty-seven who 'sought the Saviour' in just one meeting. This is a remarkably high figure, and, given what we know of the movement in Lochs, almost certainly excessive. Elsewhere, we're told of 'over forty seeking salvation' at the close of the Tarbert mission, while following three nights' meetings in Garrabost, Point, 'fifty people, most of them men, experienced life-transforming conversion.' In both cases the true figure is thought to have been somewhat lower.

In his reports, Campbell also had the (perhaps natural) habit of considering the mission in which he was currently engaged to be the biggest or greatest experienced of the entire revival. So, his Tarbert mission (May '50) was 'the most fruitful of the revival' so far; whilst that in Point in Nov 1950 he termed 'the mightiest wave of divine power that I have yet seen on the island'. Meanwhile, of his Lochs mission (Feb '51) he wrote, 'Interest was greater than in any other part of the island', while crowds in Shawbost (Mar '52) 'exceeded anything we saw in Lewis'.

Use of Word 'Revival'

Campbell frequently used phrases like 'a most gracious move of the Spirit' or 'a most remarkable move of God'[15] in his weekly reports. It is essential to understand what he meant by them. It would be natural to assume he is talking about definite outbreaks

---

15. e.g., Campbell, *Revival in the Hebrides*, p. 34.

of revival. But this would be to misinterpret him. In general, when Campbell wanted to note definite revival, he used the 'R' word specifically; his use of terms like 'a remarkable move of God's Spirit' was generally a reference to a break in the spiritual atmosphere that didn't necessarily constitute revival.

Nevertheless, one wonders if Campbell at times saw revival where it was not. On occasion he refers to revival having occurred sometime prior to his arrival in Lewis. For example, he spoke of his stint in a French hospital during First World War as a time of revival. He said that revival came to an unnamed town during his ministry in Falkirk.[16]

Campbell also made one or two intriguing references to revival occurring in diverse places on the heels of his Lewis mission. A couple of months after addressing meetings in Hastings in November 1952, the evangelist said that revival had broken out in the town, and that, among other things, 'people had been seen to fall in the streets as they came out of shops.'[17] And he spoke of revival attending his ministry in Skye in December 1953.[18] I have been unable to identify any other source specifying the occurrence of revival through Campbell's ministry in any of these locations.

Norman Maclean

Leurbost native Donald Maclean recalled 'one man who was well known in the area by name of Paddy Maclean. He had a significant drink problem. He used to convey folk in his van from all over Lochs to dances. He'd wait in his van all evening, then take them back home. He was one who went to hear Campbell preach in Leurbost.'[19]

---

16. Allen, *Catch the Wind*, p. 60.

17. *Portadown Times,* 23.01.1953.

18. Allen, *Catch the Wind*, pp. 201–3.

19. Personal communication with Donald (Dinnie) Maclean, 23.09.2002.

When the evangelist appeared to retell his very own life story, Paddy became angry with an elder whom he assumed had told Campbell about him. But the Spirit was speaking to his soul, and, frightened at the thought, Paddy got thoroughly inebriated. While driving home, he put his foot hard to the accelerator when he saw the police following him. In the safety of a friend's house, he jumped up on a chair in imitation of Campbell's preaching style.

But in coming days the '*cúram*' caught even firmer hold of him, and soon he was driving his car many miles across the lonely moor to hear Campbell preach in Arnol. 'Suddenly, in the middle of the moor, in the dusk, a light shone on the windscreen of the car. I didn't know what it was, but it forced me to stop. The sound of the engine was in my ears as sounds from hell itself, and the noise was so fearful that I would not wish a dog to spend a day there, never mind eternity!'[20]

Norman (Paddy) Maclean

As he continued his journey, Maclean met a minister, whom he stopped and asked directions to where Campbell was preaching that night. The minister told him to inquire at the police station.

20. Peckham, *Sounds from Heaven*, p. 255

A minister and a policeman! Maclean found this highly ironic given that these were the two types of men he most wanted to keep clear of! By chance he came across the home where Campbell was speaking; and as he entered, the preacher's words hit him; 'You're afraid of Christ, He who loves you more than your own mother ever did. His is a gentle loving hand and He is waiting to receive you now.'[21]

Afterwards, tea was served and then the singing began. As a young girl sang in Gaelic, *'A thighearna cuidich me, s'aithne dhuit m'fheum'* (*'Oh, Lord, help me, You know my need'*), these words, too, gripped him and he could resist no longer. When he got home in the early hours of the next morning, Paddy went out to his loom-shed, got down on his knees, and gave his life to the Lord. Heaven entered his heart and he rose a new man.

Going into his house, he cried to his family, 'Get up, get up. We're going to praise God!'[22] It was 2 am. He didn't need to tell his mother what had happened. She quickly realised that her longstanding prayers had finally been answered. Night after night for many months following his conversion, Paddy would continue to fill his grocery van with folk eager to hear the gospel, and take them to meetings in other districts.

Many came to know the Lord by this means, including several from his own family.[23] His mother's prediction that her son would go into full time service for the Lord also came true, for Paddy went on to become a Church of Scotland missionary.

Praying by the Road
A gamekeeper, Finlay Maciver, was another who played a significant role in bearing testimony to the mighty movings of

---

21. Personal communication with Donald (Dinnie) Maclean, 23.09.2002.

22. Peckham, *Sounds from Heaven*, p. 256.

23. He served for a time in North Uist, where, at a later date, he was aware of between five and ten Lewis men and women engaged in gospel work.

God in this parish. He rejoiced in the salvation of several of his children during the revival.

A popular story told by Campbell relates to him travelling early one morning by motor bike on the east side of the island to visit a minister in a district where revival hadn't yet come. He noticed a woman in her twenties kneeling in prayer by the side of the road. She had recently started a prayer meeting two nights a week with two teenagers from the area who had attended meetings in Barvas and had been converted. After praying for several months, God had given them assurance that revival was coming, and the woman was delighted to now find Campbell in the area. They prayed together by the road for some time.[24]

One of many lochans in North Lochs

Campbell goes on to tell of fourteen young men who were subsequently convicted and converted while discussing alcohol

---

24. Allen, *Catch the Wind*, pp. 81–3. The story is given added validity owing to the fact that Campbell pointed out the woman he had met by the roadside to Colin Peckham at a Stornoway convention many years later (Peckham, *Sounds from Heaven*, p. 115).

consumption outside their local dancehall. Fourteen years later, the evangelist discovered as many as eleven of these men serving as elders in the local church. Sadly, the story cannot be accepted as it stands, as none of the men have been identified; nor is there any record of anything like eleven converts going on to become elders in any Eastside church (note also the 'seven times' feature).

Seeking for Jesus

One of the most beautiful stories of the awakening in Lewis relates to a service in Lochs for which a lorry was being used to convey many anxious souls. The lorry broke down by the side of a loch several miles from their destination, and while the younger members of the group decided to carry on by foot, the older folk had no option but to reluctantly turn back. On their way home it came to them that if they could row across the loch, they would still be in time for a house meeting to be held after the service. They walked some distance to a village where they managed to secure a small dinghy; then they proceeded to row across the calm water to where the meeting was being held.

As they entered the house, Duncan Campbell, unaware of their venture, announced as his text, John 6:24: '*They also took shipping and came to Capernaum, seeking for Jesus.*' They too were seeking Jesus, and some found Him that night. As dawn was breaking, the congregation gathered by the shore to bid the joyous seafarers 'goodbye,' and a local minister led them in singing,

When all Thy mercies, O my God,
My rising soul surveys;
Transported with the view,
I'm lost, In wonder, love and praise ... ,[25]

---

25. Music: Thomas Tallis (c1567); Words: Joseph Addison (1712).

Revival Statistics: Kinloch

The church membership figures for Kinloch also include the South Lochs districts of Lemreway and Pairc, which, being part of Kinloch parish until the 1960s, was served by a mission station.

Professions of Faith: Kinloch[26]

Year	Total
1949	0
1950	**9**
1951	**4**
1952	**3**
1953	3

Stornoway

Other than individual meetings, Campbell held just one mission in Stornoway; this was a fortnight's campaign at the start of 1952. Apparently, the evangelist had pondered whether he should alter his simple gospel message – with its emphasis on sin and judgement – for the more sophisticated and southernised island capital. He felt clearly that he wasn't to alter it one bit.

At an early stage he reported, 'We are up against a good deal of opposition, and of a kind we did not experience before.'[27] The 'hard fighting' continued throughout the first week and into the second. 'Everything seemed to be against us ... and large gatherings and a few seeking the Saviour was all we could report.'

26. Kinloch church records forwarded by Rev. Iain Campbell, 16.06.2022.
27. Duncan Campbell, FM Report, 09.01.1952.

Stornoway

A breakthrough came during the second week, when 'a gracious wave of blessing' extended over the meetings. Visiting from Edinburgh, I. R. Govan of the Faith Mission wrote of one evening when 'the people stood on the last night by the Town Hall, reluctant to leave, and there at 11 pm, in the clear light of a northern summer evening, the voices of over six hundred were raised in the psalm of the revival:

Thou shalt arise, and mercy yet,
Thou to Mount Zion shalt extend.[28]

At one cottage meeting, as young Donald MacPhail was praying, Campbell recorded: 'God swept in, in power, and in a few minutes some people were prostrate on the floor, others with hands raised up fell back in a trance. We were in the midst of it until one o'clock in the morning.'[29] Despite such brief moments of victory, and a number of folk being converted, the Stornoway meetings failed to captivate the town in any significant manner,

28. Govan, *Spirit of Revival*, pp. 206–7.
29. Duncan Campbell, FM Report, 23.01.1952.

and the revival that was so prominent in country districts of Lewis bypassed the main centre of population on the island.[30]

* * *

Personal Trials

Campbell faced many personal trials during his years on Lewis, including a three-month period of inexplicable spiritual depression. In early May 1951, his mother passed away in Glasgow where she had, for some time, lived with a married daughter. At the same time, his own wife was laid up with rheumatism, and resided for a while with her daughter in Kilmarnock.

It was also around this time, the close of April 1951, that the evangelist developed a bad throat due to his constant preaching. The problem persisted, much to Campbell's annoyance. A month later and his voice was reported to be slowly improving; he travelled to Lewis, despite being advised not to, but didn't preach. The doctor's verdict at the start of June was not encouraging, and in July he journeyed to London for treatment. It was a most frustrating period for the evangelist, who was impatient to get back to his true calling. By early August, he was doing just that – preaching the gospel to unsaved souls on the Lewis island of Bernera.

A year later, in July 1952, Campbell was ordered to rest for some weeks owing to unspecified ill-health. Then in early August, he ploughed his motorcycle into the back of a lorry on a narrow single-track road, cracking one of his ribs (on a previous occasion he struck a ram). Being strapped up, he was able to get about, albeit with some discomfort. In the following month there came

---

30. It has been said that nearly as many people from Stornoway came to Christ during the Billy Graham relays in 1955 as did during Campbell's mission in the town three years earlier.

news of the sudden death of his blind brother, Donald, also a deeply committed Christian.[31]

Praying in a Barn

The story of Duncan Campbell's conversion is worth sharing briefly here. In his home parish of Ardchattan, West Argyll, in 1913, the fifteen-year-old came under deep conviction one evening while playing bagpipes at a local concert. Forced to leave the event early, and walking home in great turmoil of spirit, he passed by a hall where a Faith Mission prayer meeting was in progress.

Slipping inside, where his father was, at that moment, on his knees praying for his son, his sense of conviction became even stronger, and he had to leave the hall. Arriving home, his mother urged him to go to the barn to make peace with God. Duncan knelt on some hay in the barn and surrendered his life to Christ, peace and joy flooding his soul.

The young lad quickly connected himself to the work of the Faith Mission, and it was at a Mission outreach held in a large barn shortly after that a teenage Shona Gray committed her life to the Lord. Twelve years later, Shona became Duncan's wife.

Many years later still, Campbell informs us of a number of 'barn-praying' incidents that occurred during the revival:

1. Young Donald MacPhail in Arnol;
2. A man in north Harris during his mission there.
3. Hector MacKinnon on Berneray.
4. A woman and two teenage girls in Lochs.
5. A Barvas elder, praying for Greece.

At first glance these incidents seem wholly natural: barns were a common feature of mid-twentieth century Lewis crofting life. Many existing blackhouses even had a small barn, as well as a

---

31. Despite being blind, Donald had conducted his business across the country throughout his life, travelling alone. He maintained a Christian testimony in his home district, despite there being no Christian fellowship available.

byre, attached to the dwelling house. What better solitary space to commune with God? Yet, when you make comparisons with other Lewis revivals before and since, you find relatively few accounts of individuals praying in barns.[32]

Donald John Smith's house and old smithy, Ballantrushal

It is significant to note that each of the above stories was shared by Campbell alone; none by any of the praying individuals involved. Another unusual feature of several of the accounts is that the person praying was doing so audibly, and that someone in the vicinity happened to hear their prayers at a critical moment. While not impossible, such unusual series of scenarios seem improbable. Is it perhaps possible that at least some of these immensely appealing 'barn stories' were added to the narrative owing to the emotional attachment they held for the narrator?

32. Donald Saunders used to pray in his barn, while fellow Barvas elder Donald John Smith, *An Gobha* (the blacksmith), was often known to pray in his smithy during the 1939 revival in Barvas.

CHAPTER 12

Revival Advance: Southwest

Bernera

Bernera, located off the south-west coast of Lewis, was, in the mid-twentieth century, a small, remote island with a population of around four hundred. The community was almost equally divided between the Free Church and the Church of Scotland. The Rev. Murdo MacLennan, parish minister of Carloway, was Interim Moderator of the island congregation, in which a long pastoral vacancy reflected in the spiritual climate of the community.

Prayer and Praise

A native of Bernera reflected that in those days, 'The young people did attend church. My father was an elder and my mother a member. There was nothing else to do on the island, so we went to church ....There was an air of expectancy and a lot of prayer before (Campbell) came. He arrived a few days before the communion season ... the talk everywhere was about Duncan Campbell, the meetings and the revival.'[1]

Campbell arrived on the island in the second week of August 1951.[2] He brought with him a small team of praying men who

---

1. Donald MacAulay, in Peckham, *Sounds from Heaven*, p. 228.

2. He had been preceded, just four months earlier, by two other Faith Mission workers, who after a struggle, had reported a deep spirit of enquiry and a distinct change in the community. Campbell makes no reference to this, and it appears that revival only broke out in earnest following his own arrival.

had been specially invited from Barvas, among them young Donald MacPhail of Arnol. These men would meet with local believers each afternoon to intercede for that evening's meeting and the ensuing cottage meeting which was held in the village of Tobson. The room was usually packed.

Perhaps because of such focus on prayer, Campbell was able to report within days of his arrival, 'This is a wonderful island; one can truly say that the praises of God are heard from every village … Meetings are crowded and full of divine power, conviction and distress of soul as deep as ever … and men and women are finding the Saviour. Ever since the movement began, the Spirit of God has been at work; the young believers are growing in grace and manifesting the power of the Saviour in redeemed lives.'[3]

Campbell was particularly struck by the spirit of praise that emanated from the converts in all the villages. Such expression of worship in outbursts of song he found truly heart-warming and soul-stirring. So keen were the people to meet together that evening meetings, which began around 8 pm, often continued till around 1.30 in the morning in folk's homes, and always closed with a time of praise.

Scores of people would cross by boat from Carloway, having come by van from communities like Barvas, Ness, Arnol and Leurbost. A large crowd gathered at four o'clock one autumn morning to say farewell to all those sailing back to the mainland. Before they sailed, they stood on the shore 'singing the songs of Zion.'[4]

Momentous Moment

One afternoon during the second week of the mission, there was a special sense of God's presence at the prayer meeting. According to one who was present, 'The Lord descended upon the united prayers and fellowship of the people whose hearts God had

3. Duncan Campbell, FM Report, 15.08.1951.

4. ibid., 22.08.1951.

touched.' Campbell apparently said, 'there will be a break tonight; God is going to bless His people.'[5]

Bernera Church of Scotland, Breacleit

The group proceeded to the church, which was filled, and Campbell began preaching. However, such was the sense of spiritual bondage that half-way through the sermon, he was forced to stop. Noticing that young Donald MacPhail was moved to tears under a burden for souls, he invited the lad to lead in prayer. As he prayed aloud, the Arnol teenager referred to Revelation 4, which he had been reading that same morning. 'O God, I seem to be gazing through the open door. I see the Lamb in the midst of the Throne, with the keys of death and hell at his girdle.' Sobbing, Donald lifted his eyes to heaven and cried, 'O God, there is power there, let it loose.'[6]

At that moment, something broke in the spiritual atmosphere, causing a visible movement among the congregation. MacPhail was amazed to find that suddenly people were bowed forward in their pews; some being bent over them. There were also those

5. Peckham, *Sounds from Heaven*, p. 235.

6. ibid., p. 236.

who went into trances or fainted. The power of God was intense. It was a wonderful evening of the revelation of God's presence and power.

In later years, Campbell adds more colour to the story, and it is invariably his dramatic account that has been handed down through scores of second-hand reports. Following young Donald's prayer, 'in that moment the flood-gates of heaven opened, the congregation was struck by a hurricane of divine power, and many cried out for mercy ....There is the congregation falling almost on the top of each other; others throwing themselves back and becoming rigid as in death.' Campbell compared these to people having an epileptic fit. They remained supernaturally in this position for two hours, as did those who were slumped over each other.

Campbell was greatly struck by the moving of God at this unique meeting. He wrote that as a result of it, 'nine men came to the Saviour, seven of them heads of families, and three of them key men on this side of Lewis.' He spoke of the meeting as a 'glorious victory over hell and the devil. One man in his prayer said, "Lord, we thank Thee for this victory and for giving the devil such a sore head and we know you will not give him an aspirin to ease it!"'[7]

All Saved

It was said that during and subsequent to this service, a number of locals who didn't attend the meetings came to faith in Christ, especially from the village of Kirkibost. Campbell takes this a step or two further, claiming that many people from all over the island and even beyond who had never been near the Bernera church came under deep conviction of sin that night. 'Fishermen out in their fishing boats, men behind their looms, men at the peat bank, a merchant out with his van, school teachers examining their papers, were gripped by God, and by ten o'clock the roads

7. ibid., pp. 59–60.

were black with people seeking after God who were never near me.'[8]

In a much later address he gives details of what took place in Croir, a village located in the northern extremity of the island. Here, at the same time as Donald MacPhail was praying in church, 'God swept through the village and I know it to be a fact that there wasn't a single house in the village that hadn't a soul saved in it. Not a single house in the village.'[9]

Croir, Bernera

Another convicted during the meeting in Bernera was a schoolmaster from mainland Lewis, who felt compelled to hire a boat to take him across to the island, where around midnight and in the dark, he somehow managed to get himself to the very farmhouse where Campbell happened to be preaching.

On the same evening, a captain of a 'clan-boat' was gripped by conviction while in his cabin, sailing down the Minch, while the Spirit of God also moved upon several lobster fishermen as they worked from their boat off Bernera. They had to leave their creels and make for the island. By the morning, all were converted.

---

8. *Keswick Week*, 1952, p. 147.

9. 1968 address, quoted in Campbell, *Revival in the Hebrides*, pp. 44–5.

These are incredible stories. It is curious that Colin and Mary Peckham, in their well-researched study on the Lewis revival, make no mention of any of the above events. They do, however, provide the short testimony of Donald Macaulay. I interviewed the Rev. Macaulay in his Bernera home in 2001. Although living on this small island at the time of the revival, he said he knew nothing about any of the more unusual testimonies shared by Campbell and related above, including the story of multiple conversions of Bernera residents who hadn't been to the meetings.

Such testimonies, if true, would surely have been the talk of the community for months to come, especially on a remote island where little of note tended to happen. Sadly, no one else has testified to these outstanding events either, and I have been unable to obtain any verification for them.

'Spontaneous' Conversion London

Campbell goes on to focus on a single family from Croir, every member of which was apparently converted that same momentous evening – a father, mother, daughter and son. In addition to these, another daughter was based in London at the time, working in the medical profession. Campbell claimed that on the very night her family in Bernera turned to Christ, and at the very same hour, this daughter 'was walking down Oxford Street after leaving a patient and she is suddenly arrested by the power of God. She went into a closet and cried to God for mercy – and God saved her there; the whole family now saved!'[10]

I remember reading this delightful story many years ago, and being astounded by it. How disappointed I was, years later, to discover that things didn't happen in the way Campbell described. Certainly, the Croir family he mentions did exist, one daughter indeed lived in London, and she did indeed give her life to Christ. Other details are more suspect. No one in the family was spontaneously converted on the remarkable night

---

10. Campbell, *Revival in the Hebrides*, p. 45.

in question. The father and mother were already believers. The daughter living in Bernera had become a Christian a few months earlier. There is no knowledge of the son being converted during the revival.

The daughter living in London, Jessie Jane, was not suddenly arrested by the power of God while walking down Oxford Street. She had come under conviction a number of weeks earlier, after her sister in Lewis wrote to her telling of her own conversion. She subsequently started attending the Free Church of Scotland in London. Hearing that Duncan Campbell was scheduled to hold a mission in Bernera in the late summer of 1951, Jessie booked some holidays and travelled north so as to be on her home island for the event. She made a full commitment to Christ at one of the meetings.

Campbell was well aware of this; indeed, he noted in his weekly report for *Pilgrim News*, that a 'visitor from London got gloriously saved' towards the close of his Bernera mission in mid-September 1951. Campbell turns what is a beautiful and genuine testimony of Christian conversion into something much more sensational; seemingly, drama for dramatic effect. And he does so, insisting, 'My dear people, these are facts. And I tell you of them to honour God.'

The evangelist states further that Jessie later became the wife of a Baptist minister in Tasmania, where they lived for many years. One who knew her and was at the Bernera meeting the night she was converted has refuted this claim. 'She was a Faith Mission pilgrim in Britain for a time, but did not serve as a missionary abroad.' Nor did she marry a Baptist pastor (from Tasmania or anywhere else); rather a local Lewis believer.

Jessie Jane Mackay

Memorable Meetings

One of the 'key men' converted during the move of God in Bernera was afore-mentioned Donald Macaulay, skipper of the local ferry-boat, the *'Mairi Dhonn.'* Macaulay testified, 'My parents tried to persuade me to go to hear Campbell. Finally I went to the house where he was to hold the meeting that night. There he was in a tweed suit – how very unministerial, I thought! But there was something different about the meeting that night and I could not explain it. He said at the end of the meeting that God was working in our midst. This hit me like a sledgehammer and it made a deep impression on me. Mr Campbell only stayed for a short time, but in that period numbers were converted. Some of them made a real mark on the church and in their community later on.'[11]

The communion season on the island the following month proved a time of rich blessing. 'Crowds gathered from all over Lewis ….The spirit of conviction among the unsaved was as deep

---

11. Peckham, *Sounds from Heaven*, p. 229.

as ever, and there was great joy among the Christians in seeing men and women coming into the glorious liberty in Christ.'[12]

Mary Peckham recalls one service she attended in Bernera where Campbell drew the congregation to Calvary. In his prayer he described the scene and then said. 'I can hear the thud, thud, thud as with a hammer, they drove the nails into His hands and His feet!' He paused and then cried out, 'It was my hand that held the hammer!'[13] Many wept.

Mary also remembers attending a crowded house meeting on the island and being unable to hear Campbell speaking due to the sound of a group of teenagers sobbing under deep conviction in the kitchen next door. On that same night, a young man left the meeting, determined not to yield to the Spirit. Each time as he approached the gate, he sensed the Lord say to him, 'It is hard for thee to kick against the pricks.' He returned to the house and that same evening made his peace with God.

In another meeting, the power of the Lord was so mighty that a number of girls sitting on a bed just bent forward towards one another and wept. Duncan Campbell passed the girls and said, 'What a beautiful nest!' They were weeping their way to the Cross.[14]

An article in the local press, referring to the work on Bernera, said that such scenes had 'not been seen here for the past fifteen years, and churches which were more than half empty are now once again filling up and the weekly prayer meeting held on Thursday past had more worshippers than has often been seen on many a Sunday in past years.'[15] Clearly, the revival in Bernera,

---

12. Duncan Campbell, FM Report, 19.09.1951.

13. Peckham, *Sounds from Heaven*, p. 236.

14. ibid., p. 145.

15. *The Stornoway Gazette*, 13.04.1951, quoted in Steve Taylor, *Lewis Revival 1934–41*, in '*Skye Report,*' unpublished, pp. 7–8; Woolsey, *Channel of Revival*, p. 138.

though significantly overblown by the evangelist who led it, was nevertheless a genuine and deeply impactful movement.

Uig

Ever since his induction to the parish in July 1951, the Rev. Angus Macfarlane had been trying to secure the ministry of Duncan Campbell in his church in Baile-na-Cille, in the sparsely populated parish of Uig in south-west Lewis.[16] At last, in October, the evangelist was able to oblige, and spent around seven weeks in the area. Campbell felt the ground had been at least partially prepared for him by the labours of other Faith Mission pilgrims the previous winter. They had left behind a group of praying people, who were now able to stand with Campbell in his mission.

Ready for a Match

In Baile-na-Cille, Macfarlane commented that the atmosphere in his own church was now 'ready for a match.' A native of the parish also felt that 'revival was in the air, and there was much expectation among the Lord's people, who could be described as being in a lively state.'[17] Additionally, local believers were well aware of the wonderful movings of the Spirit of God all over Lewis and Harris during the course of the preceding twenty-two months, and this fired their expectations and strengthened their faith.

According to Campbell's biographer, little happened in the early meetings, leading Campbell to call on further prayer support – engaging his trustworthy intercessors in Barvas to get

16. A native of Dell in Ness, Macfarlane had been a Christian from his youth. He served as a lay missionary for some years before studying for the ministry. Regarded as a good preacher and a faithful pastor, Macfarlane also served as Chairman of the first Community Association in Uig. At communion times in particular, his fund of stories about worthies he had known and respected in his youth was a source of great blessing to many.

17. Peckham, *Sounds from Heaven*, p. 277.

into action, while he too gave himself to prayer. This seems to contradict Campbell's own weekly reports, where he states that 'the break came on the second night, and great was the rejoicing.'[18] This presumably, constituted a degree of breakthrough, but not full outbreak of revival, which was yet to come.

One afternoon Campbell was in his study, deep in prayer for the spiritual breakthrough he felt was so needed in the community. Macfarlane was mowing the hay on his glebe when Campbell came out, declaring, 'It's coming, it's coming – We've got through at last! We're over the top!'[19] He was confident God had heard the prayers of the saints – assurance had been given of imminent blessing.

Baile na Cille manse

That evening, while the host minister was in his pulpit leading in prayer, 'suddenly a consciousness of God came over the congregation, and we were lifted out of the realm of the ordinary, to realise a spiritual impact that could not be explained from any human point of view. Revival had come.'[20]

18. Duncan Campbell, FM Report, 24.10.1951.

19. Woolsey, *Channel of Revival*, p. 131

20. Campbell, *The Lewis Awakening*, p. 17.

Campbell's earliest record of this memorable evening is gripping. 'I find it difficult to put down on paper what our eyes have seen and our ears have heard this week. Revival has gripped the parish. Deep conviction of sin has laid hold of the people, and many have found the Saviour – as many as twenty in one meeting. Men who were never near a meeting were suddenly arrested by the Spirit of God and had to give up work and give themselves to seeking after God. People walk miles through wind and rain, and will wait through three services between 7.30 and 3.00 o'clock in the morning. We praise our faithful God!'[21]

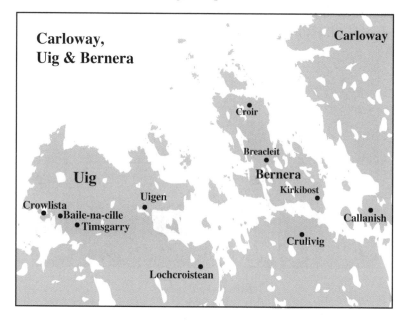

'Cross Hills and Moors

Campbell held other meetings in a village at the other end of the parish – Lochcroistean, to which lorries, vans, motorbikes and cars were used to transport folk, while many others travelled on foot. 'So,' wrote Campbell, 'they came across moors and over the hills, young men and maidens, their torches flashing in

---

21. Duncan Campbell, FM Report, 31.10.1951.

the darkness, intent upon one thing, to get peace from a guilty conscience, and refuge from the storm in their bosom, in the shelter of the Rock of Ages.'[22]

By the beginning of November, Campbell could further rejoice, given that revival had now spread 'to every part of the parish.' A number of folk awakened during the Pilgrims' mission nine months previously were now rejoicing in their Saviour. Conviction of sin was deep. 'The agony of godless men whose consciences awoke was terrible to see. Men have been found during the day praying among the rocks.'[23]

Mary Ann Morrison remembers walking with family and neighbours of all ages across the bay when the tide was out and around it when the tide was in to get to the meetings. They made a point of being at every meeting, whether it was in the main church or in one of the village meeting halls. The staff of the Youth Club in the area were all converted during the revival and the Club ceased to function.[24]

Campbell reported that meetings during one particular week were characterised by physical prostrations and swooning. Ms Morrison's recollections, in distinction, were that 'there was nothing at the meetings that would have distracted anyone. There was just the sense of awe and solemnity which surrounded us everywhere. Silent tears were shed and deep conviction was experienced, but the atmosphere was under the control of that awesome felt presence of God.'[25]

By now people were coming from all over Lewis to witness the movings of God, some from as far as fifty miles. 'Whole districts have been completely changed,' wrote Campbell. 'Social evils have been swept away as by a flood, and a wonderful sense of God

---

22. Campbell, *The Lewis Awakening*, p. 18.

23. Duncan Campbell, FM Report, 08.11.1951.

24. Peckham, *Sounds from Heaven*, pp. 278–9.

25. ibid., p. 279.

seems to pervade the whole district ....Yesterday was a day that
will never be forgotten in Uig. We began at noon and continued
until three o'clock this morning. In that time I addressed
six meetings.'[26]

Defying Difficulties

Distances were considerable in this vast, hilly parish, and there
were no buses to ferry people to the meetings. To top it all,
throughout much of Campbell's time in Uig, the weather was
particularly inclement. Rain and wind were incessant for days
on end. Things only got worse as December arrived, Campbell
noting, 'I do not remember ever conducting a mission under
such conditions.'[27]

Still, many came to the meetings. The more fortunate came in
cars or vans, though the uneven, single-track roads in this remote
district were particularly hazardous. Fortunately, four men who
owned their own cars were converted during a single week in
December, and their vehicles were made available to take people
to and from the meetings.

To add to the logistical difficulties of holding a mission
in Uig, Campbell was now suffering from a bad chill, which
caused considerable trouble to his chest and throat, and led
him to hold no more than one meeting each evening. Despite
all these obstacles, blessing attended the mission right to
the end, with 'crowded meetings, deep conviction, and souls
being saved.'[28]

One night, a whole family, father, mother, two sons and
daughter (in the Bays of Uig) were among those who put their
trust in Christ as Saviour. 'Someone started singing Psalm 103,
verses 17 to the end, and as the Spirit of God swept through the

---

26. Duncan Campbell, FM Report, 14.11.1951.

27. ibid., 12.12.1951.

28. ibid., 19.12.1951.

meeting, the cry of the unsaved could be heard, as strong men wept their way to the Saviour.'[29]

Timsgarry and Crowlista

In the tiny village of Timsgarry, very close to Baile-na-Cille, all the unconverted male members who were home at the time – several had godly widowed mothers living with them – came to Christ in a short space of time (around five or six men in total). Around twenty people from various parts of Uig joined the church on one Sunday.[30] And they continued to serve the Lord, becoming stable pillars of both church and community. When William MacLeod moved to Uig as Church of Scotland minister in 1964, he found that nearly all the office-bearers had been converted in the revival.

25th Anniversary presentation for Rev Angus Macfarlane
(front row, second from left), Uig, 1976.
Rev William Macleod is seated second from right.

In early March 1953, Campbell conducted one further mission in Uig – this time in the small communities of Lochcroistean and Crowlista, at opposite ends of the parish. Despite 'much

---

29. ibid., 12.12.1951.

30. Peckham, *Sounds from Heaven*, pp. 207, 278.

opposition' in these areas, in contrast to his earlier Uig missions, he could still report, 'a great manifestation of the power of God in the hall at Crowlista. I had to stop preaching, until the cry of the people who came under the power of God became more subdued. Some burdened sinners were greatly distressed and since then have found the Saviour.' With anxious souls turning to the Lord, day by day, Campbell was aware of 'only two left in this village unsaved.'[31]

Songs of Praise in the Valley

In one talk Campbell speaks of 'seven American ministers' coming to Uig during the revival. While walking through a valley, 'they heard singing coming from this direction, coming from that direction.' The song being sung was Psalm 72:17–19. One of the ministers turned to the other and said, 'This is heaven; heaven around us.' The suggestion was that angelic voices were resounding through the Uig glen. Woolsey refers to the experience as 'celestial melodies – angelic praise.' Campbell noted also that this was the very same night that revival reached its pinnacle in the parish of Uig.[32]

The arrival of seven American ministers would have been prominent in almost any setting. But such a group suddenly cropping up in a backwater rural parish of a remote Scottish island in the early 1950s would have stood out like seven fish out of water! The fact that no other writer mentions these trans-Atlantic visitors, and no one I have spoken to knows anything about them, is somewhat curious.

The answer appears to lie with the testimony of an overseas visitor who recalled an evening meeting in a packed two-storey house in Uig in December 1951. He and his brother sat on the steps of the staircase, as Campbell moved from room to room, challenging the people. 'They prayed, sang and praised God as

---

31. Duncan Campbell, FM Report, 11.03.1953.
32. Woolsey, *Channel of Revival*, p 173; Allen, *Catch the Wind*, p. 124.

the power of God's presence overwhelmed them.' It wasn't till around one o'clock in the morning that the people finally left the house, and slowly wound their way homeward in various directions, all the while continuing to sing their songs of praise (which would indeed have included psalms).

Road running through a Uig valley

Wrote the visitor, 'We walked about a mile home and could still hear them singing under the starry sky, in the still night air of this country village of Uig. We were weary but rejoicing.'[33] A wonderful experience to hear the sound of praise echoing through the glen, no doubt. But no reference to angelic hosts – all was explainable by natural means.

Further, there weren't seven visitors; there were rather, just two. Campbell actually makes this clear in a report to the Faith Mission at the time – one that was inadvertently missed from the Peckham's extracts in *Sounds from Heaven*. Writing from Uig,

33. Bushby, *Adventures in Revival*, p. 31.

Campbell notes, simply, 'Two American friends are with us for several days; one gave a word last night.' [34]

Also, neither of the visitors were ministers; one, rather, had recently graduated from Bible College and was considering applying for ordination. Nor, thirdly, were they American – they were two brothers from Australia (though they were at that time based in America). Campbell's description appears to have been wrong on all three counts. Instead of 'seven American ministers,' what we have is two Australian laymen!

---

34. Duncan Campbell, FM Report, 5.12.1951.

CHAPTER 13

Revival Advance: Harris

Mainland Harris

During May and June 1950, Campbell conducted several missions in Harris, in which location[1] he had already held a number of meetings. Six isolated communities were visited across the north of the district, the main meetings being held in Tarbert Church of Scotland, where the Rev. Murdo Macleod was the popular minister. In each location expectations were high and meetings were well attended, if not crowded.

Tarbert

In one township, so deep was the interest that all work was stopped during Campbell's visit, 'and the day regarded as a Sabbath.' Another day, buses brought the people a certain

---

1. Although not an actual island in itself, Harris is regarded as quite distinct from Lewis, and is often referred to as the Isle of Harris.

distance, others came by boats, but most trudged over the hill and moor on foot. At one meeting in the early hours of the morning, Campbell spoke of 'fourteen adults seeking the Saviour'; a husband and wife and a local school teacher being among them.

In one place a barn in which a man was praying was suddenly flooded by light, and assurance came that God had broken through in the village. The meeting in Tarbert was mightily blessed by God at that very hour. Campbell felt the success of the meetings in Harris 'clearly demonstrates that missions can be worked as effectively in summer as in winter, as seasons and seasonable work present no barrier when God is at work.'[2] One man converted here was Roderick Mackinnon, a young joiner from Bunavoneader, North Harris, who later went on to become a minister in the Church of Scotland. Roddy's twin brother was converted around the same time, and later became a home missionary.[3]

Roderick Mackinnon

<hr>

2. Duncan Campbell, FM Report, 31.05.1950.

3. After studying at the Bible Training Institute in Glasgow, Roddy served as a Church of Scotland Missionary in Tiree and Govan. At the age of forty he was ordained and inducted as Church of Scotland minister in South Uist. He was called to the Ross-shire parish of Kilmuir Easter and Logie Easter in 1981.

'Break' in the South

From Tarbert, Campbell moved to the south of the island, to a small *tigh-leughaidh* (reading house) in Leverburgh that had been constructed fifteen years previously. It was situated roughly equidistant from the two main Church of Scotland congregations – those of Manish on the east coast and Scarista on the west. These churches shared a minister and kirk session, but the two congregations were quite distinct and only rarely worshipped together. The Rev. Norman MacDonald, a native of Barvas, had been inducted to the charge in 1948.

The session agreed on 5th May 1950 to invite Duncan Campbell to undertake a campaign. He arrived just over a month later, on Sunday 11th June, conducting daily meetings for exactly two weeks (except on Saturdays), with two or three meetings on the final Sunday. All meetings were held in Leverburgh, due to its more central location.

Campbell noted that opposition was in evidence 'from the usual source' (a reference to elements within the Free Church), making it 'a week of hard fighting.' Thankfully, the evangelist could declare that his 'eyes are towards God, and already the enemy is yielding.' Accommodating the crowds who attended the meetings was an equally big problem; it proving necessary to transport people by bus to a larger church five miles away.

After almost a fortnight of meetings, Campbell noted that the 'real break came on Thursday, and since then we have been in the midst of a very blessed move of the Spirit. Men and women have yielded to Christ in every meeting, as many as fifteen at a time, and meetings continuing until dawn, and then buses taking the people home.'[4]

---

4. ibid., 28.06.1950.

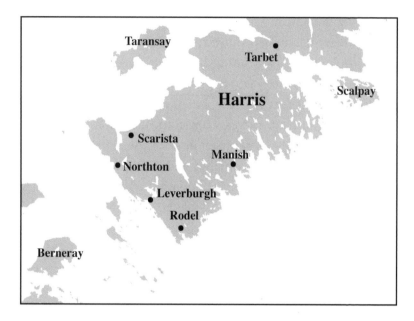

It was observed how influential was the power of worship in song in the meetings. 'Again and again a wave of deep conviction of sin would sweep over the congregation, and men and women would be seen bending before the mighty impact of the Spirit, as the heart-cry of the penitent found expression in the words of Psalm 130:

Lord from the depths to Thee I cry'd,
My voice, Lord do Thou hear:
Unto my supplications voice,
Given an attentive ear
Lord, who shall stand, if Thou, O Lord,
Should'st mark iniquity?
But yet with Thee forgiveness is,
That fear'd Thou mayest be.[5]

Campbell returned to Harris a few months later to assist in the November communion. People came not just from across Harris

---

5. Campbell, *The Lewis Awakening*, p. 13.

but also from all over Lewis, and Campbell said he 'never in my life witnessed such crowds in the Highlands.'[6] It was estimated that three hundred came for the whole period of the communion, this not including the people of the parish. No church building proved big enough for such crowds, so overflow meetings were arranged.

Conviction and distress of soul were features of the meetings, one of which, devoted solely to dealing with the anxious, went on until three o'clock in the morning. But still, there occurred no dramatic outpouring of God's Spirit as had overtaken the West Lewis districts of Barvas and Ness.

Donald Macleod

Norman and Chrissie Macleod recalled; 'There were many conversions in Harris during the 1949–52 revival. Duncan Campbell came to the parish several times. One convert was Finlay Maclean. Finlay had been a heavy drinker, but his life was transformed, and he went on to be an elder in Leverburgh Church of Scotland.'[7]

Chrissie, already a believer, urged her father to go to the services. At the close of one, Campbell asked if anyone wanted to stay behind for the after-meeting. Immediately her father, Donald, sensed what he later felt was the 'enemy' speaking into his ear and saying, 'No, you need to go home and attend to your cow in the byre!' His cow was one of the very best he had ever owned, and he was very proud of it. So he encouraged the others to go in, but he went back home.

The following year, Campbell returned to Harris for a further series of meetings. At the time, Chrissie was a teacher in Finsbay, and was walking home one evening after a busy day's work. Thankfully someone in a lorry stopped and gave her a lift. She was deeply thankful, for she knew that Duncan Campbell

6. Duncan Campbell, FM Report, 29.11.1950.

7. Personal communication with Norman and Chrissie Macleod, 12.09.2002.

was stopping at her parents' house that evening for tea before proceeding to the meeting. Her father accompanied him to the meeting. Shattered after her day's work, Chrissie stayed home, and both she and her mother went to bed early.

But they had been praying that the Holy Spirit would be working in her father's life through the meeting. They knew he had no good excuse for not attending the after-meeting this time – his precious cow, which up until recently had been in full health, had inexplicably swallowed a needle. This had the effect of puncturing the cow's heart, which led to its death. Any excuse for returning home quickly had been removed.

It wasn't until around three o'clock in the morning that Chrissie heard her father coming in the door. He went straight upstairs and, with face beaming, gave his wife and daughter a big hug. They knew at once he had been converted. He looked an entirely different man. Donald told them he was so happy he could hardly express himself, and there was no way he was going to go to bed that night! Although not naturally melodious, he began to sing praises to God, his heart full to overflowing with the spirit of joy.

Donald's wife and daughter got out of bed and rejoiced with him. Eventually he calmed down sufficiently to tell his family how God had spoken deeply to his heart at the meeting, and brought him through to peace in Christ. For all his adult life, Donald had shown a Christian respectability – always saying grace before eating, and attending church every Sunday. Now, however, his whole life was changed from one of formality to that of genuine heartfelt faith – and he became a man of earnest prayer. He later became a much respected elder in his church.[8]

---

8. ibid. Chrissie's father went to the Keswick Convention just a year or two later, where he not only heard Campbell speak but was able to converse with him in person.

'This Blessed Move'

Campbell returned for a second two-week mission to Leverburgh in November 1952. While there still occurred no outbreak of revival, Campbell felt, 'we are on the verge of another great movement.' He reported: 'God broke in among the self-righteous sinners,' causing deep conviction and confession. 'Some terrible characters have been saved. So great was their distress that we had to leave some of them lying on the floor.'[9] There was a notable ingathering of men. One young student, just home from the army, some days after his conversion heard the call of God to the ministry; his father being among nine who surrendered to Christ early one morning.

Despite references to 'this blessed move in Harris,' and 'the Spirit of God moving in a mighty way,' there is no mention in the reports of revival breaking out. Indeed, in all his missions on mainland Harris, while Campbell repeatedly uses the term 'move' / 'movement' to describe what he experienced, he never specifically refers to the breakout of 'revival,' a term regularly employed elsewhere in his Lewis reports.

Revival Statistics: South Harris

Church roll additions for South Harris during the years of the revival are as follows:

Professions of Faith: South Harris C of S[10]

Year	Manish	Scarista	Total
1949	2	0	2
1950	**2**	**4**	**6**
1951	**2**	**1**	**3**
1952	**0**	**4**	**4**
1953	0	2	2

---

9. Duncan Campbell, FM Report, 08.11.1952.

10. Figures obtained from The National Records of Scotland, 31.08.2022.

Thus, we have a total of seventeen names added to the communion roll (including one or two re-admissions) in the five-year-period 1949–53 (thirteen in the pivotal years 1950–2). In the following five-year period (1954–8), only three names were added (all in 1958), while in the five-year period prior to the revival (1944–8), the total was thirteen.

The four new members added to the Scarista communion roll in November 1950 may well have been converts of Campbell's May–June mission of 1950, and it is known with some certainty that the four added in November '52 were converts from his autumn mission of '52. All hailed from Leverburgh and one of these, Neil Martin, went on to become a Church of Scotland missionary.

Berneray

The small island of Berneray, located in the Sound of Harris, and historically part of South Harris, is actually nearer to North Uist, to which it is now joined by man-made causeway. Prior to Duncan Campbell going there, it was reported that the Spirit of God moved in a powerful manner during one particular communion weekend. One who attended testified that the sense of the presence of God was so strong upon the people that if you wanted to speak or to sing, then you had to sit down, or you would fall; such was especially true during the singing, which was most powerful.

Although no one was converted at that time, it was felt that God was preparing the hearts of the people for what was soon to follow. Even before Campbell came, it was, claimed one, 'like heaven on earth. People were open, convicted, ready to receive and ripe to be plucked. God went before and prepared the ground.'[11]

---

11. Personal interview with Colin Peckham, 21.06.2002; Peckham, *Sounds from Heaven*, p. 182; Rev. Kenneth Macdonald, *Testimony of Revival*, Duncan Campbell Lectures, Faith Mission Bible College, Edinburgh, 18.02.2000, audio tape.

Bangor Convention

Campbell was invited to speak at the Bangor Convention in April 1952. This event was the highlight of the Faith Mission calendar. People travelled by coach and car from all over Ireland to attend, while a great many also came over from mainland Britain. In all, up to 15,000 people attended.

Conducted over a long weekend, Easter Monday was the 'big' day, when five large churches were engaged for the no fewer than fifteen meetings held. 'Pilgrims meetings' were favourites; held on the Monday afternoon, these allowed Faith Mission workers to share personal accounts of the Spirit's moving in various fields of labour.

Campbell considered the Bangor Conventions to be particularly significant. From the mid-1940s up to his death in 1972, he very rarely missed one, despite the inconvenience of getting there.[12] Faith Mission President J. G. Eberstein called the 1952 Convention a 'remarkable' occasion, there being a 'depth and atmosphere about the meetings which cannot be put into words. God was certainly in the midst.'[13]

Spiritual Impulse

The account of Duncan Campbell finding himself on Berneray is another of the best-known stories of the entire Lewis and Harris revival. The thrust of it is as follows. Campbell had spoken on the Saturday evening of the 1952 Bangor Convention on the topic of laying hold of the blessings and experiences which are ours

---

12. It is known that Campbell attended the events held in 1946, 1948, 1950, 1952, 1953, 1955, 1958, 1959, 1960, 1961, 1964 and 1969; but it is quite likely he was also present during several of the missing dates here. He was also due to speak at the Convention in 1972, held from 30th March to 4th April. Sadly, he died the day before he was due to travel there, on Tues, 28th March.

13. There were 'hallowed seasons of prayer' with 'real brokenness.' A 'great longing for revival' was evident throughout the Convention, with an anticipation that 'we are on the verge of great things' (J. G. Eberstein, FM report, 1952).

by right, but as yet unpossessed. He was due to give a further message two evenings later, on Easter Monday.

Having just finished his Saturday address, he was suddenly impressed to leave the convention immediately, and make his way to Berneray.[14] Despite objections by the conference chairman, who like most at the convention had never heard of this tiny island, Campbell was certain God was speaking. So, to the chagrin of the conference committee, off he went, crossing to mainland Scotland and travelling up north, and over the Minch to Stornoway, being driven the length of the island to Leverburgh, where he caught a small boat across to Berneray; in all, a three-day journey.

Knowing no one on the island, which he had never visited before, Campbell made enquiries of a young boy, who informed him there was no minister in either of the island's two churches. The lad agreed to go and tell an elder, Hector Mackinnon[15], that 'Duncan Campbell, the minister who preached in Lewis,' had arrived. Soon the boy returned to say that Mackinnon had been expecting Campbell, accommodation was arranged, and he would be expected to preach in church that same evening!

It turned out that the day Campbell had felt called to go to Berneray, Mackinnon, the island's recently retired postman and ferryman, had spent much of the day praying in his barn. Known

14. Campbell was not due to speak on the Sunday evening, but on Easter Monday, in one of five churches where meetings were being held. His non-appearance wouldn't have been nearly as big an inconvenience as if he had been the sole speaker at one main event. In fact, Mr Eberstein, in his report of the Bangor Convention, makes no mention at all of Campbell leaving the conference early.

15. Along with two of his brothers, Hector Mackinnon served in the Navy during the First World War. Of the three, only he survived. It was his experiences during the war, particularly when his ship, *HMS Ermine*, was sunk in the Dardanelles, that brought about his religious conversion. Hector became a lay preacher and was highly respected in his community. He died two years after revival came to the island, in 1954, aged sixty-seven.

to have a prophetic gifting, he received a promise through the verse, *'I will be as the dew unto Israel'* (Hosea 14:5), that revival would sweep Berneray. Approaching the barn, his wife heard him praying that wherever Duncan Campbell was at that time, God would send to the island as His channel of revival. Indeed, so sure was he that God had heard his cry that he arranged for a mission to commence in three days' time!

The clear implication from all the accounts is that the impression Campbell got to go to Berneray was by spontaneous revelation rather than by logical reasoning. He makes this clear when he said he had never been to Berneray, didn't know anyone on the island, and had received no invitation from anyone to visit the place – the Spirit simply bade him to go.

Likewise, the impression given in regard to Mackinnon praying intensely for Campbell to suddenly appear on his island is that there was no logical reason to expect him to come at that time. Rather, he believed it by faith. It is these impressive factors that, for decades, have made the story so appealing and faith-inspiring to succeeding generations of readers.

Pre-planned Visit

But there are problems with the above story. Faith Mission pilgrims only held missions by invitation; not because of personal desire or spiritual impulse. This was especially important on the island of Lewis, where, as Campbell was fully aware, some church groups were completely opposed to him holding meetings. In any case, a Berneray believer made it known that Campbell had, in fact, been invited to the small island 'many times' previously but was only finally able to come in the spring of 1952.[16]

A short entry from Campbell's weekly reports further dismisses the evangelist's account of events. On 26th March, a fortnight *before* his Berneray campaign was due to begin, Campbell noted in his weekly report (never intended for public

---

16. Peckham, *Sounds from Heaven*, p. 281.

scrutiny), 'Berneray, Harris, will be my next mission. I go there after the Easter Bangor Convention.'[17]

So, Campbell had known for weeks, and possibly many months, that he was due to begin a gospel mission on Berneray in mid-April, 1952. The Church of Scotland charge on Berneray was vacant at the time, and Mackinnon was one of the leading elders who conducted meetings. Mackinnon would have had full knowledge of Campbell's impending visit and would have been preparing for it.

Hector Mackinnon

This lessens the impact of the story to some extent. At the same time, given Mackinnon's prophetic gifting, there is no reason to doubt that he genuinely did receive the promise that revival was coming to his island, and that Campbell would indeed arrive in time for the mission he had already arranged.

Later accounts dramatise and distort the basic series of events to even greater lengths. It is commonly reported that the Spirit urged Campbell to immediately leave Ireland for Berneray at the very moment he stepped up to give his Easter Monday address in Bangor. A popular published account has it that he quickly

---

17. Duncan Campbell, FM Report, 26.03.1952.

made his excuses to a stunned and displeased event organiser, and rushed back to his hotel, it being late in the evening. He packed his bags and got a taxi to the airport – all this despite the fact that Campbell was not in the habit of staying in hotels, very rarely hired taxis, and was not accustomed to travelling by by plane within the UK.

The misinformed report goes on to tell us that at the airport, Campbell tried to book a flight to Berneray (which tiny island has no runway). When told there were no more flights from Belfast to this destination at that time of night, Campbell was unperturbed – he simply booked himself on the next flight to mainland Harris instead (Harris has no airport either!). From there, Campbell walked, suitcase in hand, to the southern shores of the island, and paid all the money he had to hire a boat to ferry him to Berneray.[18] Anyone with even a miniscule knowledge of Scottish custom and geography will be bemused at the multiple implausibilities of this venture.

Berneray Blessing

Back to the main story. Campbell's first few meetings were relatively uneventful. Then, on the second or third evening, after the meeting had closed, and people were making their way down the road from the building, Campbell and Mackinnon could observe that the Spirit was clearly dealing with people even as they made for home. Some were being stopped in their tracks, unable to move further. Some fell by the roadside, under deep conviction; still others knelt to pray.

In no time the whole island seemed to be moved by the awe-inspiring sense of the presence of God. A minister from each of Harris and Lewis came over to assist as the movement progressed. Campbell noted that this was the most unfavourable time of the year for meetings, as the people were busy on the land. That day,

---

18. Wesley Duewel, *Heroes of the Holy Life: Biographies of Fully Devoted Followers of Christ*, Grand Rapids, 2002, pp. 32–3.

however, work on the crofts was given a secondary place. Campbell was told that on one night at least, 'every person on the island who could be out was in the church. I am dealing with anxious souls every night. On my way home last night I met a group by the roadside in great distress; others had met in a house and were there until four o'clock in the morning.'[19]

Borve, Berneray

It is worth noting that both Campbell's earliest account of the Berneray revival, found in his weekly Faith Mission report, along with the two short accounts given by locals (Mrs MacKillop and Mrs Maclean) in *Sounds from Heaven,* are more 'down-to-earth' and less sensational than what the evangelist later shared about it, making no reference to the Spirit suddenly descending on islanders in the evening open-air.

Nonetheless, there is little doubt that Berneray was touched by a genuine breath of the Spirit of God. A further surge of blessing came when the evangelist returned to Berneray a year later. The ground had been well prepared by the converts of the previous year, and Campbell found himself in an atmosphere of spiritual intensity. 'Every person that could move was out

19. Duncan Campbell, FM Report, 30.04.1952.

today,' he wrote, 'and an extra meeting had to be arranged in the church.' Campbell addressed no fewer than five meetings in the course of the day, including one at the shore before the boats ferried the Harris people home, and another one to help those in distress of soul.

'How we praise God for being in the midst of revival again,' Campbell rejoiced. 'Seeing the people coming over the hills and along the roads, others coming in boats, was a sight to be remembered, and to listen to the singing of Psalm 122 from the boats leaving the shore was soul-inspiring.'[20]

Revival Statistics: Berneray

Additions to Berneray Church of Scotland during the years of the revival are as follows:

Professions of Faith: Berneray C of S[21]

Year	July	November	Total
1949	2	1	3
1950	**0**	**9**	**9**
1951	**4**	**1**	**5**
1952	**16**	**4**	**20**

It would seem natural that few, if any, Bernera residents made the journey by boat and road to Barvas, Ness or other districts during the first few months following the outbreak of revival in Lewis; consequently, there were no additions to the church roll in July 1950. Campbell's mission in Leverburgh in June 1950, however, would have induced a considerable number to make the boat trip across the Sound of Harris to hear him. Because the mission was from mid-to-late June, it would appear that converts

---

20. Duncan Campbell, FM Report, 13.05.1953.

21. Figures obtained from The National Records of Scotland, 31.08.2022.

were too late to be added to the July communion roll; instead a remarkable nine additions were made in November.

A further five were added the following year; but most impressive of all are the sixteen who came forward to the first communion following Campbell's visit to the island in April '52. Referring to this occasion, an elder stated, 'The centre of the church was reserved for communicants, but it could not hold them; this never happened in the history of our parish before!' [22] The four people added the following November may have been converts of the evangelist's second Leverburgh mission, in the autumn of '52.

Altogether, the thirty-four additions to the Berneray church roll over the course of three years constitutes a remarkable harvest on a small remote island with a (then) population of around 300. A remarkable ten per cent of the island's population joined the Church of Scotland during those years, while many other residents were already church members. Additionally, some may have professed faith but not yet applied for membership. Unquestionably, the revival would have made a tremendous impact on the island. The Berneray revival was, without doubt, one of the most fruitful movements of the entire Lewis and Harris awakening.

22. Peckham, *Sounds from Heaven*, p. 281.

PART 4

Revival in Focus

Chapter 14

Awareness of God

The authors of *Sounds from Heaven* have stressed that every convert they interviewed was keen to emphasise the awareness of the presence of God as the outstanding feature of the revival (rather than the presence or influence of Duncan Campbell!). 'It seemed as if the very air was electrified with the Spirit of God,' noted one convert.[1]

As the movement intensified, people became convicted, not just in church, but as they worked in the fields, in the peat-banks or at their weaving looms, or even as they walked by the roadside. A few were converted before ever listening to a sermon or attending a meeting. The sense of the presence of God seemed to pervade the community.

Donald MacPhail was one upon whom conviction fell long before he attended any meetings. 'There was something in the atmosphere that affected us quite apart from the meetings – an atmosphere of the presence of God – a felt presence,' he said. Campbell also spoke of 'this consciousness of the Eternal; men moved with bowed heads, the realization of God in the midst, so overwhelming that sometimes they dared not move.'[2]

'When you came out of the church,' noted one convert, 'it seemed as if the people carried with them that awareness, and with that awareness came the fear of God on the unconverted people. People were afraid, because this was a supernatural happening.

---

1. Margaret Macleod, on *Revival in our Times*.
2. Peckham, *Sounds from Heaven*, p. 233.

This was God coming into the community. The presence of God brings solemnity; brings silence, and an awareness of the supernatural which I could not understand.' William Macleod concurred; 'The fact that people listened to us was also part of the revival; there was an awareness of God in the community.'[3]

One woman gloriously converted during the revival remained ever since a prayer warrior, with a living concern for the glory of Christ. Reminiscing on the revival, she said, 'People were adoring Christ ... . Some of the house meetings were so full of the peace of Christ that it was utterly beautiful and people would sit in the beauty of that peace in total silence.'[4]

A visitor from mainland Scotland attended a cottage meeting. Though he didn't understand what others were praying (in Gaelic), 'what I did understand,' he later reflected, 'was the presence of God, such as I had never felt before, or have felt since, and that is after nearly forty years as a Christian. It is difficult to explain. We sat there in awe and reverence in the presence of holiness. The deep presence of God fell over us like a mantle and filled our beings with an indescribable love and compassion. I could only sit there and weep in gratitude and thanksgiving that I had found this One as my Lord and Saviour.'[5]

'There were people coming to the manse to see Duncan Campbell and myself,' noted the Rev. Angus Macfarlane of Uig, 'who weren't in the services at all. Mr Campbell asked one man who came, what touched him. He replied, "What's here just now seems to be in the air. It doesn't matter where I go, I can't help thinking of things that are going on." Instances like that convinced you to believe that there was nothing else but the Spirit of God that could move people.'[6]

---

3. ibid. p. 198; Mary Peckham, in *Wind of the Spirit.*

4. Shared in personal communication with Kenny Borthwick, 10.11.2021.

5. Bill Kettles, '*The Lewis Revival: A Covenant Engagement,* unpublished, nd.

6. Angus Macfarlane, on *Revival in our Times.* Donald John Smith said it was as if there was 'an electric current running through the air.'

Jack Macarthur stated that when people say how they would love to experience revival, his immediate thought is, 'I don't think you know what you're asking for. For revival can be a terrible thing – being face-to-face with God. You're up against something completely out of this world. It's supernatural. The awareness of the holiness of God is something that is difficult for anyone to describe.'[7]

'In one sense you could say it was a revival of silence,' Donald John Smith said. 'For again and again at meetings you could hear a pin drop, such was the full attention given to Campbell as he shared the gospel to a hungry audience. Even before the meetings started, people spoke only if they had to, and then in hushed tones. Such a sense of expectation pervaded the meetings.'[8]

A visitor who attended cottage meetings on the island wrote, 'There was a deep awe and a reverence for the living God among the people. We would gather for house meetings. There was the peat fire at one side, and the room jam-packed with people (adjacent rooms and even the stairway were also packed). The preacher's back was to the peat-fire, and he would be nearly roasted before all was over! You arrived at the door, you were received, and you went in and sat down, and there was scarcely a word spoken, little more than an initial greeting. You sat in the profound silence of God. The meeting would start, they would maybe sing a psalm or two, there would be a prayer or two. The sense of God was there. And then the time to preach would come.'[9]

Donald John Smith of Upper Shader spoke of blessed house meetings, when the presence of the Lord seemed so close that he would literally shake. As people departed, they would stand in the road not wanting to go home, and arm in arm they would walk

7. Jack Macarthur, on ibid.

8. ibid.

9. Hugh Black, 'Revival: Personal Encounters,' New Dawn Books, 1993, p.43.

to another village. It was considered the best of all experiences to help lead people to Christ and then accompany them to the prayer meeting for the first time.

Catriona Macaulay remembered being at a house-meeting in Barvas police station. Duncan Campbell was preaching, and reached a point where he felt he couldn't go on any longer. Donald MacPhail was called upon to lead in prayer. 'The first thing he said was, *"Athair"* - Father. And that's as far as he got. I think almost everybody just broke down, overwhelmed with the reality of that one word.'[10]

Spiritual Aura

It has become an oft-repeated statistic of the revival, quoted by Duncan Campbell in nearly all of his later addresses, that seventy-five per cent of those who came into saving relationship with Christ entered into that experience before listening to a sermon or attending a place of worship.

It is evident from the collection of testimonies recounted in *Sounds from Heaven*, and from my own interviews across the island, that only a tiny minority of those who became Christians during the revival suggest that they did so before attending a church or house meeting. One rare example was a man who 'became so convinced of his sin, convinced of his need of a Saviour, that he fell on his knees, down on his croft, without anybody near at all, and he gave his life to Christ.'[11]

It is apparent that the vast majority of converts came to peace in Christ after hearing Duncan Campbell preach. Unquestionably, Campbell's seventy-five per cent statistic is greatly inflated – another example, it seems, of him intentionally downplaying his own role in the revival.

A number of stories have been related of people sensing the presence of God as they approached the island by boat during

---

10. Personal communication with Catriona Macaulay, 05.04.2020.

11. William Macleod, on *Revival in our Times*.

the revival. It was claimed that many sailors testified that while their ships were passing the island they would feel the presence of the Lord, without knowing anything about the revival in full flow onshore.

A woman in Lewis regularly prayed for the salvation of her son, who was a student in Edinburgh. Travelling home on vacation, he apparently sensed a divine presence on the boat, well before it had reached Stornoway. He was said to have given his life to the Lord, and went on to become a minister in the Church of Scotland.[12]

While it's possible that one or two of these stories may be authentic, they invariably come second-hand. No one has identified themselves as being the one convicted or converted after sensing God's presence as they neared the island. One wonders, rather, whether in some instances the reaction was psychological; being induced by an existing awareness of the spiritual movement underway on the island.

This has even been the case for revival pilgrims streaming to Lewis many years, or even decades after the revival had come to a close. One man visited the island in 2001 after reading everything he could on the movement. 'I felt I had landed on holy ground,' he exulted. 'Never have I had a more thrilling experience, than to walk the land where revival occurred. I found myself, at times, floating on air, and, the next moment, my knees would crumble under me.'[13]

Prayer

As prayer was, as ever, to the fore in the lead-up to the revival, so it retained its rightful place during its progress, when believers received an even greater burden for intercession. They prayed for the whole community and also for specific individuals. Loved

---

12. Personal communication with Andrew Woolsey, 17.06.2016.

13. Allen, *Catch the Wind*, pp. 69, 94.

ones away from home became the focus of many prayers, and, quite remarkably, a number of these were converted around this time hundreds of miles away, in Glasgow and elsewhere. Many converts also testified to the boldness and desire they now had to tell anyone they met how Christ had changed their lives.

Believers longed that there would be no one who would be outwith the flock of Christ at the great throne of God, and they often ended their conversation with a thought-provoking remark. Donald John Smith of Upper Shader recalled one Christian father saying to all his family one by one at his death bed, 'Goodbye, I'll see you in the morning.' But to the one unconverted son he just said, 'Goodbye.' That was a means of convicting that man.[14]

In some communities, three or four cottage prayer meetings were held weekly; some proved so popular it was with difficulty they managed to pack several dozen people into a praying believer's humble adobe! In addition to various informal cottage prayer meetings, the main weekly prayer meeting was held on a Thursday evening at 6 pm (in each of Barvas, Shader and Arnol) in the local church or church hall. Additionally, there was a prayer meeting on Thursdays at noon, and a united prayer meeting on the first Monday of each month at the same time (held on a five-location rota; Barvas CofS, Barvas Free Church, and Borve, Shader & Arnol meeting halls).

Much prayer was spontaneous. As people visited one another in their homes, they would pray and often keep praying until they felt that they had got through to God. It was sometimes noted that certain men and women known for their gift of prayer would be absent from a church meeting where some felt the going might be tough. Invariably they were to be found in a house nearby, engaged in prayer for a victorious outcome to the meeting in progress.

---

14. Personal communication, 16.09.2004.

A visiting journalist was deeply moved at hearing converts praying at one or two cottage meetings he attended. 'There is intensity in their prayer,' he noted. 'They are strong men crying to God with all of their being. They do not wave their arms around and work up a frenzy. It is supernatural prayer, having a power which comes down from heaven, and goes up to heaven. They are channels that the Spirit of God flows through. They are not themselves when they are gripped by this mighty power of God.

'There is worship as well as intercession in their prayers,' continued the journalist. 'There is adoration and praise to our Saviour, the Lord Jesus Christ. When the heavenly atmosphere of the Divine presence comes down, it can be felt in reality. One night as I was praying with these people, the Holy Spirit seemed to hover above me, and light upon my head. This was like the quiet gentle dew of heaven. There was a wonderful sense of the presence of the Lord. One of those in prayer fell prostrate before God.'[15]

Donald Saunders Jr. recalled that even though he wasn't yet converted, he could instinctively tell when a person was praying 'in the Spirit – there was a power within them that didn't belong to them.' Likewise, he observed, 'when a hymn was sung in the Spirit, you quickly got the heart of it, having a deep feeling of what it was about.' Donald was sorry when the Barvas Church was renovated, and the old pews removed to make way for comfortable chairs. 'Those pews were sodden in the tears of the saints over the years,' he reminisced, 'especially during times of revival.'[16]

'It didn't matter what you were doing during the day,' reminisced Willie Smith, 'you were dying to get to the prayer meeting! You were working away on the croft – except it didn't

15. Douglas Bushby, *Revival in the Hebrides* in *The Pentecostal Evangel,* 25.01.1953.

16. Personal communication with Donald Saunders, 04.05.2020.

feel like work at all; you were more or less floating on air the whole time. And you were praying without ceasing for the meetings and for those who weren't yet converted. And the Spirit of the Lord was pouring upon you, and you hardly knew where it was coming from.'[17]

One young girl under deep conviction went to Shader to visit her friend, Chirsty Ann, who had recently been converted. The second she walked into the house, Chirsty Ann's parents 'downed tools and both enveloped me in a great big hug, with tears streaming down their faces. "My dear friend," the father said, "maybe you've come that the Lord might have mercy on you." They were making dinner, but this was completely neglected, as they just sat down and prayed with me – this was revival.'

Chirsty Ann continued: 'A neighbour who had also been recently converted came in. And all the busy activities of a Saturday afternoon were laid aside, and the entire afternoon was spent in prayer and praise – my friends just pouring out praises and supplications to the Lord. Thanksgiving for all the Lord had done; prayers for me and for everyone living round about who still hadn't found Him. I could only think of my emptiness and desolation, while they were all so completely full of the Spirit. It was a revelation of real revival, where truly the things of the earth took second place, and only the Lord and His kingdom were seen to count.'[18]

Fellowship

One convert shared, 'We were happy to have cottage meetings any time in these days. Or gatherings for praise and fellowship. No one person led them, but elders took them in turns, and if the Lay Missionary, Callum Macmillan, was at home, he was

---

17. Willie Smith, on *Revival in our Times*.

18. Fay Macleod, on *Revival in our Times*.

always more than ready to do so. He was a good preacher with a burden for the lost.'[19]

There developed a special affection between revival converts; one said it was 'like a family bond.' Even though Lewis folk were somewhat non-demonstrative in expressing their emotions, many believers would show their mutual affection in the form of a hug, where no words needed to be spoken. Physical closeness took other forms too. The Rev. Mackay owned a small car, and he used to transport folk to meetings in other districts. Agnes Morrison recalls as many as seven believers piling into that small vehicle to be ferried to some revival meeting in a distant part of the island!

John Smith (Gobha) next to Rev Mackay's car

Donald John Smith recalled, 'There was great excitement jumping on a bus that was heading off to a revival meeting somewhere on the island. You hardly knew or cared where it was going. The singing on the bus was spontaneous and loud! And it continued virtually the whole way. There was no point in trying to make

19. Personal communication with Margaret Macleod, 03.03.2022.

conversation with the person sitting next to you – for the singing filled the bus.'[20]

The twice-yearly communion seasons were further times of heightened blessing and fellowship during the revival, Christians travelling from all over the island to participate in them. Believers ate, fellowshipped and prayed together. 'How we looked forward to them!,' said one revival convert. 'What heavenly times they were,' said another, 'and all the while remembering the Lord's death until He comes.'

We need to remember, of course, that the conversations, prayers and praise all took place in the Gaelic language. With almost everything produced on the revival having been published in English (book, pamphlets, audio tapes, video recordings, websites & blogs), it's all too easy to overlook this fact. Campbell delivered his sermons in Gaelic, public prayers were offered in Gaelic, Psalms and hymns were rendered in Gaelic, and all conversation at cottage meetings and elsewhere was spoken in that language. In context, the Lewis revival of '49-52 was an almost exclusively Gaelic affair.

Singing

The singing of praises to God took on a highly significant role during the revival and was regarded as one of its most salient features. Believers sang in the churches; they sang during times of family worship in their homes; they sang as they walked to and from meetings; they sang in buses and on boats; they sang in their shielings,[21] in the peat banks, and as they wove at their looms. Throughout the duration of the revival, the island resounded with the joyous tones of praise.

---

20. Personal communication with Donald John Smith, 19.09.2016.

21. Small huts seasonally inhabited by crofters tending cattle or sheep on high or remote ground.

Like the preaching, the singing was invariably in Gaelic, and, in line with Highland Reformed tradition, came without instrumental accompaniment. In churches, only the Psalms were sung – favourites among converts included Psalms 72, 102, 126 and 132. The custom in Gaelic Psalm singing was that a precentor would lead the first two lines, following which everyone else would join in.

During the revival, in spontaneous reaction to the liberty of the Spirit, the eager congregation would join in right from the start, and many said they never heard singing like it before or since. It virtually transported them into another realm. One convert recalled, 'You could close your eyes, listen to the singing and just float to heaven! As the meeting progressed in power, many times the singers would take over the precenting as well, so every line was sung not just once, but twice by all.'[22]

Another convert said: 'the Lord's presence was felt more deeply during the singing than at any other time during the revival. The singing during a service was an indication of the type of meeting we would have. I remember that in one or two services you felt you could continue singing throughout the whole service,' and during the singing, converts were born into the kingdom.'[23]

New Hymns
While only Psalms were sung in church services, both Psalms and hymns were spontaneously sung in the cottage meetings, or at other times. In Barvas, it was often at the close of the last cottage meeting, in the early hours of the morning, as people were leaving to return home, that a group of local converts known simply as 'the Shader girls' would stand by the road junction and lead the joyous believers in singing. At times this would continue for up

---

22. Peckham, *Sounds from Heaven*, p. 217.

23. Testimony on *Lewis, Land of Revival*, audio tape, quoted in Allen, *Catch the Wind*, p. 122.

to an hour. Often the local minister would join with them in singing newly composed hymns.

Indeed, scores of new hymns were written by budding composers during the revival, mainly on the theme of the love and wonder of Jesus the Saviour. John Murdo Smith wrote his first hymn just days after his conversion in December 1949. He titled it '*O Nach Tig Thu Fhear Mo Ghraidh*' ('*O Won't You Come My Beloved*'), and he sang it at a cottage meeting the following night. His sister, Catherine, converted shortly afterwards, also became a prominent hymn writer. She was also a popular singer of spiritual songs, including her own. An Arnol convert, Margaret MacPhail, had no previous gifting in song-writing, yet wrote several hymns during the revival;[24] her lovely songs often being sung locally, as well as being distributed to Gaels all over the world.

Katie Campbell recalled a friend who was converted during the revival who composed a lot of hymns. 'But she couldn't do it anytime she wanted to do it. The words just came to her, they were just divinely inspired. And she never ever wrote one of them down. She remembered them all by heart. And they are beautiful ….People were so full of praise, and it just poured out of them.'[25]

Former Glasgow Tent Hall pastor John Moore visited Lewis shortly after the close of the revival, and called in on a woman converted during the movement. As she was preparing the tea, John, already a prolific hymn-writer,[26] wrote a hymn. He believed such tasks become easier during times of revival. The first verse of it is …

---

24. Not thirty as has been reported. Nor is it true that as many as five people in Arnol alone were known to have written spiritual poetry and songs during the awakening.

25. Katie Campbell, in *Hebrides Revival: A Retrospective*, Video, Sentinel Group, 2012.

26. Perhaps his best-known composition is, *Burdens are Lifted at Calvary*, as popularly sung by the Gaither vocal group.

Lord Jesus I adore thee.
Thy name to me is sweet.
With all my heart I'll praise thee,
And worship at thy feet.

It was said that singing during the revival took on a form hitherto unknown and inimitable. 'I have heard stories of revival when people walking on the road would hear the singing,' noted Katie Campbell, 'and you would know that the people were revived, because of the life in the singing.'[27]

Hymns and Poems

The following song was composed by Kate Macdonald of 56 Lower Barvas during the early days of the revival. The first nine verses are presented in its original Gaelic, along with the full composition in English (translated by Alice Allan). While not always rhyming, the translation seeks to retain the meaning and the spirit of the original, as well as the many details of the Old Testament record of God's dealing with His people.

Gabh rann do Mhaighstir Caimbeul còir,
Gum fada bhios e beò;
Cuireadh pheacaich don a' chrò,
'S dhan treòrachadh gu aithreachas.

An cuala sibh an riamh na b' fheàrr,
An cunnartan air inns' do chàch;
Dìdean breuga faoin gun stà,
Chan fhagadh e aig duin' againn.

Ach an Tì a thig bho h-àrd –,
Iosa Criosd le cumhachd gràidh;
'S e troimh Spiorad Naoimh nan gràs,
Ri gabhal tàmh nar cridheachan.

---

27. Campbell, *Hebrides Revival: A Retrospective*, video.

Ged a dh'eisteadh sinn car uair,
Bho Bheinn Shinai bagradh cruaidh;
Anns an tionndadh dha mu 'n cuairt,
Bhiodh buaidh am fuil a chrathaidh leis.

Se lagh 's an soisgeul a thug buaidh,
Air an oigridh ghràdhach tha mun cuairt;
'S bithidh iad air a deanamh luaidh,
Gu ruig iad suas na flaitheanas.

Theirinnsa ri peacaich thruagh,
Gun iad bhith coimhead air mar fhuaim;
Ach iad aomadh ris an cluais,
Gu ruig orr' buaidh a theachaireachd.

Bha cuid againn mar Iònah truagh,
Nuair labhradh ris an dara uair;
S ged thugadh e a doimhne chuain,
Bha nàdur truagh cho ceannairceach.

Tha cuid eile mar eun air sgèith,
Bhios a' caoidh gu tric leoth' fèin;
Aig eascreideamh ann an grèim,
Gun tog E fèin le ghealladh iad.

Their an namhaid riu gu dian,
Cha robh do sheòrs sa chrò a riamh;
Gun cuimhnich iad air pobull Dhia,
Gun tàinig trian tro teine dhiubh.

Translation

Dear Mr Campbell, I applaud,
May he with many years be blessed;
Inviting sinners to the fold,
And guiding them to penitence.

At warning sinners unsurpassed,
Useless strongholds false and frivolous;

Without substance for good living,
He would not leave with anyone.

Rather, he'd promote One from on high,
Yea, Jesus Christ with power of love;
Whose Holy Spirit by His grace,
Would now reside in each of us.

Though he might rant perhaps an hour,
With serious threats from Sinai's Mount;
The tone he then would turn around,
While leading us to Calvary.

The Gospel's power has touched the lives,
Of cherished young folk all around;
Who've joined the ranks of God's beloved,
There to remain till Paradise.

Now my advice to sinners poor,
Please view him not as merely noise;
Rather to him an ear incline,
So that his message penetrates.

Like poor Jonah some did flee,
But rescued was from ocean's depth;
Yet when challenged a second time,
His nature still rebellious.

Some others are like bird on wing,
Who often weep and grieve alone;
Caught in the grip of unbelief,
Till His own promise rescues them.

To them the devil's constant words,
"Your likes were never in the fold,"
May they recall God's chosen flock,
A third through fire were sanctified.

As Israel's children in their need,
Received from Heaven the manna pure;
He showered us with God's own Word,
We're lost if we don't value it.

May spirit of prayer from above,
Descend upon Your flock below;
The tumbling of the barley bread,
Cat'lyst for the rout of Midian.

When Your people all as one,
Prevailed against God's enemy;
No other words were in the tale,
But *"The sword of God and Gideon."*

So that the Gospel's healing power,
Touches lives who're heavy burdened;
Bestowing blessings rich, eternal,
Blood of the Lamb was shed for them.

When John he did observe the crowd,
Gathered round the throne above;
Twas through the Word their victory won,
The Blood of the Lamb had ransomed them.

Some of us can't follow the flock,
As age has robbed us of our vigour;
But such blessings from his words receive,
Creating heaven on earth for us.

* * *

Hector Mackinnon was an officiating elder on the isle of Berneray, and became a notable convert of the revival of 1952 on that island (see Chap 13). He was previously well-known as a local bard; after his conversion most of his compositions were of a spiritual nature. His songs were always composed to well-known Gaelic

tunes, a number of which became very popular. It was said that
he died on his knees at a spot on the shore which he frequented
for his times of prayer. His songs include this one (translated
from the original Gaelic), which rejoices in the indescribable
treasure he found in Christ.

The Precious Pearl

The precious Pearl that I found myself,
I would not give up for any earthly price;
There were Three around her who sealed it above,
The precious Pearl that I found myself.

I see friends every day who are going astray,
Storing treasures on earth that can't satisfy;
How poor you are, if you have not received,
The precious Pearl that I found myself.

How poor you are if you have not found her,
The precious gift of which you've surely heard;
But time will come when you regret not having gained,
The precious Pearl that I found myself.

I see an ancient one, there in the land,
Always descending the side of the glen;
The question is: did they win their race?
The precious Pearl that I found myself.

Oh, I see young people living among us now,
With rosy cheeks You made beautiful;
The beauty You created can most nobly be found,
In the precious Pearl that I found myself.

What makes you both purposeful and jealous
The day of youth living deep in your heart?;
Drawing close to him and asking him for,
The precious Pearl that I found myself.

For death will come to us, demanding its due,
And our homeland will never return;
How good to be under the Shepherd's protection,
The precious Pearl that I found myself.

Gold will not buy it, nor anything else,
Not even the cattle on a thousand hills;
The Lamb promised not to take away from me,
The precious Pearl that I found myself.

Is it not worthwhile having life to the full?
And seeking the desires of our heart?
Is it not worth spending virtues to gain,
The precious pearl that I found myself?

It cannot be overstated, her value and price,
She is the love of the Lamb to his people forever;
How sad I didn't find, in my childhood days,
The precious Pearl that I found myself.

When the flock that did not obey the King
And the sweet voice whispering, *You are from me*;
Happy are those people with precious Pearls,
That will not be taken from them all their days.

When I have to leave, I'll take her with me,
And be carried far away in time;
She will stand by me at the Court of the Lamb
The precious Pearl that I found myself.

* * *

Revival Ballad

The following song was written by popular Scottish folk singer, Mairi Campbell – a grand-daughter of Duncan Campbell – along with her musical partner David Francis. The song was

written for a musical show performed at the Edinburgh Fringe
Festival 2012.[28]

When war had gone and peace had come,
Times were hard, I've heard folk say;
There were such sights on the Long Isle,
Folk still remember to this day.

It started on a bitter night,
As people crept to church, in fear;
That God would pass them by again,
When hopes ran high that He was near.

In the pulpit, Campbell stands,
He shakes his head, he bangs his fist;
As if to rouse them from their sleep,
Of sin, and move them to resist.

Old Satan's snares and Satan's wiles,
And Satan's plans to keep them from;
The chance to know the Saviour, who,
Could take their souls to rightful home.

Campbell thumps the pulpit hard,
The sweat it runs all down his face;
His finger points, his eyes are fixed,
On all those sinners seeking grace.

A silence fills the crowded church,
A silence broken by the call;
Of one young man, all in a daze,
Who cries as to the floor he falls.

---

28. 'Revival!': An account and exploration of the life of Duncan Campbell,
preacher and itinerant Scottish missionary. (Permission to publish courtesy of
Mairi Campbell).

And as they gathered, as they met,
Their anxiousness both wide and deep;
The people cried out to the Lord,
And sore did sigh and sore did weep.

And then the cries, and then the groans,
And prayers for mercy all did rise;
And some were weeping tears of joy,
As they received salvation's prize.

The news spread fast, the news spread wide,
Revival longed for now was near;
And people flocked to Barvas town,
In hopes that Campbell they might hear.

Across the island, tales were told,
Of meetings in the dead of night;
Of corn uncut, and yarn unspun,
And shaking walls and floods of light.

How this man, drunk for twenty years,
Had thrown the bottle in the sea;
And that man, flat upon his face,
Had cried out, *'Hell's too good for me!'*

Of this old woman's visions strong,
Of that young woman in a trance;
And how the pipers wouldn't play,
And how the people wouldn't dance.

* * *

Children

As with most spiritual outpourings, the majority of converts of
the Lewis revival were in their later teens or twenties. Presbyterian

church structure on the island meant that children aged under fifteen weren't encouraged to attend meetings, there being little expectation of them getting converted. It was theologically questioned whether such young minds could truly grasp the fundamental truths of the gospel.

It is not surprising, therefore, that only a small number of converts were aged fourteen or less. As a rule these youngsters would not apply for church membership for some time, in order that their 'fruit' be tested. An emphasis on worthiness before taking communion and on immediately attending the prayer meeting as a mark of conversion were two notable factors that mitigated against children making a response to the gospel. It was, said one, as if childhood did not count as a time for regeneration.[29]

Jack Macarthur

Jack Macarthur said that up to the age of eleven, he had only been inside a church once, and had no idea what a Sunday school was.[30] Nevertheless, he was never more aware of issues such as sin, judgement, hell and forgiveness as he was when, during Duncan Campbell's mission in Galson in 1950, he would attend the meetings with his newly-converted parents. He did not recollect any other children attending.

He remembered being conscious night after night that God was there in that small Galson hall. 'There was a searching, an awareness, a knowledge that something had to be done. I had to respond.' Initially he found himself rebelling against Campbell's message, yet knowing full well that if God consigned him to hell, He would be totally just in so doing. There was, he said,

---

29. Harry Sprange, *Children in Revival: 300 Years of God's Work in Scotland*, Fearn, 2002, p. 290.

30. Although there almost certainly was one in his home parish of Ness – albeit some considerable distance from the Macarthurs' home in Galson – where the very capable Lady Missionary Miss Jessie Macleod served.

'an amazing refusal to stay at the end of the evening. Knowing myself searched and judged and knowing the battle inside.'[31]

Jack's moment of spiritual breakthrough came a year later (1951) during quiet evening worship in his own home, through a Brethren man from Whitehaven speaking on the Second Coming. 'I was caught off guard because he wasn't preaching, and I had to leave the room and go up to my bedroom. I knew there was no alternative, and he led me to the Lord in the morning.'[32]

Jack Macarthur

This man, George Taylor, travelled around with his wife in a caravan, and a few days later, met Jack again, in the parish church at Ness. He said to the lad, 'I hope I'll see the day when you come down these pulpit steps,' which statement made a deep impression upon the boy. Sure enough, some years later, Jack felt called to the ministry. And Taylor was indeed present when he preached his opening sermon after his induction to his first charge, in Kinlochbervie.

31. Sprange, *Children in Revival*, p. 382.

32. ibid.

Norrie Maciver

Norrie Maciver lived on Lewis between the ages of eight and eleven at the time of the revival. He attended some of the midweek meetings with his parents, and he knew that God was present there, as well as in the community. He was aware the Spirit was convicting people of wrongdoing, and that he had a clear decision to make. In fact, his boyhood fear was that if his mother had a direct hot-line to God, then she would know his sins too!

Although he didn't respond to the gospel at that time, he knew that he could have. For him it confirmed the possibility of children being converted. Even at that tender age, the revival had a definite effect on Norrie. It laid within him the basis of an evangelical faith, and after he returned to Glasgow at the age of eleven, he retained that faith despite not being part of an evangelical church.[33]

Two Donalds

Donald Macdonald was one of the youngest converts of the '49 revival in Ness – he was gloriously converted at the age of fourteen. He came from a Free Church background, and sadly, was ostracised and scorned for attending Campbell's meetings. But he held fast to his new-found faith and went on to become a minister in the denomination of his youth, serving in Uist and Bernera, among other places.

Another fourteen-year-old Donald who heard Duncan Campbell was Donald Saunders. While his parents attended all the meetings in Barvas, Donald only attended the occasional one to see what all the fuss was about. He and his father had just laid the foundations of a new house. One evening during the construction, the young lad went to hear Campbell preaching in Shader. The evangelist's message was on Armageddon. Deeply impacted by the sermon, Donald went home thinking there was

---

33. ibid. p. 290. After turning to Christ many years later, Norrie went on to become a minister in the Church of Scotland.

no point in continuing with the house since it seemed the day of reckoning was so near! Although impressed with the meetings he attended, Donald did not surrender his life to the Lord at that time, naively thinking he would leave the decision till he was older.[34]

Kathleen Macleod

With her mum and next-door neighbour, fourteen-year-old Kathleen Macleod attended a couple of Campbell's meetings in Stornoway in January '52. Though not fluent in Gaelic, she understood most of what was preached. She didn't come under conviction, but at one meeting her neighbour, Cathy, like various others in the packed Town Hall, began sobbing quietly. Kathleen was sure her neighbour would be saved that night – but she remained unconverted in subsequent months.

Kathleen's mum, Morag, was married into the Church of Scotland, but had come to Christ years earlier in the Free Church. She eagerly attended numerous of Campbell's Stornoway meetings. Indeed, with a friend, she followed him to gatherings all over the island. Kathleen recalled that her mum's circle of friends seemed so on fire for God in those days, and they never stopped enthusing about Him. Kathleen gave her life to Christ some years later.[35]

---

34. Donald's sister, Alisanne, seven years his senior, reluctantly agreed to attend one service – purely because of the pleadings of her mother. She sat in the church feeling totally out of place and longing to be somewhere else – anywhere else! Yet within half an hour of the meeting beginning, she was smitten by conviction under the preaching of the Word and came to a place of peace soon after. (Personal communication with Donald Saunders, 04.05.2020).

35. Personal communication with Kathleen Macleod, 12.03.2023.

CHAPTER 15

Revival Phenomena

There would appear to be something of a curious contradiction when it comes to the topic of unusual phenomena attending the revival. On the one hand, revival converts have been in near unison in stating that little in the way of revival phenomena occurred during the '49 movement compared to the earlier 1930s revival on the island.

On the other hand, in most of Campbell's reports on the revival, there is a notable emphasis on phenomena; indeed, the majority of stories he told had this as their focus. His own explanation was that he saw more physical and supernatural manifestations in his ministry in the Highlands and Islands than elsewhere because of the problem of assurance. God granted manifestations to encourage those of weak and trembling faith to grasp the promises of life, he believed.

Campbell's fascination with emphasising the sensational is certainly more apparent in his later addresses, and barely features at all in his weekly FM reports. Curiously, those acquainted with his preaching point out that he was generally against emotional displays, and at times even sought to dissuade them at meetings.

Nevertheless, a number of cases of unusual phenomena were reported during the movement. Even those who encountered such manifestations, however, were quick to point out that they never became a central focus of the movement. Jesus Christ was central; inexplicable curiosities were peripheral.

Trances

There were a number of testimonies of individuals falling into trances or becoming unconscious during the revival. While these have regularly been highlighted in reports of the awakening, revival converts say that excepting one or two specific individuals, they were relatively rare. Perhaps the most common expression was of people raising their hands in the air and remaining in that position for an unusual period of time, occasionally extending to up to an hour.

Such was the case with a young girl from Carloway whose hands would go blue for lack of circulation. Others in the room became concerned, and gently tried to ease her arms down, but found them rigid and impossible to move. She would later come out of the trance calmly, drop her arms, and the circulation would begin to flow again. Allan MacArthur remembered seeing 'people raising their arms in the air, and others shaking at meetings, both in church settings and in houses.'[1] 'But there was not much in the way of manifestations in the '49 revival,' observed Catriona Macaulay. 'All I remember was a man from Barvas who used to raise his hands in the air.'[2]

One visitor at a cottage meeting in the afterglow of the Uig awakening watched the wife of the Rev. Macfarlane 'going off into a trance and breathing heavily.' She later testified, 'Since the Holy Spirit's power broke my heart during the revival I often get lost in the Lord. His love overwhelms me.'[3]

Then there is the (unconfirmed) story of a Christian woman who repeatedly fell into a trance, whereby she had visions concerning incidents and people of which and whom she had no natural knowledge. One day this woman informed Campbell that he should visit a lady who was in agony of soul some twenty miles

1. Personal communication with Allan Macarthur, 20.08.2009.

2. Personal communication with Catriona Macaulay, 05.04.2020.

3. Bushby, *Adventures in Revival*, p. 30.

away. Travelling to the village, Campbell found the situation just as it had been described to him. He was able to bring a word in season to the woman, pointing her to the Saviour.

Heavenly Music

There were a few testimonies to the hearing of angelic singing during the revival (in distinction to angelic sightings, which were not a notable feature of the movement). Indeed, this theme of heavenly music seems to have inspired the title of the Peckhams' book, *Sounds from Heaven.*

Chirsty Maggie MacPhail describes a house meeting where, towards the close, 'My brother and I heard heavenly music as if it came out from the closet under the stairs. It seemed that a heavenly choir was passing through! It was somehow not like voices but like an orchestra, yet more wonderful. It was simply a marvellous sound. It was heavenly! It wafted through from under the stairs and moved slowly across the foyer and out through the front door.' People looked at each other in astonishment, whispering, 'Did you hear that too?,' though not everyone present did.[4]

Catherine Smith recalls an occasion when her mother stood outside on the path one night and she called her father, saying, 'Come and hear this!' They heard the voices of angels singing. They followed the sound of the heavenly harmony to a home two doors away and there they found two women crying in distress of soul.[5] They were convinced that God had led them to that home in an hour of need.

Prophetic Words and Premonitions

Norman Campbell tells how he had been under conviction of sin for much of his life, but tried to shake it off by joining his friends in the pub, drinking. One day the Rev. Lachie MacLeod

---

4. Peckham, *Sounds from Heaven*, p. 218.

5. ibid., p. 225.

put his hand on Norman's head and said, 'This boy will yet be a good boy,' meaning a godly Christian. Interestingly, Campbell was the only boy present who went on to become a Christian and to live a life of godly witness.[6]

Another story related by Norman Campbell is that of a friend of his who had been held as a prisoner of war by the Japanese, during which time he had witnessed the most awful atrocities. He returned to Lewis an avowed atheist. He did, however, go to hear Duncan Campbell preach after his mother pled with him to do so. One evening he and a friend met Mary Macdonald of Swainbost on the road. She told them both to go to the service that evening as God was going to deal with one of them. They went and from then on, Calum's life was transformed.

There are a number of stories that testify to the spiritual sensitivity of Duncan Campbell himself. A minister with whom he once stayed related that Campbell sometimes knew in advance who was going to get converted. One day, looking across a loch to a house on the other side, he remarked, 'There's a young woman who is going to find the Saviour in that house tonight.' It happened just as he said.

Cases of physical healing during the revival were almost unknown – possibly because they were neither sought after nor expected. One unique exception, shared by Norman MacDonald, relates to the above-mentioned Mary Macdonald. Mary had been bedridden for several years, during some of which time she seemed to be in a coma. On the outbreak of the revival, remarkably, she suddenly recovered. 'She could tell us who the next convert would be,' noted Norman, 'and on hearing the door opening, although she was blind, she would greet each visitor with a very apt and suitable verse from the Word of God. Her recovery was remarkable – nothing short of a miracle.'[7]

---

6. Peckham, *Sounds from Heaven*, p. 185.

7. ibid., p. 260.

Shortly after his dramatic conversion during the revival, Norman ('Paddy') MacLean was asked to drive a coach of young people on a May Day excursion. On the way to Ness lighthouse, Norman pulled the coach to the side of the road so they could enjoy a picnic. Here, he turned to face the youngsters and began to preach. As he did so, he directed a special warning to a young lad who he believed was resisting the Spirit of the Lord. He had a conviction that the teen's death was imminent, though he didn't know when. Before the group left the Butt of Lewis, the passengers enjoyed a game of football with other visitors. Tragically, the lad to whom Norman had felt so burdened to speak went over the cliff as he chased the ball. He died later in hospital. Some of those who had been on the coach came to the Lord shortly after, when Norman preached at a house meeting nearby.[8]

Tales of the Sensational

There was a dear old man who used to warmly welcome 'revival pilgrims' from all over the world into his home over the course of many years and share with them stories of the revival. Visitors loved his warm personality and gentle Hebridean accent, his unassuming nature and his genuine love for the Lord. Long retired, and living alone, this genial gentleman appreciated the company of his guests, and enjoyed helping them in their quest for revival knowledge.

With the passing of time, and perhaps aware that visitors were increasingly clamouring for stories that were out-of-the-ordinary, some claim that the man began to focus on the more sensational anecdotes that so appealed to his guests. As such, they say, a few of his stories may have become somewhat distanced from reality. Whether this is true or not, certainly, one or two of the anecdotes he shared were rather unique.

---

8. Personal communication with Mary Anne Darragh, (daughter of Norman) 10.03.2023.

He said, for example, that one night during the revival, while a man was praying at a cottage meeting, he saw in his mind's eye a white dove resting on the heads of certain people. He named those individuals one by one, and remarkably, each one of them was converted that night. In a separate interview, the same man claimed that during a meeting in the blacksmith's house, a dove actually flew in through an open window and landed on the shoulder of the host, resting there for a time.

This man also attested that as crowds walked along the road going to and from meetings, supernatural lights would shine around them. He stated further, 'When the fire fell, you could see the lights on the houses, the barns, as people began to seek the Lord.⁹ Jehovah drew near to us. The Shekinah glory of God descended on the community, a tangible, supernatural light hovering over the farmhouses. When the glory of God shone on a house, the people would just be silent. It was like we had stepped into eternity.'¹⁰

Perhaps the most unusual phenomenon claimed by the Barvas worthy was the supernatural sighting of a 'gospel ship.' 'One night as we left (a cottage meeting), we saw in the open fields, a ship – a navy ship – all lit up between the masts. We knew it

---

9. One convert belatedly spoke of a supernatural light that shone down on a group of young converts as they walked home from meetings in dark winter nights. As one person left the group to walk the track to her house, a light would follow her to the door. (Interestingly, very similar experiences were reported during the Indonesian revival of the late 1960s.) Intriguingly, although this convert relates stories of walking home from late-night meetings in other interviews, she does not there recount any occurrence of supernatural activity.

10. Allen, *Catch the Wind*, p. 164. Alistair Petrie took this considerably further: 'There would be great big balls of fire falling out of heaven, and literally setting the houses on fire. How do bricks and mortar light up, unless there's something of the physics of God changing the molecular structure of those bricks. It's an incredible thing to behold. ... There was very high supernatural activity, because of the permeating presence of God' (Revival Lecture, YouTube).

wasn't "real" for it was on dry land. We couldn't say a word; none of us could even speak. *"Be still and know that I am God"* – that's all we could say.'

Fascinated by this testimony, author, Alistair Petrie – in a video entitled, *Supernatural Works of God in a Revival* – developed the theme further. He claimed that 'Only two times in biblical history has this revival ship ever been seen on land' (although we're not told when the first occasion was). Petrie was convinced that as 'a sign of when God's about to come and pour out His Spirit, a nautical ship is sometimes seen on land. And everybody sees it. It's breath-taking. You can hardly describe it.'

Petrie referred to several other phenomena that he claimed occurred during the Lewis revival. He noted for example, 'one person would be out singing on one of the islands. They would hear angels singing over one island, and then the angels over there would be singing on the other island, and then there'd be a response of singing (back and fore).' Fascinating as they certainly are, most of these sensational anecdotes have not been corroborated by other revival converts, and one or two individuals have questioned their authenticity.

The Paranormal

One Lewis native who became a critic of the revival shared several examples of people being negatively impacted by the movement. One case was when he and a friend, both in their early teens, attended a late-night cottage meeting in Barvas. During the course of the meeting, his pal witnessed a grown man levitating on the stairway.[11] Naturally, the young lad was both surprised and shocked by the incident, and he was said to have never attended a revival meeting again.

Another example related to a cottage meeting elsewhere on the island. The lady of the house was carrying a tray of refreshments

---

11. This friend, John Murray, went on to become an eminent Gaelic writer and head of BBC Gaelic radio.

for the visitors. As she entered the living room, she began to swoon under emotional influence. She instantly let go of her tray, full as it was of cups, saucers and a pot of tea. As the tray dropped it began to float in mid-air. Some were deeply impressed at such display of the supernatural, though others were disturbed by the incident.

The person said the story had been confirmed to him by those directly connected to it. But some who attended the meeting later insisted the incident never happened, while someone present at the Barvas cottage meeting has testified that no instance of levitation occurred, also dismissing other details of the above account. I have been unable to substantiate either of the stories, both of which were, in any case, quite unrepresentative of the revival in question.

Pentecostal Presence

The 1949–52 Lewis revival was not Pentecostal in form. Duncan Campbell was not a Pentecostal,[12] there were no Pentecostal churches on Lewis or Harris, and virtually no believer on the island was known to hold to the theological doctrines of Pentecostalism. Lewis was predominantly, indeed almost exclusively, Presbyterian. Nevertheless, as in the 1930s awakening, so too in the later movement, there were one or two individual cases of believers receiving a post-conversion 'baptism in the Spirit' and of speaking in tongues.[13]

---

12. Nevertheless, Campbell willingly accepted invitations in later years to speak in churches of all denominations, including Pentecostal. His involvement in later years with Y.W.A.M. was disapprovingly regarded by some as a personal connection with Pentecostalism.

13. Hugh Black claimed that at one time Duncan Campbell spoke in tongues. I am aware of no evidence to back this up. To the contrary, Campbell made it clear that he never spoke in tongues and that neither did he even hear anyone in the Hebrides exercise that gift (Black, *Revival, Including Prophetic Vision*, Greenock 1993, p. 100; Allen, *Catch the Wind*, p. 158).

Within twenty-four hours of his conversion, Norman Campbell was walking along the road with some church elders when he became aware of a bright light shining down from above. Looking up, he saw a vision of the face of Christ, who also told him, 'I love you all.' Norman was elated and assumed this sort of experience must be common to every new Christian! Strangely no one else in the group saw or heard what he did, and for a long time he told no one. That same day Norman also experienced a 'baptism in the Spirit' and found himself speaking in an unknown language, though he had never read or heard of such an experience before. He became a powerful witness and a gifted prayer warrior.[14]

A 'Phenomenal' Visit

When Hugh Black visited the island with the purpose of 'taking the message of Pentecost to Lewis,'[15] he led house meetings in various locations, during which a number of people experienced 'the baptism of the Spirit' accompanied by speaking in tongues. Black relates a number of other unusual phenomena experienced by himself and others in the afterglow of the revival. These include:

1. 'A being of tremendous spiritual power' standing behind him during a cottage meeting; tugging Black's jacket to indicate that he was to sit down. When he did, 'the glory of God fell upon that company.'[16]
2. Clear supernatural words of knowledge about a Christian woman on the island.
3. A supernatural light filling the room (terrifying another person present), and with it an intense sense of the presence of God.

---

14. Black, *Revival: Personal Encounters*, pp. 65–8; *The Baptism in the Spirit and Its Effects*, Greenock, 1987, pp. 59–60.

15. Black, *Revival: Personal Encounters*, p. 40.

16. ibid., p. 44.

4. Supernatural fragrance and sound filling a room.
5. The spontaneous outbreak of 'holy laughter.'
6. The visible manifestation of demons at a prayer meeting.

Even more out of the ordinary (if such is possible) was what happened late one evening after a house meeting in Stornoway. Three people left the meeting but returned hurriedly a short time later. Though not excited or hysterical, they were for some time unable to speak. It transpired that as they walked down the street, they all saw a band of light in the dark sky, forming into the shape of a cross. Out of the cross, a luminous cloud appeared, from which a figure of Christ emerged, hand stretching forward. All three went down as one to the pavement.[17] The group was profoundly blessed by the experience.[18]

17. ibid., pp. 54–6.

18. There was opposition to Black's meetings by some on this strictly Calvinist island, and it was claimed that the friction resulted in a split in at least one congregation (Rev. M. Macaulay and Rev. M. A. Macleod, *Discussion on Revival*, audio tape)..

CHAPTER 16

Revival Visitors

As news of the remarkable revival taking place on the island spread outwith Lewis, people began to stream from the mainland of Scotland and further afield with a desire to witness unusual goings on for themselves. Visitors were most common in 1952 and '53, by which time news of the revival had disseminated widely across the country.

Campbell spent time with many of the visitors, recounting the beginnings of the movement and some of his favourite stories for the umpteenth time. He acted as a gracious host, often taking visitors to meet revival converts in their homes, conducting interviews, and inviting them to meetings in churches and halls.

Early Arrivals

One of the first visitors was Duncan Campbell's wife, Shona, who met with her husband on the island in June 1950.[1] By the autumn of that year, the revival was attracting more and more curious pilgrims. One was James Clark of the Drummond Tract Society (who later used revival stories to address evangelistic meetings on the mainland). Another was Dwight Wadsworth, an American journalist living in Germany (Nov 1950). At one point several students from the London Bible College established

---

1. Shona had worked in Africa for several years as a member of the Algiers Mission Board, before marrying Duncan in 1925.

253

links with Campbell, and some made the long journey north in hope of seeing a 'real life' revival in progress.[2]

Duncan & Shona Campbell with the parents of Mary Morrison

A number of leading figures connected to the Faith Mission went over to witness what they'd been hearing from their evangelist colleague ever since revival first broke out; these included J. G. Eberstein, President of the Mission and Editor of *Bright Words*; G. E. M. Govan, and Willie Black, District Superintendent for the Highlands and Islands. Regarded as a 'spiritual giant-heart for whom all felt such a spontaneous affection,'[3] Black visited Lewis several times during the revival (sometimes with his wife), supporting Duncan Campbell, engaging in preaching, and supervising the local Prayer Unions.

In the autumn of 1951, twenty-eight-year-old Arthur Wallis, an evangelist from Bristol, made the long trip north to witness the revival in progress. He was given the opportunity to spend some time with Campbell, and was 'greatly impressed by this godly Scot, a man whose self-effacing humility marked him out as one of God's truly great saints.'[4]

2. Ian M. Randall, *Educating Evangelicalism: The Origins, Development and Impact of London Bible College*, Carlisle, 2000, p. 7.

3. Peckham, *Heritage of Revival*, p. 69. Black died suddenly in Ireland in 1967.

4. Jonathan Wallis, *Arthur Wallis Radical Christian*, Eastbourne, 1991, p. 92. Wallis retained a life-long passion for revival, later becoming a leader in

1952 Visits

One visit from 'several minister friends' of Campbell coincided with that of perhaps the foremost itinerant evangelist serving in Britain at the time, Tom Rees. Both parties spent valuable time with Campbell and fired a host of questions at him relating to the awakening.[5] Additionally, in 1952, Dr George Johnstone Jeffrey, Moderator of the General Assembly of the Church of Scotland, paid a visit to Lewis, where he attended a conference in Stornoway. Jeffrey spoke of 'the warmth of feeling, and the evangelistic zeal and fervour of the people.'[6]

Another young man who travelled from afar to visit the revival was Douglas Bushby, a champion Australian runner, then based in America, who later entered the ministry. Ambitiously, he and his brother, Max, decided to engage on a world tour to learn more about revivals. The two Australians stayed in Lewis for a month, travelling around and meeting those caught up in the awakening. Day after day they cycled seven or eight miles to attend prayer meetings.

Douglas Bushby

the fledgling charismatic movement, also producing the book, *In the Day of Thy Power* (foreword by Duncan Campbell), still considered a classic on the dynamics of revival.

5. Rees' outstanding career is ably outlined in the biography, *His Name Was Tom*, written by his wife.

6. Campbell, *The Lewis Awakening*, p. 10.

In Uig, 'the sight of a two-storey home filled with people downstairs and up was unforgettable,' records Bushby. 'We sat on the steps of the staircase as Rev. Campbell went from room to room challenging the people. They prayed, sang, praised God as the power of God's presence overwhelmed them.'[7] Bushby met dozens of believers during his stay on the island, including 'many Presbyterians to whom God had shown remarkable visions of future events that actually took place ….My questions rattled out like machine gun bullets. I was convinced after a month with these people that God wrote the Book of Acts to be our experimental textbook on revivals.'[8]

In 1952, Bill Kettles, a young recently-converted student, was invited to Lewis by a friend from the island. At that time the Rev. Macfarlane of Uig was still holding cottage meetings virtually every night of the week. Although, the meetings were held in Gaelic, Kettles attended as many as possible. The minister would ask the elders to pray in turn, and Kettles sat in amazement as they prayed with fervour for 'half an hour each.'[9]

Post-Revival Pilgrims

While the revival had largely died down by 1953, visitors were flocking in increased numbers to the island. Campbell wrote in August, 'There is much need of prayer, as the enemy is at work, causing division. Preachers from churches with different emphases have been here, from Brethren to Pentecostal, causing confusion.'[10]

---

7. Bushby, *Adventures in Revival*, p. 31.

8. ibid, p. 32. After returning to America, Bushby became a U.N. War Correspondent for Korea. He witnessed for Christ on the front lines in the Korean War, and played a vital role in getting Syngman Rhee, first president of the Republic of Korea, to sign the truce which eventually brought peace in this conflict.

9. Kettles, *The Lewis Revival: A Covenant Engagement*.

10. Duncan Campbell, FM Report, 26.08.1953. The Pentecostal reference appears to relate to Hugh Black, whose visit carried the focused objective of

People on mainland Europe were also excited to hear of the gracious showers of blessing falling on Lewis and Harris. In 1956 a wealthy Swiss lady made the lengthy journey to the Western Isles in the hope of meeting Duncan Campbell and confirming first-hand accounts of the movement she had recently heard about. She shared her experience with friends, the Vischers, on her return to the continent.

Excitedly, Mr Vischer related how he had served with Duncan Campbell during a six-month stint with the Faith Mission in Oban in 1920. This led to a close friendship developing between the Vishers and Duncan and Shona, one eventual result of which was that the Visher's son, Karl, proposed to the Campbell's daughter, Sheena and they married soon after.[11]

Even during his years based in Edinburgh as Principal of the Faith Mission, Campbell continued to receive visitors from far and near. One who made the long journey to meet the evangelist – in October 1958 – was Wesley Duewel, an American writer and missionary who had served in India for twenty-two years.[12]

Duewel spent time with Campbell, both at the Faith Mission Bible College and in Campbell's home, and again some years later in Duewel's American home during Campbell's first visit to the States, for which the American organised several meetings for the Scot to speak at. Reflecting on his times with the evangelist, Duewel wrote, 'I treasure most sitting by his side as he told me revival stories.'[13]

'taking the message of Pentecost to Lewis.' A revival convert also shared that 'In the mid fifties some folk with different traditions came to the area and although not preaching in churches, made clear in house groups that they thought what we had was insufficient. It had a very unsettling effect in the congregation. It was not pleasant for us at the time' (personal communication 18.07.2018).

11. Personal communication with Sheena Campbell Vischer, 15.03.2020.

12. Duewel went on to author numerous highly acclaimed inspirational books on persevering prayer and the power of victorious living.

13. Wesley Duewel, *Heroes of The Holy Life*, Grand Rapids, 2002, p. 36.

CHAPTER 17

Revival Conduit

Channel of Revival

We've noted that during the first year of revival in Lewis, Campbell was out of the island for around half of that time. What is fascinating to observe is that during those twenty-six weeks, there was no fresh appearance of revival in any locality.

It is easy to argue that the revival wasn't dependent on any one man, and continued without him. That statement is only half true. Certainly, revival continued in Campbell's absence in places where it had already been ignited under his ministry. But there is no documentation of revival breaking out anywhere in Lewis and Harris between 1949 and '52 until or unless Campbell visited the area to hold a series of meetings.

We have already noted that to be true of Barvas (p.*); the same is true of other districts. For example, in Arnol, situated only a few short miles from Barvas Church (and officially part of the parish of Barvas), revival only arose several months after it did in Barvas-Shader, and only following meetings begun by Campbell in (and following concerted prayer for) the district.

Precisely the same is true of the movements that commenced in Lochs, Bernera, Uig and other districts across the island. In each of these places, the faithful preaching of God's Word week by week did not result in the breaking out of revival. From each of these places, many visitors had attended revival meetings in Barvas and elsewhere after revival had begun under Campbell's ministry. Still revival failed to take hold of these communities in earnest, and it appeared to many that it wasn't going to.

Duncan Campbell

It was only directly following campaigns by Campbell in each of these localities that revival broke out – sometimes dramatically – in these districts. Conversely, areas where revival failed to take root tended to be districts where there existed strong opposition to Campbell, where there was no Church of Scotland presence and to which the evangelist was never invited; areas such as North Tolsta and Back to the north of Stornoway (where there existed a predominantly Free Presbyterian and Free Church presence, respectively), and Lemreway in the south – though even here a successful mission was held at the invitation of some Free Church people (being strongly opposed by some others).

It is quite apparent that Campbell did not follow revival around the island. Rather, revival followed Campbell. Revival, or revival-like scenes, broke out wherever *he* went, rather than him going where revival had already been ignited. Furthermore, revival appeared to await him patiently; coming to Uig, for example, in October 1951, nearly two full years after it first broke out in Barvas. In Berneray it was two-and-a-half years after.

Revival in these places waited, not just for Campbell to do his round of campaigns elsewhere on the island, but also for his return from numerous trips to mainland Scotland or from his lengthy missions to places like Partick, Glasgow and Monaghan, Ireland. It seems quite possible, if not likely, that revival would have broken out considerably earlier in places like Uig and Berneray had Campbell held missions in them sooner. It is therefore also quite possible that revival on the island would have faded sooner but for Campbell's prior commitments, and his obvious lack of haste.

Uig

Let's consider one or two locations where Faith Mission evangelists other than Campbell held campaigns during the revival. Pilgrims MacArthur and Coulter commenced a mission in Uig in October 1950. Intensive visiting and helping with the potato harvest helped increase attendance.

A brief visit from Duncan Campbell led to the 'first break,' when 'two young women sought the Lord, with much brokenness, to save them.' But numbers declined following an outbreak of measles in the community, and only one other person was noted as having 'come through for salvation' in the entire mission.

Moving on to nearby Lochcroistean in December, attendance averaged fourteen for the first week. MacArthur was laid off with the flu for a while, and although some were reported to be 'near the kingdom,' a concluding report in February 1951 states simply, 'no break at Lochcroistean.'[1]

---

1. FM Report, 14.02.1951. One man converted from this district was the headmaster of the small local school. He later moved to a larger school on the island.

At the very same time, elsewhere on the island, Campbell was 'in the midst of revival' in Point. 'What scenes – the whole district is stirred,' the evangelist wrote. And when he went to conduct his own mission in Uig the following winter, a spiritual break came on the very second night, and continued for weeks. Campbell was quick to acknowledge the preparatory work of Coulter and MacArthur a year previously, leaving behind 'a group of praying people'; but the contrast between the two Uig missions is quite remarkable.[2]

Bernera

Following arduous campaigns in Uig in October 1950, pilgrims Coulter and MacArthur moved on to Bernera, where forty attended the opening meeting. There had been no minister for the past four years, so the two men had to take the Sunday services also. This allowed the building of relationships with church members, while many opportunities also arose through house-visiting. Coulter had to take several weeks off due to illness; his colleague being forced to continue alone. The meetings were described as 'good,' but no break came.

Yet when Duncan Campbell joined MacArthur for the closing meetings at the end of March, suddenly, a change occurred. 'The Lord graciously blessed the meetings,' which were now 'full of grip and power.' Campbell stayed on to conduct the communion services. MacArthur wrote:

'Interest has been growing and this last week we have been in the midst of revival. Seventeen souls openly sought the Saviour.

---

2. One might agree with Coulter and MacArthur that, occurring in mid-winter, the inclement weather they faced was a primary reason for the low attendances at their meetings. Yet there were blizzards and gales during Campbell's Uig mission too. He noted, 'Yesterday was so terrible that one would hardly expect anybody to come out, yet the church was crowded' – prompting one elder to exclaim, 'Only God could have done this!' (Duncan Campbell, FM Report, 05.12.1951 – one of the very few weekly reports from Campbell that were missed out of *Sounds from Heaven*).

Meetings were packed, and there has been a very gracious sense of the Lord's presence and power in the midst. Packed cottage meetings have been going on until after midnight, at which most of the island is represented. The most stirring thing of all is the way that the Spirit of God is gripping the people. Before the revival started, everything was dry, dead and quiet. Now the echoes of praise sound through the valley as the young folk recently saved make their way to the meetings. As revival has broken out, I am now staying here another week ....'[3]

The change in the spiritual atmosphere following Campbell's arrival is dramatic. Almost immediately, the formerly mediocre meetings were charged with power, and revival broke out. Oddly, Campbell makes no mention of this significant breakthrough in his own weekly reports. More unusually, he also fails to refer to it when he begins his own mission in Bernera just five months later. Presumably, the movement didn't expand further at that earlier stage.[4] Yet, undoubtedly, this earlier movement helps explain the spiritual liveliness encountered by Campbell almost immediately on his arrival in the summer of '51, when a deeper and more extensive move of the Spirit took hold of the community.

Crulivig / Callanish

Perhaps a yet more notable contrast between Campbell's meetings and those organised by other Faith Mission workers occurred early the following year. In February 1952, Brother Jamison opened up a mission in the scattered, neglected community of Crulivig in north Uig. The meetings struggled, partly because of the small population, but equally because a more popular speaker was operating in a neighbouring parish.

While Jamison's mission was 'losing interest,' just eight or nine miles further north Duncan Campbell's meetings in Callanish

---

3. FM Report, 04.04.1951

4. When another FM pilgrim held meetings in Bernera early the following year, they were again marked by poor attendance (FM Report, 12.02.1952).

were crowded to capacity, and revival was gripping the parish.[5] It is interesting to note that people travelled from Crulivig by van and boat to Campbell's meetings, at least some of whom had already heard Jamison speak in their home district: Campbell notes several who had come under conviction there, and who 'came out brightly on the Lord's side' at his own meetings.[6]

Campbell's presence, preaching and personal dealings were clearly important factors to the revivals that broke out in different parts of Lewis. Despite his own humble protestations to the contrary, and irrespective of the theological positions that people on the island adhered to which seem to counter this reality, the controversial evangelist from mainland Scotland was indeed the catalyst that set off revival fires in many parishes across Lewis and Harris between the years 1949 and '52.

Leave of Absence

As we know, during the years of his missionary endeavours in Lewis and Harris, Campbell spent much of his time deeply engaged in intensive evangelism across the island. What is fascinating to discover is that during these same years, he was living something of an impressive 'double-life.'

Campbell took numerous well-earned breaks from the Lewis mission field. These were not purely times of rest. Yes, he was able to spend time relaxing with his beloved family at home in Edinburgh. But invariably, the evangelist found himself officiating at meetings in various locations.[7] Indeed, for significant periods, he was travelling all over the country, speaking at prayer meetings, communions and conventions, as well as holding short-term campaigns and full-scale missions.

---

5. FM Report, 12.02.1952, 12.03.1952.

6. Duncan Campbell, FM Report, 19.02.52. Campbell noted one young man as being an 'outstanding case.'

7. During his break in late October/early November, for example, Campbell conducted the funeral service of a Faith Mission stalwart, Miss Tickner.

Early Revival Publicity

We've already noted Campbell's two-week break from Lewis in the immediate aftermath of revival igniting so spectacularly on the island in December 1949 (see p. 84). It was Christmas, and he wanted to be home with his family. But he also spoke at several church functions during this period – how many cannot be ascertained, for clearly, intimations of such events were not always promoted in the local press. But we know of at least two, advertised in *The Scotsman* and *The Berwickshire News*, respectively.

The first was a regular united prayer meeting held in Edinburgh's Goold Hall on Thursday 29th December. Campbell had addressed this same prayer meeting just two months previously, on 27th October. On that occasion he gave a report on his recent Skye mission. It would not be unreasonable to assume that his December message focused on the success of his recent mission in Barvas.

Then again, just four days later, on Monday, 2nd January 1950, Campbell spoke at the Faith Mission New Year's Day Conference in Duns, in the Scottish Borders. We're told that in his message, he 'stressed the need for sanctified Christian lives,' and reported on one particular mission where he had been invited to help in crowded churches.[8] It requires little imagination to guess what mission he was referring to, although, given the movement was in its infancy, it seems that he wisely chose not to specify the location.

And so it transpires that within just a couple of weeks of revival breaking out in Barvas, and still before the close of 1949; indeed less than half-way through his opening mission in that parish, news of the 'Lewis revival' was already being broadcast to groups of believers at the other end of the country.

---

8. *Berwickshire News and General Advertiser*, Jan 1950.

Information on the awakening continued to be disseminated by the man at the forefront of the movement throughout its duration, as Campbell was invited to speak at missions and prayer meetings, Faith Mission conventions and other conferences the length and breadth of the United Kingdom. Quickly 'the Lewis revival' was becoming famous across the land, paving the way for it to become one of the most well-known revivals in the world.

Revival Pause

It's a remarkable truth that during the first twelve months of revival in Lewis, Campbell was out of the island for almost half of that time. This included a single period of almost four months in the summer and autumn (July to October), when he left Lewis to conduct missions elsewhere in the UK and Ireland.[9]

Just as with his Christmas break of '49, such a lengthy absence after six months of witnessing dramatic bursts of revival on different parts of the island seems somewhat surprising. With the Spirit moving so powerfully, and with Campbell as the predominant 'revival conduit,' one might have expected him to have remained 'on site,' before, or in case, revival fires began to fade. But once again, Campbell's calm intuition served him well, and his absence from the island proved no hindrance to either the spread or the intensity of the ongoing revival.

Monaghan and Partick

Campbell's first full mission during the summer and autumn of 1950 was in the small town of Monaghan in Ireland. Held during the last three weeks of August, the mission was an outstanding success. Campbell wrote of one meeting starting at 7 pm and going on until two o'clock in the morning, men and women openly confessing their sins to one another. Meetings

---

9. Additionally, he was out of the island for the first three weeks of February 1950 (home to Edinburgh); the first three weeks of April; and two weeks from end of May to mid-June.

were invariably large, and attended by numerous conversions, including some outstanding cases.[10]

In October, while the movement in Lewis was progressing in his absence, Campbell led meetings at Gardner Street Church of Scotland, Glasgow, where the Rev. Kenneth Gillies of Applecross was minister (and in which church he served for no less than fifty-two years). Here, Campbell was invited to hold a two-week mission, which, owing to its popularity, had to be extended to three. Many in the congregation were deeply touched, and there was even occasional fainting and, more rarely, the occurrence of 'trances.'[11]

Rev Kenneth Gillies

Campbell's own diary for this period records that one night no fewer than fifty-three people went to the inquiry room in spiritual anxiety, while there was an average of twenty-five each night after that.[12] During the last week, Campbell preached as many as five times on the Sabbath. As a result

10. Duncan Campbell, FM Report, 18.08, 23.08 and 30.08.1950.

11. K.A .Gillies, *Gillies of Partick: The Life and Ministry of an Applecross Man*, Aberdeen, 1999, p. 43

12. Duncan Campbell, FM Report, 11.10.1950.

of the mission, there were twenty admissions to church membership over three communion seasons, the most in twenty years – many of whom continued to worship in that church for the rest of their lives.[13]

Partly due to problems with his throat, which prohibited him from preaching for several months in 1951, Campbell attended fewer conferences and campaigns outwith Lewis during that year. 1952 proved much busier in this respect, particularly from August onwards, which period saw him criss-crossing the southern half of England, holding powerful meetings in East Anglia, Hastings and Exeter, to name just a few locations.

1953 missions

By this time, news of the remarkable revival in Lewis was becoming increasingly well-known. With it, Campbell's popularity also increased, and people flocked to hear him wherever he travelled. One newspaper billed him as 'the Church of Scotland minister whose name is appearing in almost every Christian paper.'

In January 1953, 600 turned out to hear Campbell preach in Ballymena, Northern Ireland, where some youths, unable to gain entry to the meeting hall, 'secured ladders and listened at the open windows.'[14] A one-day convention at Southport, which normally drew around eighty people and was held in a café, was moved to a much larger venue and attracted around 400.[15]

---

13. Further good was accomplished when Campbell preached at a crowded meeting in this church two-and-a-half years later, in May 1953 (ibid., p. 70). At an earlier date, he also spoke in the nearby Gaelic congregation of Partick Highland Free Church, under the ministry of Calum Morrison.

14. Duncan Campbell, FM Report, 21.01.53

15. ibid., 23.09.53.

The following month, as many as 2,000 crowded to hear Campbell speak at the Calvary Holiness Church Annual Convention in Manchester.[16] And in November '53, 'God broke through' during a mission in Duirinish, Skye, after which, 'we were daily in the midst of men and women seeking the Saviour (as many as fourteen adults making public confession of Christ at one meeting),' and 'a sudden change that came over the community.'[17]

Advert for Revival Mission, 1953

The years 1953, '54 and '55 were the busiest for Campbell in terms of speaking engagements, before accepting the role as

---

16. ibid., 21.10.53. The Calvary Holiness Church was a holiness denomination founded in 1934 by evangelists Maynard James and Jack Ford. This marked the beginning of a close association between Campbell and holiness groups in the UK. Ironically, James was in Scotland at the time of Campbell's visit, but the two men met on subsequent occasions and a deep bond of friendship was formed (Paul James, *The Story Of Maynard James: A Man On Fire*, Derby, 1993, p. 93).

17. Duncan Campbell, FM Report, 18.11.53

Principal of the FM Bible College in 1956 restricted his travels considerably. The engagements of these years took him all across the British Isles, and included several return trips to the Western Isles. In particular, a mission in Lerwick early in 1954 saw deep blessing, as did one in South Wales the following month. Both places, Campbell felt, were 'near to revival.'[18]

18. Duncan Campbell, FM Report, 18.02.1954, 04.03.1954.

CHAPTER 18

Revival Hope: National

People who turned out to hear Campbell were delighted and awed by the wonderful and often dramatic stories he shared of revival happening now, within their own country. It quickly became apparent that there existed a growing hunger for revival across the land. Indeed, in some places there occurred notable stirrings of the Spirit.[1]

The Influence of Keswick

It was at the Keswick Convention in Cumbria in 1952 that the greatest hope for a national revival was raised. Record attendance marked the convention in 1951, with over six thousand attending some meetings. Among the many speakers in 1952, Fred Mitchell (who died in a plane crash the following year) spoke on Psalm 86, *'Revive us again,'* while Alan Redpath insisted that 'present methods of evangelism have failed: unless God the Holy Spirit works, the battle is lost.'

But to Douglas Bushby the early morning prayer meeting was 'artificial; human leadership usurped the place of the Holy Spirit. I contrasted this with the Hebrides. There was a divine harmony in the holy confusion. Here was a divine discord in rigid routine.' Duncan Campbell, another visitor at the convention, was apparently equally discouraged by the prayer meetings, which just under a thousand people attended. 'We agreed that

---

1. ibid., pp. 69–70.

the Convention was a monument to tradition,' noted Bushby, 'and cramped by English conservatism.'[2]

With a deep conviction that Campbell should speak at the gathering, Bushby approached the Committee, but was told the programme was complete, although some members expressed a real interest. That evening, four of them (including a Church of England rector) gathered in an empty barn they came across just outside Keswick. Here, perhaps deliberately reminiscent of the Barvas pre-revival 'barn' meetings, they spent the whole night pleading with God 'to break through in revival and use Campbell to encourage the people for an awakening to spread over England.' According to Campbell, who wasn't present at this all-night meeting, God 'came down in mighty Holy Ghost power,'[3] and as he walked home to bed, Bushby felt his burden lift, receiving in its place an assurance his prayers were being answered.

The following morning Bushby bumped into Campbell, who intimated that a special meeting had been arranged, whereby he was to speak in the 'second tent' on the last evening of the Convention. Despite the awkwardness of the hour (5.15 pm), the tent was not only filled, but some hundreds stood around outside.[4] As Campbell spoke of the momentous happenings on Lewis over the previous two-and-a-half years, the audience drank in the

---

2. Bushby, *Adventures in Revival*, pp. 34–5. Bushby spoke with Canon Barham from Rwanda, who felt that the problem with Keswick was, 'The blood of Jesus has not been given its rightful place; this is almost a bloodless Convention, its power has not been released by faith.'

3. Duncan Campbell, FM Report, 23.07.1952.

4. S. J. W. Chase testified that 'when the convention was over and folk contemplated the whole set of meetings, the one by Rev. Duncan Campbell in the small tent was unanimously acclaimed the best of all' (S. J. W. Chase, *Let It Come O Lord*, Madras, n.d.).

story with wonderment. 'God met (with us), and his power was manifestly felt,' Campbell later enthused.[5]

Entrance to Keswick Convention, early 1950s

As well as this meeting, Campbell spoke at no fewer than nine 'house parties' during his brief time in Keswick, and 'in every group God was manifestly present' (especially in the George Duncan and Emmanuel Bible College groups).[6] Altogether, a new expectancy was created that revival might spread throughout the British Isles in the months ahead, a conviction that Campbell apparently shared.[7]

The Keswick committee enthused that revival had been the dominating note of the Convention. 'It was sounded again and again, but even more potently it made itself felt in a spirit of yearning manifest in all the gatherings; it was freely expressed in the prayer-meetings and in house-parties, and in countless conversations.' In particular the Keswick leadership later

---

5. Duncan Campbell, FM Report, 23.07.1952.

6. ibid. After resting for a few days, Campbell returned to Keswick, to minister to a conference of Chinese students from various universities in Britain.

7. Bushby, *Adventures in Revival*, p. 31

noted that after hearing Campbell talk, 'very many came away convinced that the Convention was a prelude, a vital preparation for it (revival). For if one thing is clear it is this, that ... laying hold upon God in earnest, prevailing prayer, always precedes it.'[8] They did acknowledge, however, that revival did not break out at that year's gathering.[9]

One who heard Campbell's Keswick address was Owen Murphy, a former journalist who entered the ministry in 1932. Murphy had never heard of Campbell or the Lewis revival at that date, but testified that he 'sat spellbound listening to the most thrilling, faith-inspired message I had ever heard ....Never in its many years of history had the Keswick Convention been more mightily stirred, as it listened to the report of the amazing events that had taken place just a few hundred miles away.'[10]

Murphy bumped into Campbell after his talk and engaged with him in conversation. The Highlander's closing words to him were that when he returned to America, he should 'rouse the people. Tell them what God is doing.' Campbell explained that 'every church could have what Lewis and Harris had recently

---

8. Charles Price and Ian Randall, *Transforming Keswick: The Keswick Convention Past, Present and Future*, Carlisle, 2000, p. 182. Despite the remarkable response to his Keswick address, Campbell was never invited to the convention again.

9. Rev. Graham Scroggie had often expressed his longing for 'a widespread and heaven-sent revival of true religion' (Govan, *Spirit of Revival*, p. 12). Yet, in his own series of talks at Keswick in 1952, he insisted that Keswick was primarily a teaching Convention, and conveyed disapproval at Douglas Brown's emotive Keswick address in the wake of the Lowestoft revival of the early 1920s. Perhaps Scroggie was acutely aware that division could ensure over the phenomena of revival. Perhaps, also, he was fonder of revival in theory than he was in practice.

10. Murphy, *When God Stepped Down from Heaven*, pp. 19–21. Price and Randall question pertinently whether Keswick-goers would have been quite so enthusiastic about reports of prostrations and other unusual phenonena had they taken place in the Convention tent! (Price and Randall, *Transforming Keswick*, pp. 181–2)

experienced. 'If God can find a people over there, prepared to pay the price as they have over here, He will visit them in the same revival of power.'[11]

Every word Campbell spoke burned into the heart of the young American, who instantly realised that the Spirit of God was imparting to him a new commission. Cancelling his scheduled evangelistic campaigns, Murphy returned at once to the States. (See p. 284 for his work there).

Scotland

Events most resembling those associated with the revival in Lewis occurred in Glasgow in the autumn of 1950 (see p. 267). But there were stirrings elsewhere, too. Joe Creelman was a young believer from Northern Ireland who studied at the Faith Mission College in Edinburgh from 1951–53 – during which years Campbell was still ministering in Lewis. His first mission on leaving the college was in the vast expanse of the Borders. The region was spiritually very needy, and often neglected by evangelists. Missions of varying duration, but usually at least a fortnight in length, were conducted in numerous villages during 1954 and '55. Indeed, throughout the wider district, something of a mini spiritual awakening was in progress.

In particular, Joe remembers many packed meetings being held in Allanton, Berwickshire, and entire families being wonderfully brought to the Lord. Duncan Campbell came several times to speak, preaching with great effect to spiritually hungry audiences. Joe and his colleagues enjoyed wonderful times of fellowship with Campbell, as they ate, prayed and preached together.[12]

---

11. Murphy, *When God Stepped Down from Heaven*, p. 21.

12. Joe also spent two months each summer over three consecutive years ministering with Campbell in Oban, where the F.M. concentrated their efforts during the college holidays. Large children's rallies, afternoon outreach sorties, and open-air addresses in the evenings kept the pilgrims ever busy. Campbell preached at the main evangelistic service held each Sunday night, to which hundreds gathered.

Other efforts were yet more successful. Revival came to North Uist towards the close of 1957, following a visit from four female missionaries from the Faith Mission, (one of whom, Mary Morrison, was a convert of the Lewis revival). Revival came after a lengthy struggle in the main village of Lochmaddy. The blessing spread to Sollas, Tighgarry and Bayhead in subsequent months. A great boost came with the fearless and uncompromising preaching of Duncan Campbell, who made several visits to the island, as did Joshua Daniel from India, a man of deep prayer who had witnessed revival in his home country some years before. Both men were gripped with the solemnity and power of the meetings.

England

Spiritual stirrings occurred in churches the evangelist never went near. Hundreds of miles from Lewis, as early as the summer of 1951, news of the Lewis revival was trickling through to members of Etloe Road Brethren Church in Bristol. They were half-way through a hectic two-week evangelistic mission in their neighbourhood. After the Sunday evening gospel service, and despite considerable fatigue, around thirty remained for a prayer meeting, having been provoked by a desire to see God move in their own area as He was doing in the Hebrides.

Several hours later the numbers had reduced to seven, all young men, but the Holy Spirit came upon them in an unusual and powerful way. All feelings of tiredness disappeared and they prayed, praised and quoted Scripture with barely a moment's intermission for over four hours. They only broke up after being interrupted by a passing policeman who, seeing the lights and hearing the singing, was amazed to find a prayer meeting in full flow. It was one of the most remarkable prayer meetings these men had ever experienced.[13]

---

13. Wallis, *Arthur Wallis*, pp. 87–8.

Another group of believers in the south of England deeply influenced by accounts of the Lewis revival consisted of some young believers from Richmond who, disenchanted with the apathy in their denominational churches, cordially left them and began meeting on their own. Through various sources they heard captivating accounts of the two old ladies from Barvas and the seven men who met in a 'barn.'

Greatly inspired by their persistent prayers, Lance Lambert and his colleagues came together every evening from 1st September to 1st December 1952 to pray that God would pour out His Spirit upon the Thames Valley, realising from the Lewis accounts that 'it was possible to get on one's knees and pray until God lifted the burden.'[14] The group witnessed many amazing answers to their prayers, not least the procurement of the commodious Halford House at a crazily low price (which was still being used for Christian purposes half a century later).

A number of people most certainly influenced by Campbell's talk at Keswick were those attending from London Bible College, during the principalship of Ernest Kevan. Keswick had greatly influenced the college's spirituality over a number of years, and several Convention figures served as its directors or advisors. As a result of Campbell's dramatic testimony, revival became a prominent theme at the college and revival prayer meetings were convened.

The hope of an imminent revival, even though backed by keen desire and a willingness to step out in faith, didn't necessarily lead to the expected outcome. In the south-west of England, a young preacher returned from a visit to scenes of revival in Lewis with a vision based on Isaiah 43 which he had received there, that God was going to do a 'new thing' which involved the outpouring of the Holy Spirit 'to bring waters to the desert.'[15]

---

14. Personal communication with Lance Lambert, 11/06/2009.

15. Wallis, *Arthur Wallis*, pp. 90–92

The young evangelist was invited to lead a mission in Whipton, Exeter. In prayer in advance of the meetings, he believed he received a promise from God that He would break out in revival power on the third day of the conference. Highly embarrassed when nothing happened, Arthur Wallis later had to apologise to the elders of the church, realising that he had acted presumptuously and over-enthusiastically.[16]

Campbell held a series of meetings in Oxford in June 1952. On the evening of the first day, 'the Holy Spirit came into our midst' and 'God broke us down in His presence. Ministers left the meeting, not to rest, but to spend the night on their faces before God.' Fourteen met in a rectory, where the rector and his wife 'came into deep blessing' at two o'clock in the morning.

'Yesterday, half-way through addressing the Young People's convention,' noted Campbell, 'we witnessed a scene similar to that so often witnessed in Lewis. I had to stop the meeting and just leave God to move as He chose. I never listened to such confession of sin in my life, especially among the student classes. We were dealing with souls right until midnight. One feels that we are very near revival.'[17]

Ministers blessed at the Oxford meetings later released a circular highlighting the main lessons learned from Campbell's teaching.[18] When Campbell returned to Oxford six months later, he found 'men truly seeking after God.'[19] And when he made a third visit in May '53 to what he termed a 'most remarkable convention … God came down upon us and quite a

16. ibid., pp. 87–95

17. Duncan Campbell, FM Report, 15.06.1952.

18. These included, 'leading us into true "Revival fellowship" with each other and Himself … learning how to "pray through" to the answer to our prayers, and … discussing together some of the "controversial" issues (e.g., Healing, Judgement), thus giving us the urge to get "over the Word" and seek His face.'

19. Duncan Campbell, FM Report,10.12.52.

number remained to pray all night.' The following evening, the testimonies of a number of Lewis converts from London made a deep impression. 'Unsaved men stood up in the meeting and asked us to pray with them as they were seeking the Saviour.' Leaders were still dealing with souls 5½ hours after Campbell had given his message.[20]

A favourite destination of Campbell's in these years was Birmingham, to visit Harry Bonsall. An Englishman living in Canada in 1935, Bonsall had received a powerful vision telling him to return to his homeland to prepare Bible colleges for thousands of people who were going to be converted in a powerful spiritual revival which was going to overtake the country. By the mid-1950s Bonsall had begun the Birmingham Bible Institute.

Campbell's repeated visits here 'introduced a new spiritual dimension to Harry and Dosie and their young students. He spoke effectively to them on the power of the supernatural over influence, reputation and academic qualifications. Harry would listen with rapt attention and mounting excitement, as Duncan Campbell shared inspiring stories of revival to staff and students alike.'[21]

On one memorable visit, Campbell made the comment, 'It only needs one committed person to bring about revival.' That was enough to prompt Dosie to fast for thirty days with this end in mind. Campbell was regarded by the Bonsalls as 'very much a Highlander and in some ways a mystic, but there was also a very gentle side to him – a kind of child-like innocence.'[22]

Northern Ireland and Eire

A seemingly independent movement began in Ballyrobert, a small village in County Antrim, at the start of 1960, following

---

20. ibid., 27.05.53.

21. Ruth McGavin, *Running For Revival: The Life and Times of Henry Brash Bonsall,* Fearn, 1999, p. 183.

22. Duncan Campbell, FM Report, pp. 204–5, 317.

a mission led by Frank Marshall of the Irish Evangelistic Band. The whole campaign had been soaked in prayer and in time was marked by a spiritual breakthrough among believers, with a spirit of deep repentance and restitution evident, and an earnest desire for a level of holiness they had never before experienced. With this, scores of young folk in the district began showing interest in the meetings, and over the course of the campaign, which was continued on an almost nightly basis for a remarkable forty-three weeks, over a hundred teenagers were hopefully converted.

Maynard James was one who visited the scene of events, while Duncan Campbell also spoke here. The phenomenon of heavenly singing was a feature of the movement, and Campbell is on record as stating that the blessing in Ballyrobert was the nearest he had experienced thus far to the Lewis revival with which he had been so closely identified.[23]

When Campbell spoke at a gathering in Lisburn, also in County Antrim, in 1964, an unusual enveloping sense of God's presence descended on the meeting hall and remained throughout the day. Following his closing address, the benediction was pronounced, when, said one present, 'God took over.' The organist was overcome and unable to play her instrument; a holy hush fell on the congregation so that, for over half an hour, everyone sat in profound silence. During this time several people heard definite otherworldly sounds, inaudible to others. The Spirit worked deeply in people's hearts, and numbers wept and prayed.[24]

Duncan Campbell is one of many evangelists credited for the openness to the gospel that developed in the Republic of Ireland from the 1960s onwards, with a great number of Bible study groups and Christian fellowships coming into existence.

---

23. Dr William Fleming, *If My People*, Fearn, 1999, pp. 40–1; James, *A Man on Fire*, p. 115.

24. Campbell had described, earlier that day, a vision he had in which he saw revival coming to Ireland, through small bands of praying people in country districts.

The Scotsman is known to have visited Dublin on at least two occasions – probably visiting other locations in the republic too. It was said that his visits 'helped extend the vision for revival' in the south.[25]

Wales

Samuel McGibben was a Scottish Christian who moved to South Wales in 1957. After five years as a coalminer he enrolled in The Apostolic Church International Bible College in Penygroes. One day while attending a lecture on missiology, the class listened to a tape of Duncan Campbell relating events of the 1949–52 Lewis revival. 'At the end of his report,' noted McGibben, 'we quietly waited in God's presence and the Holy Spirit fell upon all of us. Finding ourselves prostrate on the floor we became aware that God was meeting us individually in a supernatural way. Some students were praying; some were worshipping, some were silent.'[26] During this time McGibben heard the Spirit's voice speak to him directly about deepening his relationship with God. His life was thoroughly changed as a result, and he went on to become a pastor, apostle and pioneer in the Apostolic Church for over half a century.

A series of meetings was arranged in Aberdare. Following the second service a prayer meeting was held, which continued till three in the morning. Expectancy ran high, and many came to pray throughout the following day. That evening, after Campbell had spoken for an hour, six young men seated together saw 'the glory of God' come down upon them. A great fear gripped them and they fell to the floor weeping. Fear also gripped the congregation; many were overwhelmed by a sense of sin, and

---

25. Fleming, *If My People,* p. 68.

26. Samuel McGibben, *The God of the Miraculous: Amazing Things Can Happen When we Believe*, Bloomington, 2013, p. 17.

scenes of repentance and restoration followed as one and another made things right between themselves and God.[27]

Elsewhere in Wales, Campbell also visited a small fellowship located high in the Swansea valley. The Mission Hall in the colliery village of Cwmtwrch, some fifteen miles to the north of Swansea, had placed revival as its central focus ever since its inception in 1912. George Griffiths, a nineteen-year-old collier converted in 1904, was the pastor of the church since it opened.

In the mid-1950s Griffiths and a few in his congregation began to meet every night for a week to pray for revival. The week passed, but still they carried on meeting together, sometimes right through the night, and hardly having time to rest before setting out for work in the morning. It was during these years of intense prayer that the Mission Hall received 'chance' visits from several noted revivalist preachers, one of whom was Duncan Campbell. Campbell's talk on the move of God's Spirit on Lewis and Harris just a few years earlier served to greatly encourage the Cwmtwrch believers. During the year 1958 the floodgates were opened; there occurred scenes reminiscent of the great Welsh revival of 1904, which some had personally witnessed, and significant numbers were converted.[28]

There were few places that Campbell enjoyed visiting more than the Bible College of Wales, on the outskirts of Swansea, founded by that remarkable man of faith, Rees Howells. Campbell found a particular rapport with the then principal, Rees's son, Samuel Howells, and they loved to spend time over a pot of tea, chatting about what God was doing across the country.

Brian Halliwell spent seven years at the College – first as a student, then as a member of staff. He recalled that Campbell visited the place almost every year while he was there, sometimes

---

27. Woolsey, *Channel of Revival*, pp. 181–2.

28. George Griffiths, *Our Fathers Have Told Us: A Record of the Last Fifty Years at Tro'r Glien Cwmtwrch Mission Hall*, Cwmtwrch, 2012.

twice a year. He was given a hectic schedule. Arriving by train on Friday afternoon, he would lead a meeting that evening, another on Saturday morning, Sunday meetings in the Conference Hall, and a further one in the evening, and again on Monday morning in the chapel – six meetings in all!

Duncan Campbell at the Bible College of Wales (c/o Mathew Backholer / BCW)

But the students loved hearing from this intrepid Scotsman, who spoke with such authority, and carried such anointing in his preaching. Brian readily recalled that it was in a Monday morning chapel meeting during one Campbell visit that 'the glory came down. I was sitting at the back of the chapel, and felt compelled to fall flat on my face on the floor. Apparently almost everyone else did too! As for Duncan Campbell, I don't know – I couldn't see him! There was such a strong sense of uncleanness before God. Feeling unworthy in His presence. It was an incredible feeling, accompanied by a deep conviction of sin. Gradually, ripples of cleansing washed over us, followed by a spontaneous overflowing of joy and praise. We had no desire but to give Him all the glory.'[29]

Revival Hope: International

We must remember that accounts of the Lewis revival were not the only factor stimulating believers at this time. As we noted at the start of the book, an increased sense of spiritual expectancy had in fact been gathering momentum across the UK as well as in America since the end of the war. Some historians in fact emphasise that the Lewis awakening was part of a worldwide outpouring of the Holy Spirit, Billy Graham and Duncan Campbell being two of many spokesmen for God in differing spheres of influence during the global movement.[30]

America

On his return to America, as early as June 1953, when revival embers were still burning in parts of Lewis, Owen Murphy was sharing accounts of that revival in Long Beach, California. He was variously advertised as an 'international evangelist, Bible teacher and radio speaker,' a leader at 'healing services,' a 'personal friend of Duncan Campbell' and one who had 'visited the scene of the Hebrides revival.' (One writer refers to him, anonymously, as a 'popularity seeking, religious showman ... impersonating the Scottish evangelist.')

---

29. Personal communication with Brian Halliwell, 12/09/2017. Campbell came to the Bible College one last time during a period of recuperation following serious illness. He had a very full itinerary that weekend. Brian believes it was his last series of public meetings anywhere in the UK, as he died in Switzerland not long after. Brian credits Campbell as being 'the reason I came to the Bible College of Wales in the first place,' being drawn to come and hear the Scots evangelist after hearing he had been invited to speak. After leaving the college, Brian and his wife went on to become missionaries in Peru and other countries, working with Christian Literature Crusade International.

30. e.g. Hanspeter Nuesch, *Ruth and Billy Graham: The Legacy of a Couple*, Ada, 2013; Towns & Porter, *The Ten Greatest Revivals Ever*.

GREATER SPOKANE CHURCHES CONTINUE
DYNAMIC MESSAGE OF REVIVAL CHALLENGE

"When God Stepped Down From Heaven"

The Message that has stirred the churches of America and caused hundreds to turn to Christ! Colored pictures will be shown, entitled "Where the Fires Have Burned," also pictures recently taken in the Holy Land.

Rev. OWEN MURPHY

and Evangelistic party present this message and program one night only in each of the following churches:

This Week's Schedule
Sunday, March 21, 11 a. m.—Lidgerwood EUB,
E228 Gordon

A City-Wide Mass Meeting
Hear This New Challenging Message for Spokane
"Spokane--The Hour of Decision"
Sunday, March 21, 2:30 p. m.—Fourth Presbyterian, Baldwin and Dakota

Owen Murphy 'revival challenge' advert

Remarkably, by the close of 1955, Murphy had spoken at as many as 500 services in nearly as many churches up and down the west coast of America – predominantly on the theme of the Lewis revival. He continued his travels in subsequent years, and in 1966–7 he embarked on a mammoth 50,000-mile tour that took in Russia, Egypt, Palestine, Germany, France and twenty-two other countries. By this time he had also spoken at more than 2,500 churches in the United States and had addressed more than fifty colleges and seminaries.[31]

As a result of his ministry, he claimed, 'Powerful prayer groups have sprung up everywhere. In many churches the all-night prayer meeting has been introduced, resulting in real movings of the Spirit of God in conviction of sin, confession, and re-consecration— upon the part of both ministers and congregations ....Camp meetings, Bible Colleges, and Conventions have been challenged and stirred ... many have witnessed gracious

---

31. Progress Index, 10th June 1967, p. 2.

manifestations of God among their congregations such as they had not known before.'[32]

Papua New Guinea

Meanwhile, a written account of the Lewis revival – most likely that composed by Murphy – helped spark off a time of spiritual quickening on the other side of the world. In 1953, missionaries working for the United Fields Mission – an international organisation set up in 1931 – in New Guinea were impressed on reading of the Hebrides revival. At a regular missionaries' conference shortly after, 'there came a spirit of prayer, an intense conviction of sin, and a response of confession, restitution and reconciliation, with not a few professions of faith – a consummating revival.'[33]

Canada

Freed from his leadership duties at the Faith Mission, Campbell made a number of journeys to Canada and America to speak at church meetings and conventions. Indeed, at this same time, elsewhere in the States, Owen Murphy was also criss-crossing the country, still on his *'Hebrides Revival'* themed mission. In the summer of 1969 Campbell visited a number of churches in Canada.[34] It was here that the closest link between the Scots evangelist and stirrings of international revival came. Only segments of the story of Campbell's link to this

---

32. Murphy, *When God Stepped Down from Heaven*, pp. 11-2.

33. J. Edwin Orr, *Evangelical Awakenings in the South Seas,* Minneapolis, 1976, p. 199.

34. One of these was intimated in a tiny box advert in *The Winnipeg Free Press* for June 7th, 1969. It declared that he was to be guest speaker at both of the following weeks' Sunday services in the city's 1,600-seater Elim Chapel, while he also led meetings there on the first four weekday evenings of the ensuing week.

movement are recorded in each of the several histories of that Canadian awakening.[35]

Bill Macleod, pastor of Ebenezer Baptist Church in Saskatoon, Saskatchewan, had longed for a genuine move of the Spirit, and knowing of Campbell's involvement in the Hebrides revival, had prayed for three years that God would send the man to his church. Campbell duly arrived for a single service in 1969. Though preaching to a congregation of around seventy-five, he was not discouraged, and as he spoke, desire intensified. As he had done in several other Canadian churches, Campbell told of how shocked he had been, on his arrival in the country, at the moral degradation of the people. He began to pray for a mighty outpouring of God's Spirit on the land.

One night as he was on his knees praying, he received a vision of Canada 'ablaze with revival from coast to coast.' What he did not say publicly was where the revival was to begin. Keith Macleod (a brother to Bill) later made clear that Campbell told him the revival would begin in the Ebenezer Baptist Church in Saskatoon. Keith did not mention this to his brother until after the revival had begun in Ebenezer.[36]

Two years later, in October 1971, a remarkable revival broke out in Macleod's church, when evangelist-twins Ralph and Lou Sutera came to hold a mission there. A deep spirit of repentance gripped the congregation, and attendance grew to the extent that they eventually hired the 2,000-seat Civic Auditorium, which soon became filled to capacity. Love, confession and restitution marked the seven-week campaign, while 'Afterglow' services following the regular meetings often continued till two or three

35. Erwin W. Lutzer, *Flames Of Freedom*, Chicago, 1976, pp. 37–8; Bernard and Marjorie Palmer, *The Winds Of God Are Blowing*, Wheaton 1973, p. 12; Kurt Koch, *Revival Fires In Canada*, Grand Rapids, 1973, pp. 20–21; K. Neil Foster, *Revolutionary Love*, Minneapolis, 1973, p. 20.

36. Lutzer, *Flames of Freedom*, pp. 37–8.

in the morning. The revival quickly spread to other churches in Saskatchewan, and even across the border into America.

Some have noted that while a degree of renewal subsequently came to one or two places in eastern Canada, such as Central Baptist Seminary in Toronto after Macleod spoke there, the country hardly became 'ablaze with revival from coast to coast,' as Campbell predicted. Erwin Lutzer has pondered whether this prophecy has still to find true fulfilment.[37] In any case, an interesting afterword to this story is that even before news of the outbreak of the awakening in Saskatoon, Campbell had apparently felt led to spend two hours praying for Canada at his home in Edinburgh, during which time he received a distinct impression that God was moving there.[38]

Switzerland

The influence of Duncan Campbell, and of the Lewis revival, extended all across Europe as a result of a chance meeting in Rockford, Illinois during Campbell's US trip of 1968, when the evangelist was introduced to Loren Cunningham. The young American had founded the Christian youth mission organisation, Y.W.A.M. (Youth with a Mission) a few years previously. Keen to set up a School of Evangelism in Europe, Cunningham received from Campbell much encouragement in his vision. The result was that a former hotel was acquired by Y.W.A.M. in Chalet-a-Gobet, just outside Lausanne, in 1970, and Campbell was one of those invited as a regular visiting speaker (others included Francis Shaeffer and Leonard Ravenhill).

For two or three weeks over the course of three years, Campbell's inspirational talks – including many 'stories of the supernatural and far-from-normal dealings of God with people he had seen' – had a marked impact on the Y.W.A.M.

37. ibid., p. 38.
38. Woolsey, *Channel of Revival*, p. 184.

students, who were hungry to receive from one so experienced in the workings of God's Spirit. Not least to have a profound respect for the Scotsman was the Y.W.A.M. founder himself, who named Campbell as one of the main influences on his life.

With the greatest admiration, Cunningham often referred to 'that silver-haired man of God' in subsequent addresses and books. Among his 'vivid memories' of Campbell are the following quotes:

'I want to be known in Heaven, and feared in hell.'[39]

'Revival is not churches filled with people but people filled with God.'[40]

'Everything is real in evangelism but God' (i.e., we often focus on a lifeless evangelistic plan rather than a demonstration of the power of the Spirit.)[41]

Greece

Campbell told of visiting one of the praying elders of Barvas during the revival, and overhearing him praying in his barn for the nation of Greece.[42] Many years later, in 1970 or '71, Y.W.A.M. sponsored Campbell to fly to Greece and hold a series of meetings. He spoke both in Athens and the nearby resort of Porto-Rafti on the Aegean Sea. Many were deeply moved by his preaching, and several young married couples later became leaders of Christian ministries in different parts of Europe. Years later, Sheena Campbell met a Greek visitor to Switzerland, who

---

39. Loren Cunningham, *Making Jesus Lord: The Dynamic Power of Laying Down Your Rights,* Edmunds, 1997, p. 69

40. Loren Cunningham, *Mobilizing Young People for World Evangelization,* Lausanne speech, 1974.

41. ibid.

42. The Barvas elder was apparently a butcher – yet there was no butcher in Barvas at the time. Also, one revival convert shared a quite differing account of this story.

told her of the wonderful work that had developed from her father's ministry in his country.[43]

---

43. Campbell was accompanied by his wife on this trip, and their daughter Sheena remembers that they travelled on from Greece to visit her and her husband in Nazareth, where they were then serving with the Edinburgh Medical Missionary Society Hospital.

PART 5

Revival Controversy

CHAPTER 19

Revival Theology

Revival Preacher

Though not a trained theologian, Campbell knew his Bible well and quoted from it frequently during his sermons.[1] While not regarded as an exceptional preacher, he was 'an out and out evangelist,' as one islander put it, and the work of evangelism is what he threw himself into, body, soul and mind. Campbell was uncompromising in his message, ruthlessly exposing sin and pronouncing God's judgement on that sin, yet always ready to point in the direction of God's remedy for it. To many, that was the message of the revival – a message of judgement and yet of God's great mercy.

Whether it came from Campbell or one of the parish ministers, the preaching of the Word had priority over everything. One convert quoted a verse from a spiritual song that her neighbour wrote during the revival: *"He showered us with the Word of God and we shall be lost if we neglect it."* That was how it felt. Surrounded by the Word of God, night after night as we listened to the faithful preaching detailing man's lost condition and the offer of salvation in Christ.'[2]

---

1. According to his daughter, 'He was not an expository preacher, in the sense that my husband, or my father-in-law were, or as my two sons are. My father didn't have that kind of preaching. In Lewis, at least, he was called to preach the gospel, and that is what he did' (personal communication with Sheena Campbell Vischer, 15.03.2020).

2. M. Macleod, quoted in Afrin, *Critical Analysis*, p. 40.

'Duncan Campbell was full-on when he was preaching,' noted one convert. He knew his message could change people's lives and he shared it in a dramatic, lively style, his clothes regularly getting soaked in sweat in the process. He did not always enjoy the best of health during his time in Lewis. However, it was noted how his physical health was repeatedly quickened to meet the demands placed on him as awakening spread from district to district.

Campbell in the pulpit (c/o Alec Stevens)

On many occasions Campbell would address at least five or six meetings in a day – many of them cottage meetings, which often ran into the early hours of the morning. With such a hectic schedule of preaching and personal counselling, the evangelist often became physically and emotionally weary. Entering a believer's house, he was known to flop down in the chair and say to someone, 'Would you pray, please?' In no time, the prayer of faith would revive his mind and spirit, and he'd be able to carry on his duties again.[3]

Although he often had no option but to use the same message repeatedly, he did not use a clinical, routine formula. Rather, steeped in prayer, Campbell was especially sensitive to the moving of the Spirit in his prayers and addresses, and words that spoke directly and remarkably to his listeners were not uncommon. It was said that there were many times when Campbell was so busy that he did next to nothing in the way of sermon preparation. He would simply take a text from some hymn or testimony that was given, and preach.

It was noted that when a spiritual break came in a mission, the very presentation and communication of his message would change. Even his voice would alter and one could tell he had liberty in the Spirit. One convert observed that during the revival it was, 'easier to say things and do things than in an ordinary service. I don't know what an ordinary service is, but in times of revival the Word is more effective, and the hearing is more effective, believing is easier and for many.'[4]

Campbell's Theology

Being born and raised in a Christian home in the Scottish Highlands in the early twentieth century, Duncan Campbell was steeped in the Reformed tradition. Family prayers, Bible reading and daily worship were regular features of the Campbell family, as was weekly attendance at services in Ardchattan parish church to the north of Oban (and Sunday school for the children).

Such devout lifestyle was also a result of the influence of the Faith Mission. Both of Campbell's parents, along with an older brother, had been converted at a meeting conducted by Faith Mission pilgrims near their home in Benderloch in 1901, when Campbell was just a toddler.

---

3. Personal communication with Donald John Smith, 19.09.2016.

4. W. Macleod, in Afrin, *Critical Analysis*, p. 40.

So, from his youngest days, Campbell's life was influenced both by the strong Calvinist traditions of the Highlands and by the work of the Faith Mission. From his mid-twenties he seems to have come under the increasing influence of Keswick theology and subsequently the Holiness movement.[5] Indeed, among his favourite writers in later years were Scottish Holiness author Oswald Chambers, American Holiness preachers J. D. Drysdale and G. D. Watson, and Stuart Holden, former chairman of the Keswick Convention.[6]

Yet nearly everyone I spoke to who knew Campbell personally insisted he could not properly be labelled 'Arminian.' In practice, one person believed, Campbell 'did not have any fixed theological position. He was not a five-point Calvinist … but he was not a rank Arminian either ….There are degrees of both. Mr Campbell preached a biblical message. No one who ever heard him doubted that.'[7]

God's Sovereignty *and* Man's Responsibility

Throughout his life Campbell fully believed in the sovereignty of God, but as he said on many occasions, 'I don't believe in

---

5. For a fascinating historical study on these doctrines, see Andrew David Naselli, *No Quick Fix: Where Higher Life Theology came from, what it is and why it's harmful,* Bellingham, WA, 2017.

6. Though among them also were Presbyterian stalwarts Robert Murray McCheyne, David Brainerd and James S. Stewart, along with former minister of Westminster Chapel, Campbell Morgan.

7. Personal communication with Colin Peckham, 21.06.2002. Colin Peckham, who was Principal of the Faith Mission for seventeen years, stated that the organisation has no specific stance on Arminianism versus Calvinism, and that Faith Mission candidates hold to a variety of theological viewpoints. (See also Peckham, *Sounds from Heaven,* pp. 121–2.) But the Rev. Dr John S. Ross feels that 'Taking up a position of neutrality on a matter that is evidently a part of the revelation of Scripture and which is so formative of the thinking of the people you are ministering to appears badly flawed. It certainly struck Campbell's opponents in the Western Isles as being so' (personal communication, 09.04.2019).

any type of sovereignty that nullifies man's responsibility.'[8] Campbell believed that in a community where one aspect of divine sovereignty / man's responsibility is emphasised above the other, then it is proper to draw focus on the other side to provide a balance. This is what Campbell did in the Western Isles, where a strong tradition of Calvinism prevailed (in some places bordering on hyper-Calvinism).

Campbell particularly disliked the hyper-Calvinist approach of one Free Church minister who organised a meeting in his Lewis church to coincide with Campbell's in the parish. There he said, 'If you're here and you're not in the elect, then the sooner you stop coming to church, the better.' Understandably, the statement caused considerable confusion among a number of younger folk present who were anxiously seeking the Lord.

The need, Campbell felt, was to understand that being religious was not the answer. Thus, he taught, along with God's sovereignty and human responsibility, another tenet of Calvinism – the total depravity of man; that man's propensity is to sin, and he has to secure a new nature to be right with God. He also stressed the covenant-keeping side of sovereign God, a further feature of Calvinist theology.

Nevertheless, in practice Campbell operated largely outwith the Calvinist-Arminian paradigm. He generally preferred not to involve himself too deeply in the doctrinal issues concerned.[9] While many attacked his theology and sought to hamper his efforts, he was not in the habit of attacking theirs. He never spoke of those within the Free Church as 'Calvinists' per se. Indeed, he wasn't generally in the habit of viewing the opposition against him as centring on the Calvinist-Arminian debate.

---

8. Campbell, *Revival in the Hebrides*, p. 59.

9. In this, he was like A. W. Tozer, who, when asked if he was a Calvinist or an Arminian, replied that he was a Calvinist when he prayed and an Arminian when he preached (John Hobson, *On the Trail of A. W. Tozer*, Frome, 2015, p. 256).

Regarding the requisite for revival, Campbell's theology was simple: 'When people will come to true repentance and loathing of sin, God will come down in presence and power.'[10]

Spirit Baptism

Campbell believed in the baptism of the Holy Ghost as a separate and distinct occurrence following conversion. However, he did not view this as a Pentecostal experience accompanied by tongues and other signs and wonders. He saw it rather as a 'new, deeper revelation of Jesus Christ,'[11] and he spoke of the evidence of such baptism as the life of Christ reproduced in that of the believer.

Such teaching never became a central focus of his preaching in Lewis. Indeed, it is questionable whether Campbell ever preached on Spirit baptism in any Lewis church, and it is significant that not one of the testimonies that have been recorded from that revival make any mention of these teachings. Nor, indeed, in my own conversations with numbers of revival converts have any mentioned the influence of these teachings of Campbell's in their lives.

During the revival's progress on the island, at least, it is likely that few people in Lewis had knowledge of Campbell's thoughts on Spirit baptism. One convert shared that it was only sometime after the revival, while she was a student in Glasgow, that she 'first heard preaching on baptism of the Holy Spirit as a second blessing. Having said that,' she said, 'we had always acknowledged and relied on the work of the Holy Spirit, both in the lives of believers and in awakening and bringing sinners to faith.'[12]

Nevertheless, there is plenty of evidence that Campbell spoke openly on the baptism of the Spirit at meetings *outside* of Lewis, prior to, during and following the revival itself. Speaking at a convention in Cheltenham as early as 1946, Campbell 'stressed

---

10. Wadsworth, *The Pentecostal Evangel*, 01.04.1951.

11. Allen, *Catch the Wind*, p. 158.

12. Personal communication, 01.02.2022.

the great need for individual consecration and the filling of the Holy Spirit.'[13] At a conference in Ireland in September 1950, the evangelist reported: 'five came out for the baptism of the Holy Spirit' (as separate from those who 'came out' for salvation).[14]

At the FM Perth Convention of 1951, at which Campbell spoke, 'definite blessing' was noted, with 'many entering into the fullness' (of the Holy Spirit). After addressing the Calvary Holiness Church Convention in Manchester in 1953, Campbell led a meeting for ministers, at which he 'spoke on the baptism of the Holy Spirit.'[15]

Entire Sanctification

Though not widely recognised, there is no question that Campbell adhered to Holiness teaching and Keswick theology. But he held such teaching in balance. He agreed with Presbyterian Rev. Dr McKennal who wrote that 'Holiness is imparted to the soul of the believer by the direct gift of God.' He said he regarded 'contentment with sinful imperfection' to be 'more dangerous' than 'holding to sinless perfection.'[16] Yet while reflecting on some who 'got it into their minds that I was teaching absolute perfection or sinless perfection,' he insisted it was 'a thing that I never did, nor could I ever believe in.'[17]

Campbell believed that 'by His grace it is possible not to sin.' He liked to quote Charles Wesley, who wrote of his longing for a heart '*perfect and right and pure and good, a copy, Lord, of thine.*'[18] Yet, to someone who boasted he hadn't sinned for forty years, Campbell replied, 'You've just broken your record!' He also

---

13. *Gloucestershire Echo,* June 1946.

14. Duncan Campbell, FM Report, 27.09.50

15. ibid., 12.09.1951; 21.10.1953

16. Personal notebook of Duncan Campbell, courtesy of his grandson, David Heavenor, 29.03.2023.

17. Campbell, *Revival in the Hebrides,* p. 46.

18. Charles Wesley, '*For a Heart to Praise my God,*' 1742.

testified that the nearer he came to God the more he discovered things in his life which he never suspected before, requiring forgiveness and cleansing.

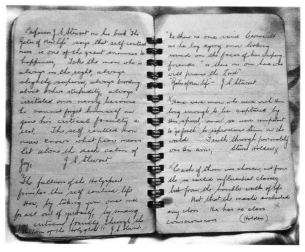

One of Duncan Campbell's notebooks

The important issue in regard to revival in Lewis is that while he appeared to embrace 'entire sanctification' as being neither a formality nor a result of a one-off event, but 'a life-long process of going from purity to maturity,'[19] Campbell did not teach any of these distinctive Higher life or Holiness doctrines in Lewis, where he stuck, rather, to preaching the gospel message of salvation in Christ.

Appeals

As already noted, and despite many accusations to the contrary, all who knew Duncan Campbell insisted he was no rank-and-file Arminian. He did not use the methods employed by well-known evangelists like Dwight Moody, R. A. Torrey, Billy Graham and so many others, of encouraging their hearers to make on-the-spot decisions for Christ. In that sense, his methods did not follow

19. Personal notebook of Duncan Campbell. (See also Woolsey, *Channel of Revival*, p.165.).

that of the 'typical American revivalist' as MacRae claimed. Campbell made no public appeals.

Rather, it was not unusual for Campbell to leave a church meeting with the building packed and with many people crying out to God for mercy. The evangelist felt quite comfortable leaving anxious sinners in the hands of God, whom he considered the Supreme Counsellor. He was also known to say, 'People under deep distress of soul may not find God tonight, or the next night, or next week, or next month. But he who searches for God will find Him, when he searches for Him with all his heart.'[20]

Even in the after-meetings, where Campbell would offer further instruction to, and prayer for, the anxious, it was claimed he never personally counselled an individual under spiritual distress, for fear he would interfere with God's dealings with that person. Mary Peckham, who attended a great many house meetings, wrote that in line with Lewis tradition, Campbell 'never made an appeal, believing that God would bring those who were seeking Him through to salvation.'[21]

The after-meetings usually took the form of two or three men being called upon to pray, after which Campbell would preach for fifteen minutes on the way of salvation from such texts as Isaiah 1:18; Isaiah 55:6 and, his favourite gospel verse, John 10:27. He would shed light on the fact that seekers should be sincere in this solemn and personal matter – that they must believe the Word of the Lord and be obedient to it.

It was in these after-meetings that the more tender, pastoral side of the preacher came out. 'The thundering prophet became the tender shepherd,' as one put it. Campbell would remind the anxious of Christ, the loving Shepherd who spoke gently to them, wooing them, calling them to Himself. This contradicts

20. Allen, *Catch the Wind*, p. 151.

21. Peckham, *Sounds from Heaven*, p. 102.

MacRae's further allegation that Campbell called for 'immediate and unqualified profession of conversion.'[22]

Ms Macdonald put her trust in Christ after attending one of Campbell's meetings in Stornoway. Still feeling affected by a sense of guilt, she later attended an after-meeting in someone's home. 'So, I went through, and he prayed and then he spoke and read John Chapter 10:27: *"My sheep hear my voice. I know them and they follow me":* and he talked a little about that. And of course, during that time, the light flooded into my soul, and I felt just like the Christian from *The Pilgrim's Progress;* the burden had gone from me. I remember going home that night and reading my Bible, and the thing I remember most clearly was, the Bible became a living Word. I could understand what I was reading, which I could never before.'[23]

It could possibly be claimed, however, that attending the 'inquirer's meeting' was taken by others present as a profession of faith. At one such meeting Campbell asked each seeker in turn, 'Do you want the Saviour? Do you really want Christ?' Then he knelt beside them and prayed. Mary Morrison was one of the spiritual seekers at that gathering. When she reappeared with her two friends, ministers came and shook hands with them, while others grabbed them and led them outside, where they formed a large circle and gustily sang out praises to God.

At this stage, however, Mary was still unconverted, and only came through to peace in Christ four months later. Similarly, when Kenny Macdonald stood up during a cottage meeting to go to the 'inquiry room,' someone said 'we don't need to pray for Kenny anymore,' taking his act as a profession of faith in itself.[24]

---

22. MacRae, *Resurgence of Arminianism,* p. 29.

23. Afrin, *Critical Analysis,* pp. 32–3.

24. Macdonald, *Testimony of Revival,* audio tape.

CHAPTER 20

Revival Denied

Opposition from Within

Few are the revivals that do not attract opposition. I can think of few revivals in the western world in the past century, or considerably longer, that attracted more obloquy than the Lewis revival of 1949–52. At times the opposition was staunch,[1] and Campbell makes reference to it again and again in his weekly reports.

Most of the opposition came from within the evangelical church. One of the few exceptions was the occasional jeering school-kid. Andrew Woolsey related the story of a schoolboy at the Nicolson Institute in Stornoway who was a believer, and whenever he spoke, an unconverted 'friend' struck him.[2] Such behaviour was exceptional. 'The three senior classes in the Nicolson were not large and we all knew each other – and the young converts also tended to know each other,' noted one revival convert. It was very rare for any pupil to get a hard time because of their new-found faith.

Although few in number, there were a few unlikely critics of the revival. Some of those converted during the 1930s movement, as well as some more longstanding believers, spoke against the latter awakening. Some had genuine concerns. Others, having lived through revival, were certain as to how it should begin and

---

1. On very isolated occasions it was extreme. A revival convert swore me to secrecy before relating in hushed tones one such instance.

2. Personal communication with Andrew Woolsey, 17.06.2016.

how it should progress, and the '49 movement didn't fit with their ideas. There were also some people within congregations where Campbell was invited to preach who disliked his style or methodology, or were resistant to change.

The preponderance of opposition, however, came from ministers and office-bearers of the island's two other main denominations. The Presbytery of the Free Presbyterian Church warned its congregations in June 1951, 'to have nothing to do with the so-called revival activities of the present day.' Their prayer and desire was that 'the Western Isles would be purged from this Arminian canker.'[3] As such, the principal publication of the FPC referred to the movement as 'the so-called Lewis revival.'[4] Such remarks apart, this denomination made little in the way of public comment about the revival.

'No General Movement'

The Free Church also remained aloof from the movement, and hit out strongly against both Duncan Campbell and the revival meetings. Numerous revival converts testify to the reality of this feature.[5] The Free Church Presbytery of Lewis recognised 'no general movement of the Holy Spirit' on the island, and issued a statement against Campbell's meetings, which, they felt, threatened to weaken allegiance of Free Church people in areas of 'revival stronghold' to the gospel preaching under which they had long been hearers.[6] Principal spokesman of Free Church disapproval was the Rev. Kenneth MacRae of Stornoway.

Rival meetings were set up by the Free Church in some areas (e.g., Arnol) to keep their flocks from straying into forbidden territory. One or two ministers spoke out against the movement in strong and unequivocal language, also claiming that Campbell

3. Taylor, *Skye Report*, periodical, p. 7.

4. *Free Presbyterian Magazine*, July 1954, p. 92.

5. Peckham, *Sounds from Heaven*, pp. 146, 151,171, 183–84, 215, 267, 274.

6. Murray, *Diary of Kenneth MacRae*, p. 445.

had come to steal members from the Free Church for the Church of Scotland.[7] Yet there is no evidence of any Free Church minister going to hear Duncan Campbell speak, so they had no personal knowledge of what Campbell said. Those Free Church members or adherents who did attend revival gatherings would have been unlikely to have informed their minister of such action.

Some in the Free Church found it difficult to conceive that God might pour out spiritual blessing upon the Church of Scotland, a denomination they considered thoroughly liberal and steeped in Arminianism, and with which they had felt compelled to part ways a century previously. Jealousy was also said to have been a significant motive for some of the opposition.

The great irony here is that the very agent through whom such signal blessing attended Church of Scotland congregations in Lewis held similarly biased views himself! Duncan Campbell had long been associated with the United Free Church of Scotland. When proposals had been made for a merger with the Church of Scotland in 1929, Campbell thoroughly opposed the scheme on theological grounds and later became an ordained minister within the breakaway United Free Church.

Of course, he was more than happy to preach in Church of Scotland congregations in Lewis, almost all of which were thoroughly evangelical in doctrine. Nevertheless, he was said to have held a degree of prejudice against that denomination (and continued to throughout his life). Even when his daughter Margaret married a Church of Scotland minister in the late 1940s, it was some time before Campbell felt at ease with the arrangement.[8]

Free Church Defection

The evidence from Campbell's weekly reports and from countless testimonies is that very significant numbers from a Free Church

7. Peckham, *Sounds from Heaven*, p. 121.

8. Personal communication with Sheena Campbell Vischer, 15.03.2020.

background attended the revival meetings in their home and
neighbouring localities. Free Church leaders would have been
well aware of this, though it is unlikely they had any idea just
how many from their own congregations were attending.

It was no doubt partly because of such defection that many
Free Church ministers reacted with such alarm. For not only were
many attending Campbell's meetings, but significant numbers
from within their flocks were also coming under conviction and
getting converted. In some areas with a predominantly Free
Church presence, it was even claimed that many more were
converted from that denomination than from the Church of
Scotland.

Aware of the opposition from their church leaders to the
meetings, many in the Free Church became confused. Some
withdrew from the meetings. Some were saddened and silenced,
and others took the minister's part and became bitter opponents
of the revival.[9] In some places, the Christian community was
divided with rifts that took years or decades to heal. People who
had been great Christian friends before the revival were now
barely on speaking terms because of the criticism that had split
their community.[10] On the other hand, there were some who,
initially hardened against the revival meetings, came to publicly
express remorse for such opposition, and from then on threw
themselves behind the work.[11]

The opposition took a variety of forms. One evening, a recent
convert of the revival with Free Church connections attended
her local church in Ness. On leaving, a woman elbowed her as

9. Allen, *Catch the Wind*, p. 195.

10. It was said that opposition to the revival even indirectly led to a
commotion in one Free Church congregation. A service became disrupted,
and the police were called to try and bring a degree of order. As a result,
several disgruntled members left the church and joined the Church of
Scotland.

11. Peckham, *Sounds from Heaven*, pp. 122, 183–4, 218.

she was going out the door. On another occasion she was spat at outside church.[12] Some mischievously suggested that Duncan Campbell was selling Bibles with chunks taken out of them! 'We didn't like talking about the opposition at all,' said one convert; 'we knew it would only get us down. We still don't like talking about it today.'[13]

Some Free Church converts were not allowed to sit at the Lord's Table for the simple reason that they had been converted through Duncan Campbell. They were forced to leave the church of their upbringing to find fellowship elsewhere. Others had to wait a considerable time before being admitted as members of their congregation – leaders being suspicious of their conversion, and thus desirous of testing their fruit. Still others voluntarily left their denomination to join the Church of Scotland, concerned that their own ministers were publicly opposing what they personally saw as an obvious work of grace in their communities.

Influence of Opposition

In regard to some objections to his practices, Campbell, with hindsight, wholly concurred. He readily accepted he had been unwise in agreeing to hold inter-denominational prayer meetings in one or two areas where active Free Church prayer meetings were already taking place. He also felt he could have used his influence more to stop people bypassing regular prayer meetings to attend revival services. Campbell, for the most part, sought to ignore the accusations made against him, making no public response to them. He felt he was called to simply preach the gospel message, and he sought to retain that focus, fully aware that the Lord was blessing the preaching of His Word.

The revival was so spoken against by some Free Church leaders that a great many in their congregations simply took their word for it and didn't for a moment consider whether there was any

---

12. Personal communication, 16.08.2008.

13. Personal communication with Agnes Morrison, 19.09.2016.

truth in their charges. One young man growing up in Lewis at that time, later to become a well-respected Free Church minister, said he only began to appreciate the revival after watching the documentary video, *Wind of the Spirit,* released in the early 1990s. Only then did he realise that a genuine spiritual movement had occurred on the island in his youth, and that the fruits of it were real and lasting.

As a result of the opposition, Campbell was not able to preach in parishes where other denominations had a stronghold but where there was no Church of Scotland presence. In one parish, the minister declared from his pulpit that if Campbell came to the area, he would set his dogs on him! (though he was in fact later invited to that community). Indeed, on several occasions Campbell did go to speak in areas with a Free Church stronghold, having been invited there by members of that denomination.

The Resurgence of Arminianism

The main mouthpiece of Free Church opposition was the Rev. Kenneth MacRae of Stornoway. MacRae published a booklet in 1954, entitled *The Resurgence of Arminianism* (written on a long boat voyage to Australia). Penned in part as a response to Campbell's meetings, which he viewed as clearly Arminian in nature, MacRae outlined what he believed to be the main characteristics of Arminian teaching – the universal extent of the atonement, rejection of predestination, denial of man's total depravity, self-willed faith, and the denial of the perseverance of the saints. These he contrasted to the essential tenets of Calvinism – total depravity, unconditional election, limited atonement, irresistible grace, and perseverance of the saints.

Historical Insights

MacRae firmly believed the Arminian system to be 'definitely not scriptural.' Certainly, he acknowledged that Arminians could have the grace of God in their hearts, and be ably used in the conversion of souls. Yet this was possible, MacRae believed, solely because the doctrines of Arminianism were mingled with those of grace – the Arminianism system itself was immensely harmful.

MacRae believed that the Church in Scotland had remained essentially Calvinist ever since the Reformation of the 1500s and right up to the arrival of American evangelists Moody and Sankey in 1873. For centuries prior to that date, MacRae stated, Calvinism was 'so firmly entrenched in the religious life of Scotland that no serious challenge appeared to be possible.' Moody, he believed 'succeeded in shaking the whole religious world to its foundation.'[14]

Since that time a plethora of Arminian evangelists had traversed the length and breadth of Scotland, holding lengthy campaigns and claiming great success. Among their number were Torrey and Alexander, and Wilbur Chapman. MacRae remembered some of these names from his own youth.

Indeed, in 1908, as an unconverted sixteen-year-old, he had attended an evangelistic rally led by an unnamed evangelist. On invitation, MacRae made a 'decision' to accept Christ in his heart, and although he believed it to be sincere, it proved not to be a deep and permanent work of the Holy Spirit in his soul. He quickly fell away from faith – though just over a year later, on the 9th of August 1909, after further deep spiritual searching, he came to a place of profound spiritual liberty, and 'the whole outlook of my life was changed.'[15]

MacRae ever after looked on Arminian-based evangelism, with its emphasis on man's 'decision,' with distrust and even disdain. Instead, he aligned himself to the Free Church, and quickly imbibed Calvinist theology, which position he ever since regarded as the one that alone was faithful to biblical truth.

---

14. MacRae, *Resurgence of Arminianism*, p. 12.

15. ibid., p. 11.

Following the Union of 1900, when most believers who favoured the new measures left the Free Church to join the new United Free Church, Calvinist doctrine was again at the fore of Free Church teaching and belief. These were fine days, MacRae believed, when a 'warm, earnest spirit prevailed within the church.' Lewis, in particular, had long remained a bastion of Reformed teaching.

Arminian Intrusion

Hence MacRae's alarm to find, in the late 1940s, a preacher invade the isle who he clearly saw as adopting a teaching system 'distinctly dishonouring to the Holy Spirit.'[16] MacRae insisted that his contention was not with Campbell in particular, but with the theology and methodology of the Faith Mission.

Another spiritual movement had occurred in Barvas just two-and-a-half years prior to Campbell's arrival – in the spring of 1947 – arousing considerable excitement. MacRae was deeply suspicious of what he had heard of it. He might well have been writing of Campbell's meetings when he noted in his diary:

'Buses are now going there, not only from Town, but also from Point; and late prayer meetings in houses seem to be the order of the day. The outcome of this will inevitably be another outbreak of the "jerks," and to induce it seems to be the great object with some. Eight are said to have come under exercise of soul. It is difficult to conceive of anything worse for them, than their being made the centre of all this publicity and fuss.'[17]

MacRae might have had this mission in mind, as well as, clearly, Duncan Campbell's campaigns, when he later complained when 'strangers come in who imagine that they have a God-given right to bid our people lay their principles aside and come out that they may be taught something different. To them the testimony of the Free Church of Scotland is nothing ….The

16. ibid., p. 8.

17. Murray, *Diary of Kenneth MacRae*, p. 423.

shepherd resents anything that may be hurtful to the flock; so do we resent most emphatically this attempt to sow Arminian doctrine among our people.'[18]

Rev Kenneth MacRae

MacRae believed that religion in Lewis was in a much worse condition than it was prior to the advent of the Faith Mission, for Arminian teachings had been propagated 'and ill-feeling and unkindly heat generated among congregations and churches which hitherto had enjoyed peace and were able to live together in harmony.'[19]

A Ministerial Matter

Some have argued, however, that much of the 'ill-feeling and unkindly heat' came, not from the revival itself, or from those who supported it, nor from the general mass of Free Church members and adherents, but directly from a few opposing church officials, notably MacRae himself. For among the laity there was generally little division.

---

18. MacRae, *Resurgence of Arminianism*, p. 31.

19. ibid., p. 27.

According to Colin Peckham, 'It did not matter what church
you belonged to. The blessing of the Lord was enjoyed by all
who knew Him. There was no distinction in the meetings. They
loved one another in the wave of mighty blessing that enveloped
them all, whether they were of the Free Church or the Church
of Scotland.'[20]

But so wary was MacRae of Campbell's missions that he made
it clear as late as 1954, several years after the revival had reached
its peak, that it was still unwise 'to pass hasty judgement' in
regard to professions of faith, knowing that 'converts, in the
modern use of the term, do not necessarily mean saved souls.' The
most he could say was that 'Souls *may* have been saved.'

In conclusion, MacRae questioned whether this was a genuine
revival at all, and stated, 'One may well stand in doubt of any
revival that is propagated' by what he believed were Campbell's
distortions and exaggerations.[21]

North-South Divide

MacRae was in no doubt that the Faith Mission, along with
the Keswick Convention and other groups, were 'thoroughly
Arminian in doctrine, and in practice unmistakeably in the
school of Finney.'[22] Yet he knew also that many, especially younger
ministers and members within his very own denomination, were
becoming increasingly influenced by Arminian theology. This
caused him great distress.

In particular there appeared to be a growing north-south
divide. Evidence of this showed itself when at the very time revival
was underway on Lewis, a Free Church minister from mainland

20. Peckham, *Sounds from Heaven*, p. 121.

21. MacRae, *Resurgence of Arminianism*, p. 29.

22. ibid., p. 24. Colin Peckham stated that the Free Church had supported
the work of the Faith Mission over a great many decades, and ministers from
that denomination had regularly taught at the Faith Mission Bible College
(personal communication, 20.08.2003).

Scotland agreed to visit Stornoway to speak at a meeting led by the Faith Mission. MacRae vigorously opposed such visit.

Again, a year later, Dr A. M. Renwick, Professor of Church History at the Free Church College in Edinburgh, wrote to the Free Church minister in the north Lewis parish of Ness, urging him to hold special services in his district, and suggesting a Faith Mission preacher, who was gifted in evangelism. MacRae was horrified at the proposal. Clearly, MacRae was at odds even with colleagues in his own denomination.

It is only with these background insights that we can understand MacRae's strong distaste of Campbell coming to Lewis. Yet while he may have been cognisant of the beliefs and practices of the Faith Mission, he appeared to know very little about Campbell himself. Not only had he never attended any of his meetings, it is possible he had never spoken to anyone who had.

Indeed, everything MacRae 'knew' about Campbell appears to have been plucked from a single source – the evangelist's 1952 Keswick address – this being the only reference cited in regard to him in his entire *Resurgence of Arminianism* publication. Such account, of course, says little of Campbell's theological views, or of his evangelistic methodology, and nothing of the man himself.

Other Reformed Viewpoints

Calvinist Critics

Author and co-founder of the Banner of Truth Trust, Iain H. Murray, was dismissive both of the revival in question, and also of Woolsey's biography of Campbell (such criticism being in contrast to the views of Murray's former mentor, Dr Martyn Lloyd-Jones – see below).[23] Murray claimed that 'the most prominent feature' in two early revival accounts is 'the phenomena – visions, prostrations, outcries, etc.'

---

23. Murray, *Diary of Kenneth MacRae*, p. 444 fn.

However, a careful read through of these documents reveals that there is no mention of any vision (let alone visions) in either report. A couple of instances of physical prostration are recorded – in each case in the context of people bowing low before God; believers crying out to Him in intercession. Outcries were a result of people coming under deep conviction of sin, a great many of whom soon went on to find peace and joy in believing.

Professor Donald Macleod of the Free Church College, Edinburgh, said he could find 'little of a positive nature' in the 1949 revival. Certainly, he recognised a great stir on Lewis at the time – but there had virtually always been a revival somewhere on the island from the 1820s to the late 1950s. In any case, he noted, 'Lewis people in the 1940s were generally of a more mystical nature than they are today ... and most were theologically articulate.'

'It was into this type of biblically-savant and emotionally-charged atmosphere that Campbell came – indeed, he walked straight into a revival situation.' In any case, Macleod expressed, 'one has to ask, did the experiences that occurred within that scenario happen spontaneously? With Campbell, they often happened in people's homes late at night.' Late night meetings, Macleod felt, were not to be encouraged.[24]

The Professor also believed that Campbell's focus on spiritual manifestations was 'unhealthy. Campbell was the first person to write about these phenomena.' Overall, Macleod was of little doubt that 'Campbell caused division within the Church in Lewis – particularly on the isle of Bernera, where whole families became divided.' Nevertheless, he felt the Free Church made a mistake in urging its members not to attend the revival meetings. 'This just made them want to go all the more!' Best, he felt, to

---

24. Personal communication with Professor Donald Macleod at the Free Church College, Edinburgh 24.05.2006.

just ignore them, in hope that the fuss surrounding them would
soon pass away.[25]

A New Religion

In his review of *Sounds from Heaven,* Professor MacLeod wrote,
'What Campbell brought was a new religion; preaching that
majored on sin and judgement; late-night cottage meetings that
began at 10 pm and sometimes went on till six in the morning;
lorry-loads and bus-loads of groupies who followed the preacher
everywhere; people swooning and groaning and going rigid
and falling into trances and singing on the shore in the dead
of night;[26] a constant eye on statistics regularly reporting to
Headquarters the number of conversions and professions;[27]
and a whole new language as unknown to the Bible as it is to
the Highland people.'[28] Brian Wilson, founding editor of the
newspaper which printed Macleod's review, termed Macleod's
statement a 'single, brilliant paragraph.'

And it certainly packs a punch. However, it might be regarded
as natural that Campbell would major on sin and judgement, as
well as on the hope of eternal life in a risen, crucified Saviour. These
are the main themes of any evangelist. Regarding the holding of
after-meetings in houses, people travelling to meetings in other
districts of Lewis and the occurrence of physical manifestations,

---

25. ibid.

26. Seemingly a reference to the shoreside testimony of Mary Morrison and
friends on the night they were converted (Morrison, *I was Saved in Revival,*
pp. 45–6).

27. For the years 1949–52, the main period of the revival, one observes a
few examples of Campbell stating the number of anxious who were actively
'seeking the Lord' as a result of his meetings. But there are in fact very few
instances during that entire three-year period when he refers specifically to
the number of professions of faith, or actual conversions.

28. Donald Macleod, review of *Sounds from Heaven* in *West Highland Free
Press,* 2004, quoted in Malcolm Maclean and Iain D. Campbell (Eds), *The
People's Theologian: Writings in Honour of Donald Macleod,* Fearn, 2011, p. 68.

all are regularly observable practices during times of revival –
certainly all were common to the revival on the same island just
a decade previously.

In that sense, one might question in what way Campbell
brought a 'new religion' to Lewis. Or indeed a 'new language'; the
Faith Mission and other groups had been active in the Western
Isles for many decades and a great many all over the island were
familiar with their operations.

Reformed and Refined

Other Reformed commentators have offered a more nuanced
take on the revival. Dr Martyn Lloyd-Jones had no hesitation in
classifying it as true and genuine, and he urged readers to pray
for a similar move of God in their own communities. Lloyd-Jones
also wrote a warm commendation of the authorised biography
of Duncan Campbell, published in 1974, which he termed a
'carefully and judiciously written book.'

This popular volume was penned by Andrew Woolsey, who
first heard Duncan Campbell speak at a Christmas conference
held in a mission-hall in Northern Ireland in 1960, just a year
after his conversion to Christ. Woolsey joined the Faith Mission
the following year, and first visited Lewis in 1963. He remembers
that he benefited greatly from times of fellowship with Campbell.
He later went on several missions with the renowned evangelist.

'Fire indeed did fall,' the Rev. Iain D. Campbell wrote.
'Without doubt, the awakening in the Hebrides was a
significant movement of the Spirit of God. Many were saved,
the Church was encouraged, and the Lord added to His people.'
He opined, however, that 'for purity of doctrine as well as for
breadth of influence, some other (Lewis) revivals were much
more significant.' [29]

---

29. Iain D. Campbell, 'Revival: A Scottish Presbyterian Perspective,' in Haykin
(Ed.), Pentecostal Outpourings, Grand Rapids, 2016, Chap 4.

For example, there was the Ness revival of 1923, which Iain D. Campbell termed 'one of the most significant in Lewis in the twentieth century.'[30] And there was also the 1934 Carloway revival, which, Iain felt sure, was 'the kind of revival that only the Spirit of God can produce,' those who were converted during it being 'deeply stirred in their feelings.'[31]

In his pioneering analysis of the Lewis revival,[32] Norman Afrin notes that a theological clash over Campbell's views on Arminianism and Calvinism had occurred at a very early date, and led to an article being submitted in the local paper in April 1950, entitled '*Anti-Calvinism Runs Riot*.'[33] Afrin quotes a few select statements by Campbell, which, he believes, leant strongly towards Arminianism, e.g., God 'cannot save a man from his sins if that man wills to hold on to his sins with both hands.'[34] Afrin felt such comments showed that Campbell disputed the doctrine of election in its fullness, a doctrine central to Calvinism.

He also claims that for anyone to declare that Campbell was not a Calvinist but that he was a biblical preacher, would not have, and would still not, make sense to those who hold to Reformed theology. Nevertheless, Afrin confirms that from 1949 to '53, 'a movement swept across the island that had major impacts and ramifications ... the evidence for the revival is irrefutable ...

---

30. For an account of this movement, see Lennie, *Glory in the Glen: A History of Evangelical Awakenings in Scotland 1880–1940*, Fearn 2009, pp. 316–20.

31. Campbell, in *Pentecostal Outpourings*, Chap 4.

32. Afrin, *A Critical Analysis of the 1949–1953 Lewis Revival*, MRes thesis, Glasgow University 2018.

33. Anonymous, *The Stornoway Gazette*, 21.04.1950, p. 59.

34. Duncan Campbell, *The Price and Power of Revival*, Edinburgh, reprinted 2015, p. 27. Afrin also quotes Campbell as saying, 'Remember that revival has got to do with God's people. We do not pray for revival in order that souls may be saved, but souls are saved in their thousands when we have revival; when the thirsty are satisfied, then the floods come on the dry ground. If you want revival, get right with God' (Afrin, *Critical Analysis*, pp. 28–9).

a revival, which has left its mark on individuals, communities, an island and the globe.'[35]

* * *

Most of the denominational tension caused as a result of the revival has melted over the years, and today Free Church ministers have no hesitation in accepting that a genuine outpouring of the Spirit occurred on their island between 1949 and '52. Along with it, in general, less distinction is placed on the Calvinism / Arminianism debate within Presbyterian circles in the North. Free Churchman Kelvin Moller perhaps sums up the current attitude of many Scottish evangelicals when he posits, 'It is not the resurgence of Arminianism we need to fear, but rather, the re-emergence of paganism, Islam and rampant atheism, coupled with an indifference to anything that smacks of Christianity.'[36]

Banner in the West

Introduction
With his book, *Banner in the West,* published in 2008, journalist John Macleod has provided a truly magisterial study on the spiritual history of Lewis and Harris. While early chapters ably chart the development of Neolithic settlers, Celtic missionaries and the Mediaeval Church, more than half the book is taken up with the island's remarkable evangelical heritage over the past two centuries. Macleod has gathered an abundance of historical and anecdotal information to present to the reader a fascinating and highly illuminating picture of the progress of evangelical religion on the island, and his writing style is consistently sharp and witty.

---

35. Afrin, *Critical Analysis*, pp. 65, 70.

36. Kelvin J. Moller, *A Reed Shaken with the Wind*, Kintyre, 2010, p. 36.

No Lewis Awakening!

In the very opening pages of his book, Macleod makes the shocking statement that there occurred no 'Lewis Awakening' in the post-war years of 1949–52; rather this is merely a legend, which he seeks to 'bust' for once and for all.[37] The author is not simply averse to using the term 'awakening,' given that in a more general sense Lewis had been 'awakened' to Christianity more than a century previously; for he is happy to use the word 'awakening' in reference to the 1930s revival on the island.[38]

Macleod feels his personal opinion finds only occasional expression throughout his 400-page treatise, but this is certainly not the case in regard to seven pages within Chapter 12. For here the author expands on his early assertion of no significant revival in Lewis between 1949 and '53; and out of over 3,000 words, provides only one positive statement in regard to the movement – that out of the 'many' professions of faith, there were 'some genuine conversions' (of these, he refers to just two).[39]

Rapid Decisions and Hysteria

Macleod makes a series of allegations against Duncan Campbell. He states, for example, that the evangelist encouraged 'much hysteria' at his meetings; that he also encouraged 'rapid decisions for Christ,' and that Church of Scotland ministers on the Westside 'actively encouraged Free Church people to attend' his meetings. One may as well reply simply, 'He did not' to each one of them, as this would be to supply as much counter-evidence as the author provides supporting documentation – i.e., none.

The latter allegation seems most unlikely given there was little interaction on Lewis at the time between Church of Scotland ministers and Free Church adherents.

---

37. Macleod, *Banner in the West*, p. 6.

38. ibid., p. 261.

39. ibid., pp. 262–3.

The charge that Campbell positively encouraged 'much hysteria' is similarly lacking in evidence, though it shouldn't be a problem to the author, who, in a previous book wrote, 'mass hysteria always seems to accompany the symptoms of genuine revival.'[40]

In regard to his oft-repeated allegation of the occurrence of physical manifestations – which he claims were a hallmark of the revival – the author omits any reference to similar phenomena attending the dramatic religious awakening that attended the Rev. Alexander Macleod's ministry in Uig in the 1820s, a movement which he describes in some detail, and of which he appears to heartedly approve.

'Sounds from Heaven'

The author claims the Peckham's book *Sounds from Heaven* is 'profoundly misleading.' He states that 12 out of the 24 conversion stories do not belong to the 1949–52 revival at all. My own count is that only two testimonies do not provide important information about the revival in question. One of these gives many illuminating details of the 1936 revival in Tolsta Chaolais. The other offers insight into the Harris revival of 1945–6, but still in the immediate post-war period.

The author has a problem with the nature of many conversion accounts, and records that the Peckhams repeatedly use the phrase 'broke through with God' to describe converts coming to a place of spiritual peace after weeks of misery. This appears to Macleod as if to say 'their quest were sadistically resisted, and salvation had to be earned by prayer and anguish.' This is in much contrast to his unsupported claim of 'rapid decisions' just two pages earlier.

---

40. John Macleod, *Highlanders: A History of The Gaels*, London, 1996, p. 231.

Again, also, Macleod offers no citations. In fact, I cannot find the phrase 'broke through with God' anywhere in the Peckhams narrative; nor, either, in any of the first ten testimonies (at least) recorded in the book (after which point I gave up my search). In distinction, an expression that does find repeated use is, 'God broke through,' in reference to revival blessing upon island congregations.[41]

'Less than Candid'

As well as accusing Campbell of being dishonest, Macleod also charges the Peckhams with telling unfounded 'tales' and says that some of their explicit statements are 'less than candid.' (Elsewhere he makes the same accusation against the Faith Mission, which he also claims is only 'vaguely evangelical' – a charge unlikely to ring true with anyone who knows much about this organisation.) Yet when Macleod makes a few factual errors of his own, he is guilty of the very thing for which he accuses Campbell – but fails to realise that this, in itself, does not make him a liar.[42]

The author dismisses a number of the Peckhams 'tales' on the grounds that 'not a single shred of documentation is offered' for them. He refers particularly to their chapter *Opposition to the Revival*, where he overlooks the fact that the authors were withholding people's names on the principle of confidentiality and sensitivity. Yet, again and again in his own seven pages, Macleod makes rather striking claims for which he offers 'not a single shred of documentation,' though without similar grounds.

---

41. Peckham, *Sounds from Heaven*, pp. 60, 65, 67, 70, 72.

42. e.g., he quotes remarks Campbell made in 1968 as being 1952, and incorrectly says the comments were made in Keswick. Macleod, however, is rightly wary of the faulty information presented on a 'Legion' of American websites where their originators did not take 'the trouble to check (their) facts' (*Banner in the West*, p. 264).

One of the earliest of these claims is that Campbell was a 'carpet-bagging mainland evangelist.'[43] But that he had any selfish motive in coming to Lewis is given no support from Macleod – nor has it, indeed, from any other writer. It is well known that Campbell initially had no intention of going to Lewis at all, being at the time engaged in fruitful evangelistic ministry in Skye, where he felt his efforts were most usefully employed. He only agreed to cross to Lewis when it became clear to him that he was being led there providentially.

Other Allegations

Macleod finds the Peckhams' claim that Free Church ministers 'stated that the devil had sent Mr Campbell to the island' to be yet another of their 'fabrications.' No evidence is offered by either writer. We do know, however, that a letter written by the Rev. Maclean of the Free Presbyterian Church and printed in the *Stornoway Gazette*, railed against churches where Arminianism abounded, urging that youth be warned against such 'doctrines of devils.'[44] And a letter written in response identified the revival of 1949–52 as the 'Devil's work ....Any new thing (even a revival of religion), in any section, must be branded as "the work of Satan" by those in the other camp.'[45]

In a number of instances, the author appears to simply extrapolate from arguments made by Kenneth MacRae and Iain H. Murray decades before him; for example in quoting Campbell as suggesting that Stornoway was a spiritual 'black spot' on the island during the revival. Campbell is nowhere on record as sticking any such label on the town. Similarly,

---

43. Carpet-bagging refers to an outsider moving in to an area to take advantage of a situation which he believes will yield him gain of some nature.

44. Maclean, 27.04.1951, quoted in Afrin, *Critical Analysis*, p. 53.

45. *The Stornoway Gazette*, 17.08.1951.

Macleod naively accepts Murray's assertion that the Faith
Mission 'clearly teaches a universal atonement'; a notion that is
patently untrue.[46]

---

46. Macleod, *Banner in the West,* p. 265; Iain H. Murray, *Diary of Kenneth
MacRae: A Record of Fifty Years in the Christian Ministry,* Edinburgh, 1980,
p. 444.

CHAPTER 21

Revival Falsified

Disdain of 'Biased Reporting'

One of the most curious and ironic features of the Lewis revival is the fact that despite Campbell's habitual distorting of many of the facts of the movement throughout and following the revival,[1] he maintained a strong antipathy towards anyone he believed to be falsely reporting any aspect of its progress. As early as 1950, a reporter expressed his great success in obtaining a personal interview with 'the man God is using.' He said Campbell was 'reluctant to speak to most people about it,' for 'he is afraid of distortion of fact.'[2]

Campbell was also quick to point out, in 1954, the 'exaggerated statements' that appeared in the press, carrying such lines as '*Revival Sweeping the Hebrides.*' Revival, he insisted, had not swept the Hebrides, 'There are many parts of the Western Isles still untouched by the movement.' He felt, rather, that Lewis and Harris had experienced 'times of refreshing from the presence of the Lord,' and that the wilderness had been made to 'rejoice and blossom as the rose.'[3] Campbell seemed unaware of the irony of

---

1. Curiously, he wasn't known for inflating stories of other spiritual movements he played a part in, such as in Skye in 1949 and North Uist in 1957. Indeed, he rarely mentioned these movements at all in his public addresses.

2. *The Pentecostal Evangel*, 19.11.1950.

3. Campbell, *The Lewis Awakening*, pp. 19–20.

his rebuttal, for in his Keswick address two years earlier he had specifically stated, 'God is sweeping through the isles.'[4]

The curiosity here is not so much the exaggeration of Campbell's statement, but the fact that he called out someone else for saying almost the same thing. In reality, the statement wasn't completely wrong. Prior to his arrival on Lewis, Campbell had been in the midst of a glorious move of God in Breakish on the island of Skye. There was plenty of evidence that great swathes of both Lewis and Harris, including the smaller islands of Bernera (Lewis) and Berneray (Harris) had been caught up in a great spiritual stirring during the years 1949 to '52. To many believers there was no question – the Spirit of God had very much swept through many of the Hebridean isles.

Objection to Owen Murphy

Campbell's concern over exaggerated reporting increased markedly following the publication in the States of a booklet by Owen Murphy,[5] the young minister who had heard him speak in Keswick. Campbell reacted scathingly to the American's account (though he never publicly named him).

Murphy's booklet – running at just forty-seven pages – was, according to its author, based largely on 'personal interviews with participants of the revival,' and on 'investigative reports that appeared in outstanding Christian publications.'[6] In reality, the information appears to have been taken largely from Campbell's Keswick address.

Murphy insisted he made no attempt to minimise or exaggerate any details of the revival. This is clearly not always true, for he

---

4. Campbell, *Revival in the Hebrides*, Keswick address 1952, p. 147. It appears to have been a one-off statement, for Campbell nowhere referred to God 'sweeping through' the Western Isles again.

5. Date of publication is not stated in the first edition, but is prior to 1955, when a revised edition appeared.

6. Murphy, *When God Stepped Down from Heaven*, p. 23.

significantly distorts the truth in stating; 'not a home, not a family, not an individual escaped fearful conviction ... the town was (also) changed.'[7]

This quote apart, it is with difficulty one can find anything in Murphy's account that is a significant misconstruction of anything Campbell himself wrote in connection to the movement. Indeed – and most ironically – one gets the sense that Campbell might have written this account himself, so in line does it appear with his own style and content. In his 2016 booklet on the Lewis revival, Wayne Krauss attempted a 'rebuttal' of Murphy's work. Despite his earnest efforts, he was unable to pinpoint a single inaccuracy in Murphy's report, leading him to conclude that any error could only have been 'minor.'[8]

Presence and Holiness

Towards the close of his account of the revival in Lewis, Murphy includes a short chapter entitled, *'Presence and Holiness.'* Here, he relates a story from Campbell's Keswick address about a young man who comes under conviction and begins to shake. He goes to a pub to drink his way out of the *cùram*; then to a dance, in attempt to dance his way out of it. Both attempts fail, and the man surrenders his life to Christ. The story is innocent and sounds plausible, although no other revival convert has referred to it, and it doesn't appear in any of Campbell's later addresses.

But Murphy takes it a step further, following the above story with four similar pithy testimonies of ungodly men who fell under conviction of sin during the revival, each going on to surrender his life to Christ. The most powerful involves a man convicted of his godless life, and unable to get peace of mind. Rushing down to the seashore and hiding among the rocks, he prepares to take his own life. At that very moment, a young woman, while kneeling in prayer in her home, has a vision of

---

7. ibid., p. 36

8. Campbell, *Revival in the Hebrides*, p. 94.

this man; the Spirit showing her exactly where he is and what he is about to do. Quickly rising to her feet, she calls her minister, and instructs him where to find the unfortunate gentleman. The minister arrives just in time to save him, not only from physical death, but from an eternal hell.

All four are gripping stories. But like Campbell's own anecdote, no context is provided for any – no names, locations, church affiliation, etc. They are tagged on at the end of Murphy's overview of Campbell's Keswick address. None of the four are included in that talk, nor in any later address given by Campbell.

The story related above is so remarkable that, if true, would almost certainly have become one of the best-known of the entire Lewis revival. One can, further, only wonder how Murphy managed to obtain these testimonies, given that he never visited Scotland, let alone Lewis and Harris, and he knew no one on the islands.

Each of Murphy's four stories is the type of contextless testimony that could easily be dropped into almost any revival narrative. Like Campbell's dancehall anecdote, it is of course impossible to *disprove* them. But, apart from the fact that no one has ever been able to confirm them, they do not have the ring of truth; they are just too neat, a little too perfect. Did Campbell have concerns about Murphy's four add-on tales, fairly innocuous as they are? Even if he did, was that reason enough for him to warn against Murphy's booklet as strongly as he did?

Covenant Theology

Then again, Campbell may have objected to Murphy's seeming preoccupation with covenant theology. While the Scotsman also strongly believed in covenant praying, Murphy placed an even greater emphasis on it. It's not difficult to see why. He testified that as a young man he was suddenly struck with polio, being paralysed from the waist down. Five London specialists pronounced him incurable.

Hearing one day of the power of covenant prayer, Murphy and his wife decided in desperation to seek the Lord according to that pattern. Lying in bed at home one foggy morning in prayer, suddenly the room was filled with the presence of God. New life surged through his helpless body, and Murphy rose from his bed completely healed. Overjoyed at God's goodness, he keenly espoused covenant praying, and began to proclaim it everywhere.

In his retelling of the story of revival in Lewis, Murphy again places a repeated emphasis on the covenant – by insisting that the biblical verse 2 Chronicles 7:14 acted as the central 'covenant' verse which the praying Barvas elders pleaded thrice-weekly in the 'barn' prior to the outbreak of revival. He also erringly explains Campbell's personal re-consecration to vibrant evangelical ministry a year or two prior to coming to Lewis in terms of covenant engagement.

Was it Murphy's near obsession with God as covenant keeper, and in particular his distortion of Campbell's pre-Lewis testimony, that annoyed Campbell so much? Or was it the overall combination of inaccuracies in Murphy's account? Whatever the truth, Campbell took a strong aversion to Murphy's publication, and even went to the extent of demanding its withdrawal from public circulation.

The book was not withdrawn; rather, it continued to receive widespread distribution across the States. As late as 1968 – ironically in the very same address that led to the most serious accusations against Campbell of gross exaggeration – the Scottish evangelist was still complaining about a man 'going about the States, telling stories about the revival and writing books about it, and I regret to say that statements have been made by him and written in his books that are not true to fact.'[9]

Because Campbell did not name the author or the publication in question, the American public had no idea he was referring

---

9. Campbell, *Revival in the Hebrides*, p. 54.

to Owen Murphy and his book, *When God Stepped Down From Heaven*. And so the popular title continued to sell. As recently as 2016 a revised and expanded edition of the book was published under the title *God, Fire and Revival*, being enthusiastically endorsed by the likes of Mike Bickle, Lou Engle, Floyd McClung and George Otis, Jr.[10]

Campbell's Sensationalism

Numerous are the individuals converted through Duncan Campbell who have retained a strong admiration for him ever since, but who yet concede to the evangelist having a strong tendency to exaggeration.[11] Campbell's biographer, who knew him well and held him in high regard, sought to partly explain Campbell's 'misleading statements' on account of his 'failure to record incidents on paper' and his 'readiness to accept second-hand reports.'[12]

It is significant that during the progress of the revival, few, if any, who spoke against Campbell did so on the grounds of exaggeration. This is largely because none of his detractors at that time had ever heard him speak. In any case, it would appear that exaggerated statements were not to be found in his day-to-day preaching during the revival, which focused purely on a strong gospel message. Rather, his distorted stories only cropped up in his retelling of accounts of the revival when invited to speak at meetings throughout Scotland and beyond.

---

10. John Wesley Adams, who edited the new edition, wrote that out of the nearly 3,000 books in his library that have helped shape his thinking and spiritual life, 'none have profoundly impacted my life more than Murphy's original booklet. It is spiritual dynamite, a kingdom gem!' (Murphy, *When God Stepped Down from Heaven*, p. 9).

11. Similar claims have been made of various other revivalist preachers, including Erlo Stegen, who was accused of exaggerating stories in the Kwasibantu revival in the late 1960s, and even John Wesley, who is thought to have overstated the size of his audiences.

12. Woolsey, *Channel of Revival*, p. 145.

In particular, accusations of exaggeration followed the evangelist's Keswick address in 1952 (by which time the Lewis revival was drawing to a close), which was published in the *Keswick Week* journal towards the end of that year. This message acted like a red rag to Kenneth MacRae, who later accused Campbell of issuing 'propaganda' to an 'extraordinary extent,' filled with 'gross exaggerations, unscrupulous distortion and absolute falsehood.'[13]

Similar accusations emerged following Campbell's three-week mission to Gardner Street Church of Scotland in the Partick area of Glasgow in May 1953. There were many Lewis natives in the congregation, linked to both the Free Church and the Church of Scotland. Some of these, surprised at several of the stories Campbell related, and questioning their veracity, wrote to friends and family back home, relating the accounts as Campbell had shared them.

This led to an outcry from a number of Lewis believers, which resulted, remarkably, in one or two Church of Scotland meetings at which Campbell was due to address on the island being cancelled. Clearly, Campbell would have been made aware of the concern and disquiet caused, which should have prompted him to ensure he took extra care in what he said in the future. It's unclear whether he accepted the charges, or whether they resulted in any changes on his part.

Mary Peckham heard Campbell when he came to speak in Canada in the late 1960s, while she was based at the Prairie Bible Institute. Shocked and disturbed by some of the things he said from the platform, she later spoke to Andrew Woolsey about it. Woolsey wondered if it was a result of Campbell being 'confused and ill, and beginning to get old' (he was then in his late sixties).[14]

---

13. MacRae, *Resurgence of Arminianism*, p. 29.

14. Some converts noticed that when Campbell returned to Lewis some years after the revival, 'he wasn't quite as clear as he used to be. He seemed to be getting things a bit mixed up.' (M. Macdonald, quoted in Afrin, p. 55).

Woolsey also told of an occasion when just prior to a meeting where Campbell was invited to speak, he had related to the evangelist the news that several people had recently been converted during a communion service in the Lewis community of Back. 'Between the door and the platform,' Woolsey stated, 'the numbers shared had significantly increased and what the Rev Campbell shared with his audience was a different story to what he had been told fifteen minutes previously'![15]

Possibilities Explored

Several reasons have been suggested in an attempt to explain why Campbell might have spun such tall tales. He may have begun to show symptoms of dementia or other form of memory loss in the years prior to his death. Family members have denied this as a possible explanation, as too, have others who knew him.

Perhaps Campbell was simply 'a first-rate story-teller who possessed a lively Celtic imagination.' This was the view of his daughter, Sheena. It also corresponds with the opinion of Mary Peckham, who referred to Campbell's 'flights of imagination.' Andrew Woolsey makes a similar (albeit more wordy) claim in suggesting, 'Many seeming inconsistencies were unavoidably caused by the intense manner in which Duncan entered into the awareness of God's work in times of spiritual quickening, which impinged upon his imagination a more vivid and arresting picture of souls in conflict than the more objective viewer would receive.'[16]

Or, Campbell may have deliberately embellished and fabricated stories for effect. In essence, was he a deliberate and habitual liar; something of a charlatan, an imposter, a fraudster? I'm aware of only one writer who has publicly pointed in this direction. Everyone I spoke with who knew Campbell personally has declared their inability to conceive that he was a deliberate

---

15. Personal communication with Andrew Woolsey, 17.06.2016.
16. Woolsey, *Channel of Revival*, p. 145.

serial liar. Instead, they have vouched for the evangelist's absolute integrity and singular desire to give glory to God.

Keeping the Peace

It is only natural to question why those who have known of Campbell's distortion of facts for many years didn't call him out sooner, rather than allow his false reporting to remain in wraps for decades on end. The answer would appear to be a combination of deep respect for the man, mixed with genuine confusion and embarrassment. Lewis converts had the deepest of respect for the visiting evangelist whose ministry had transformed their lives; standing in awe of this formidable yet modest minister.

At the same time, his exaggerations and fabrications caused them enormous confusion. They found his distortion of facts impossible to comprehend, and were deeply embarrassed that the man at the centre of a revival could make up such fanciful stories. They preferred not to let their minds dwell on such things, choosing to focus instead on the great good Campbell accomplished, or better still, not to focus on the evangelist at all, but on the remarkable works of God in their midst.

Knowing they weren't personally present at every gathering, some converts may have assumed that some of Campbell's more sensational tales perhaps did truly occur. It is also the case that many converts were never truly aware of the extent of the evangelist's exaggerations; not everyone listened to the many audio tapes of his messages, nor did they trawl through the plethora of websites devoted to his revival teachings. Thus, they had no way of knowing. Of course, there is also the possibility of converts not wanting to play into the hands of Campbell's opponents; those who would have jumped at the chance of exposing the evangelist as a fraud and the revival as inauthentic.

In any case, one must remember that the writing of *Sounds from Heaven* was very much an attempt to take the emphasis away from sensationalist anecdotes, and present in their place a more factual record. Sadly, the various falsehoods that the authors commendably bring to light seem to have been overlooked by many revival enthusiasts.

Mythomanic Addiction

A plethora of websites reveal that the telling of compulsive, habitual lies is known as mythomania or *pseudologia fantastica* – but is commonly referred to as pathological lying. Although not a recognised condition, some common characteristics of this behaviour resonated with me as being true of Duncan Campbell. These include:

Lying without any obvious benefit or reason. This might help explain why Campbell told outlandish tales about the revival, when in fact the movement required no exaggeration or embellishment at all; the wonderful truths of the awakening were remarkable enough.

An inability to control the impulse to lie, even when it brings the individual into disrepute. For years I simply couldn't believe that Campbell could have shared entire stories with no basis in fact. The possibility that he might have been addicted to lying, and hence hardly able to control the impulse, greatly helps to understand this aspect of his behaviour.

We observe a similar trait regarding the location of Campbell's addresses. It is one thing exaggerating stories of the Lewis revival in far-flung places like rural America and South Africa, where nobody knew him, and people could not verify the facts. But on home soil, one would expect him to be much more careful, knowing that many going to hear him in, for example, Glasgow and Edinburgh, would hail from the Hebrides, and might easily check details with relatives or friends from the isles. Instead, we find the evangelist relating the very same myths all over Scotland as he did in more distant places.

Telling lies that are dramatic, outlandish and detailed. A number of Campbell's stories are not just implausible – they're fantastical, making one wonder how anyone could have possibly been taken in by them. But he had a habit of mixing elements of myth with actual true events, which helped make the stories appear more credible. He was also an extremely good storyteller, relating his stories with remarkable conviction and flair – highly adept at capturing the hearts and imaginations of his audiences.

Believing (or seeming to believe) one's own lies. This undoubtedly helps explain why countless Christians worldwide have been taken in by Campbell's untruths for over seven long decades. He didn't at all come over as if he were lying – rather, he seemed utterly convinced of the reality of his stories, which is why he told them with such ease and with such frequency, leading multitudes of others to be convinced of them, too.

Indeed, how else could Campbell have moved from church to evangelical convention to gospel hall, month after month, year after year, for over twenty years, sharing fabricated stories of the Lewis revival, yet often also preaching potent messages on repentance, the Cross, righteousness and holiness? Surely, it would have played so strongly on his conscience that he could potentially have cracked under the convicting strain – unless, that is, he was personally convinced of the untruths he was telling.

Surely, only this explanation can also account for Campbell's repeated use of phrases like: 'I am talking about fact that cannot be gainsaid' (a favourite saying of Campbell's);[17] 'Now, dear people, that's true, that's true!' (immediately after telling a story that was not true); 'That is the story of the revival that can bear the light of examination' (at the close of an address, the truth of which does not bear the light of examination).[18]

Compulsive liars tend not to exaggerate stories in order to make themselves appear more interesting (because they are often told for no good reason). Campbell's tales have the

---

17. *Keswick Week,* 1952, p. 146.

18. Campbell, *Revival in the Hebrides*, p.53.

effect of aggrandising, not himself, but the revival movement in which he played so large a part. Each one of them makes the revival sound more dramatic, more sensational, than it truly was, thus making the movement come over as more remarkable and appealing to listeners. Indirectly, one could argue that this gained Campbell admiration; but that this was consciously a motive seems unlikely given his own understated role.

Addictive liars do not generally intend to harm others and are by no means necessarily bad people. Those who knew Duncan Campbell and who were thoroughly aware of his tendency to exaggerate still found him remarkably likeable, unassuming in nature, friendly, courteous, and especially, having a genuine love for God and a true passion to see His name glorified.

*   *   *

Campbell's addiction to lying may have been connected to a profound enjoyment of the acclaim his public addresses on the Lewis revival brought him. The fact that from the very earliest date, and for the remainder of his life – a period of over twenty years – he accepted almost any invitation to go and speak about the Lewis revival shows his true love of this lifestyle.

Another motive (if, indeed, there was one) may have been Campbell's delight in the obvious effect his talks had on his hearers. Everywhere he went, sinners were brought to Christ and believers were profoundly stirred by the stories he shared; leading many to deeper spiritual consecration and to more earnest prayer for a move of the Spirit in their own communities and in their nation generally. All of this may well have confirmed to the evangelist that his tall tales (if he saw them as such) were productive of immense good.

Ultimately, we don't know why Duncan Campbell told untruths about the Lewis revival. Over half a century after his death, there's no way we can get into his mind. I'm simply offering a possible explanation; one that refuses to ignore or diminish the reality of his ongoing myth-making, but which at the same time takes into account the above-mentioned factors; and which is ultimately helpful in maintaining the overall integrity of the evangelist at the focus of our attention. The reader will need to decide for him or herself whether such explanation is felt to be satisfactory.

PART 6

Post Revival

CHAPTER 22

Revival Decline

Effectively, the Lewis revival began to subside from around the spring of 1952, following Campbell's mission on Berneray. Certainly, there does not appear to have been any fresh revival outbreak anywhere subsequent to that date. Indeed, after April '52, Campbell held only one further mission on the island that year (in Harris in November), spending the majority of his time outwith the island. While he continued to attract large crowds to his meetings in various places – especially Barvas – few conversions accompanied them. The revival proper was effectively over; in its place, a period of revival afterglow was very much apparent.

Gravir

Many maintain that revival continued, not only throughout 1952, but right up to the summer of '53. They offer as strong evidence of this, a campaign that Campbell conducted in Gravir in the Park district of South Lochs, in the east side of the island, towards the close of August 1953; a full three-and-a-half years after his first mission on the island in December 1949.

It wasn't the first time Campbell had held a mission in the Gravir area – indeed he had spent some time elsewhere in the district just five months previously.[1] Campbell wrote that 'a bus full of converts from Gravir' attended those meetings. These were

---

1. He had also attended an evangelistic meeting in Gravir Free Church at an earlier point, but he didn't speak at it (personal communication with A.M. [2001], who attended this meeting).

presumably converts of Campbell's earlier missions in other parts
of Lewis over the previous three years.

Duncan Campbell at Gravir

Of the later Gravir meetings, which began on August 21st in the
small Church of Scotland meeting house, it appears that initially
they were not remarkable. That soon changed, however, for on
day five of the ten-day campaign, Campbell could exult, 'We
are witnessing a gracious move of the Spirit, similar to what we
saw in other parts of Lewis; crowded meetings, deep conviction
of sin, and souls seeking the Saviour.' Many people, old and
young, walked four miles over the hill from Lemreway to the
Gravir meetings.[2]

Campbell occasionally uses the word, 'revival' in his narrative,
and his direct comparison of the Gravir blessing to what he had
witnessed in other districts in Lewis, such as Barvas, Ness and
Uig, suggests he saw it as a very significant movement. He goes

2. Colin Macmillan was one who was converted through Campbell during
the Gravir mission, later becoming an elder in the parish.

on to say, 'Now that God is moving, buses and vans are bringing the people from other parishes.'[3]

This implies that visitors weren't coming in significant numbers from other areas until they heard that God was moving in power. This in turn suggests that revival had broken out in Gravir at least a night or two earlier, in other words, on at least the third or fourth evening of the campaign.

Gravir, South Lochs

Campbell goes on to provide a few more details. 'Another headmaster has been added to the number already witnessing for Christ ....Our meetings continue each night until midnight. I am arrested each night by a group of ministers from the south of England who are rejoicing in seeing revival.'[4]

Was it revival?

Hugh Black, a schoolteacher from Greenock, visited Lewis in the summer of '53. He wrote, 'As a young man keenly interested in revival … I had a distinct urge to go to the Hebrides. I found myself there just as the revival was deemed to be over. I had the

---

3. Duncan Campbell, FM Report, 26.08.1953.

4. ibid.

privilege of chauffeuring Duncan Campbell for about a week of what I think was his last campaign on the island (in Gravir) … But the revival by that time had largely passed, and it did not break out when I was there.'[5]

If Black is correct with what he relates (he was reminiscing in 1993), then he was present around a week after the meetings began – i.e., shortly after the time that Campbell dates as the beginning of the move of the Spirit. Yet rather than exult in the mighty movings of God he was witness to, Black found the Gravir gatherings rather unspectacular. 'They were good meetings,' he said, 'but not what would be called revival meetings.'[6] Black provides no details, and stopped attending prior to the mission closing.

Hugh Black

As a young man fascinated with the concept of revival, if Black had witnessed the Spirit of God moving powerfully at these gatherings, he would surely have been the first to enthuse about

---

5. Foreword to Kathie Walters, *Bright and Shining Revival*, Macon, p. vii. Hugh Black, *Revival, Including the Prophetic Vision of Jean Darnall*, Greenock, 1993, p. 25. Black goes on to say that his only personal experience of revival was some years later, at a school camp.

6. Black, *Revival, Including the Prophetic Vision of Jean Darnall*, p. 96.

them – not least because he had never witnessed anything of the kind before. The fact that he states, quite categorically, 'revival did not break out when I was there,' suggests that however good the Gravir meetings were, they were not attended by the flow of revival that Campbell depicted.

'Fathers' of the Revival

A hugely popular story relating to the Lewis revival appeared on a mass-distributed cassette tape in the mid-1990s. *Revival Fire* consists of a compilation of short audio clips (interspersed with evocative worship music) from popular revivalist preachers, including Leonard Ravenhill, Duncan Campbell and Steve Hill. The tape was offered to thousands of believers attending the 'Brownsville Revival' in Pensacola in 1995–6. Included around half-way into the recording is a story related by the then leader of a community church near Portsmouth, who states that a friend of his was once engaged in research into revivals. He continues;

'As part of his research, he went to the Hebrides to research the history of the Hebridean revival. He booked into a guest house, which was run by an elderly couple, and the father of the house was actually one of the "Fathers" of the revival. So he found himself, without trying, sitting right at the feet of someone who could tell him quite a lot of information. This man said to him, with tears in his eyes, "There were six of us who fathered the revival who are still alive. We meet together occasionally when our wives are in bed. We sit down and talk about those days and we can't stop crying."

'He said, "The reason the Hebridean revival failed was this; the leadership didn't know what to do with it. They didn't know how to structure it. They didn't know how to prepare a wineskin for what God was doing. And it faltered and it failed."

'And this old man got hold of my friend, who was about thirty years of age, and grabbed him by the collar, looked in his eyes;

his piercing eyes looking up, and he said, 'Son, when you get it, whatever you do, don't let go of it.'"

The *Revival Fire* tape has inspired literally hundreds of thousands of believers in America and across the world since it was first produced.

The audio-clip in question, like others on the tape, is indeed deeply moving and on first hearing might seem quite reasonable. But a number of problems emerge. Anyone researching the Lewis revival of 1949–52 invariably concentrates their focus on Barvas, the starting place and main centre of the movement. Yet I am reliably informed that none of the office bearers at the time of revival in Barvas subsequently ran a B&B or guest house.

Further, none of the elders in Barvas or anywhere else on the island were subsequently referred to as 'fathers of the revival.' Revival converts I spoke to had never even heard the term being used before. Nor is there any record of any elder having spoken of 'fathering the revival,' an expression that appears presumptuous and awkward to older Lewis believers.

The idea that these six men met up in one of their homes after their wives had gone to bed has been deemed 'comical' by others who lived through the revival. 'I cannot imagine that happening,' noted one. 'People don't go to bed early here and the men always conduct family worship before they do. The idea of them then sneaking out about 11 pm is rather far-fetched!'

The idea that the so-called 'fathers of the revival' couldn't stop crying when they met to reminisce about bygone days, while sentimentally appealing, also seems quite unlikely. Certainly, there are next to no documented instances of such overt collective emotional display among Christian men on the island, this being especially true in the years and decades after the revival had subsided.

Why did the Revival Stop?

I've never heard anyone from Lewis suggest that the Hebrides revival in any way 'failed.' The idea that it was a flop is especially anathema to anyone who was in any way connected to it. Among island believers in the Church of Scotland, the Lewis revival was universally regarded as a glorious outpouring of God's Spirit, a divine visitation that swept hundreds of needy souls into the kingdom of God. It is quite illogical (and to many, almost scandalous) to suggest that a move of God's Spirit that led to an abundant – and lasting – fruit somehow 'failed.' Even those who opposed the revival didn't make this claim.

Nor is any church elder in Lewis on record as blaming congregational leadership for not knowing how to 'manage' or 'structure' the revival – a notion quite alien to the Christian community in Lewis. Almost everyone on the island, and certainly all believers, had enormous respect for their local minister (who effectively *was* the church leadership). In Barvas, this was the Rev. James Mackay, a man loved and respected by all his parishioners, and who earned nothing but their praise for his tireless work in the revival.

Surely, with such a remarkable history of spiritual awakenings, if any group of people anywhere in the western world knew how to prepare a wineskin for what God was doing in revival, it would have been the church-going people of Lewis. The wineskins had already been prepared in the form of entire communities ready and open to receive from heaven.

Other reasons have also been offered as to why the revival ended prematurely; a common one being that it was owing to the opposition that came against it. It is argued that without the opposition, the revival would have continued much longer. It is true that intense opposition can falter the progress of a spiritual movement, or even bring it to a close. Yet, opposition regularly goes hand in hand with revival; true revival often continues to prosper even in the midst of opposition.

The suggestion that because the revival came to an end after several years, therefore it 'faltered and failed,' is also quite alien to both the theology and practice of the church in Lewis. As believers on the island are thoroughly aware, revivals never continue indefinitely – nor are they meant to. The Lewis revival continued on and off in different parts of the island for two-and-a-half years – much longer than most revivals endure. No one connected to the revival saw that as a faltering or a failure.

It's probably more realistic – and helpful – to consider the Lewis revival as an overall movement of spiritual awakening, consisting of a series of separate, though inter-linked revivals. While the movement as a whole lasted nearly two-and-a-half years, the individual parish revivals were more typically of a few weeks' – or occasionally a few months' – duration. Those occurring in smaller communities, such as Arnol or Berneray, consisted of short, sharp bursts of heightened revival activity; people spoke of Berneray's 'week of revival,' for example. Even in larger parishes like Barvas, where revival was more sustained, the main season of revival was the four-month period from mid-December 1949 to April of 1950, corresponding to the period when the majority of conversions took place.

When you Get it, Don't let Go of it

The Reformed culture of Lewis did not hold to the theology of 'getting' revival, or 'keeping hold of it,' making revival to be some commodity that you can grab on to. No Lewis elder of the day would have used this phrase, or anything resembling it. Rather, the Church in Lewis fully believed that revival comes and goes; God is sovereign and He alone determines the timing.

As for the story of a Barvas elder grabbing an unknown young man by the collar and staring him in the face, Lewis converts I spoke to found it not just unlikely, but quite unbelievable. Such abrupt and unseemly action was quite anathema to island culture of the time (and even still today).

When shown a copy of the above story, one Lewis revival convert shared, 'Nothing in that transcript makes sense to us!' Somewhat grieved by its contents, and clearly shocked that stories like these were in circulation, he added, 'Every time we think we have heard all the erroneous or exaggerated tales, another appears.' The above story did not happen and is clearly a fabrication. It appears to be a case, like so many others, of someone seeking to read back into the revival theories or elements that they particularly want to be true.

Societal Transformation?

A variety of claims has been made in recent times to the effect that Hebridean society was radically altered by the Lewis revival. A renowned researcher into societal transformation achieved by moves of God's Spirit has contended that the Lewis awakening may be 'the last undisputed example of (community) transformation in the Western world' – a community 'whose values and institutions have been overrun by the grace and presence of God ... a culture that has been impacted by the full measure of the Kingdom of God. A society in which supernatural power flows like a river of molten lava, altering everything and everyone in its path.'[7] Another author exulted that 'the social landscape changed dramatically for the better in community after community.'[8]

Similarly, a Scots-Canadian writer saw what occurred in Lewis during the years 1949–52 as not just spiritual awakening, but *absolute* transformation. 'The consistent testimony from Lewis,' he wrote, 'was that when God's presence entered into the community through the prayer and witness of the revived local Church, it permeated every aspect of life ... the presence of God began to influence and change every part of society –

---

7. George Otis (Jr), quoted in Murphy and Adams, *The Fire of God's Presence*, Kansas, 2004, pp. 1, 80.

8. John Wesley Adams, in ibid, p. 81.

politically, economically, educationally, morally and ethically, ecologically and spiritually.'[9] What's more, the author contended, half a century after such spiritual transformation, the island of Lewis 'continues this process of being changed from one degree of glory to another.'[10]

No evidence is provided in support of any of the above claims, although they may be in part inferred from Campbell's own exaggerated reports. The statements ignore the fact that Lewis and Harris was *already* an overwhelmingly Christian community long before the '49 revival ever graced it.

As we have noted, hundreds of individual lives were transformed by the Lewis revival, and with lasting effect. This indeed would have had a significant impact on societal life in many communities across the island. More people were now attending Sunday services and weekly prayer meetings. There were fewer young people going to the cinema, or the pub, or engaging in other forms of worldly amusement. But, deeply influential as it was, it is not the case that the 1949–52 Lewis revival achieved anything like the societal transformation suggested by the above writers.

Last Revival in Western World?

The Lewis revival is widely regarded as one of the last significant moves of God's Spirit in Great Britain, and even in the western world. This point has been stated repeatedly in revival literature; most notably in the Foreword to a popular study, which notes, 'The last recorded revival in the British Isles ended just half a century ago' – clearly referring to the Lewis revival of 1949–52.

Yet that same volume makes note of a revival occurring on that same island just five years later (Point 1957), a widespread

---

9. Alistair Petrie, *Transformed: 10 Principles for Sustaining Genuine Revival*, Lancaster, 2003, p. 29. The author makes the same claims of absolute transformation regarding a number of other (more recent) revival scenarios, such as Cali (Columbia), Almolonga (Guatemala), the Eastern Arctic of Canada and Uganda.

10. ibid., pp. 29–30.

move of the Spirit in North Uist the same year, and a more localised movement in the east Lewis township of Lemreway in 1969. These revivals did not differ in essence from the '49–52 awakening, having the same fundamental characteristics.

Other revivals have since occurred elsewhere in Scotland too, as well as in other parts of the United Kingdom, and indeed other locations across the developed world. Admittedly, most have been localised, or at best regional – but then so was the Lewis revival – confined, as it was, to one Scottish island. The 1949 revival is far from being the last revival to have occurred in the western world.

CHAPTER 23

Revival Afterglow

Lasting Fruit

Rarity of Backsliding

If the late spring of 1952 was indeed the time when the revival began to come to a close, it served as a suitable moment for the evangelist to pause and look back on the past two years plus. Following a tour of several districts in May of that year, Duncan Campbell expressed his 'deep gratitude to God for allowing me to labour in the midst of revival' throughout that period. He also spoke of his 'great joy to find the converts going on so well,' with 'practically no backsliding; only four of the hundreds who professed' conversion across the island.[1]

Five months later Campbell made a similar report from places in Harris touched by the movement. And the following year, after meeting with converts in Uig, Bernera, Barvas and Arnol, he was 'greatly cheered and encouraged to find them all going on and growing in grace, and to God's glory we can report that no-one in the districts mentioned has gone back' (though one might question how this was ascertained).[2] Around the same time, the Rev. James Murray Mackay also said he knew of no cases of backsliding in the Barvas area.

These are astonishing claims. They amount to what is surely less than a one per cent fallout rate – a remarkably low dropout

---

1. Duncan Campbell, FM Report, 28.05.1952.

2. Peckham, *Sounds from Heaven*, pp. 70–71.

percentage. Backsliding is an almost invariable consequence of periods of multiple conversions, though much more common following evangelistic campaigns than spontaneous revivals. Writing decades later, however, one journalist asserted; 'there was widespread recidivism' generally across the island. 'Many early Campbell converts eventually turned their backs on religion.' To back up his assertion, he refers to two notable revival hotspots – Arnol and Bernera – both of which districts were, he claimed at the time of writing in 2008, 'among the least religious on Lewis.'[3] However, even if one accepts that the contentious assumption is true, to what extent such vague evidence – from over half a century after the revival – is relevant, is debatable.

Certainly, none of those who provide testimonies in *Sounds from Heaven* makes mention of significant backsliding in the years or decades after the revival. On the contrary, several have spoken of the continuation of most converts in their new-found faith. Mary Peckham called it a natural 'characteristic of revival – that very few go back into the world. The work is genuine.'[4]

It is certainly apparent that in the years immediately following the revival, cases of backsliding across the island were fairly rare. This was especially true of Barvas. Looking back seven decades after the movement, one convert stated of that parish, 'There were few backsliders that I can recall. Perhaps there were some temporary lapses but these were generally followed by years of bright witness.'[5] The paucity of backsliding cases in the Lewis revival has been regarded in part as a consequence of Campbell and other ministers allowing the Spirit to deal with people rather than coercing them into making decisions.

---

3. Macleod, *Banner in the West*, p. 266.

4. Personal communication with Mary Peckham, 16/08/2008.

5. Personal communication with Margaret Macleod, 02.05.2020.

Growing in Grace

In the afterglow of the revival itself, both Campbell and the Rev. Mackay of Barvas testified to over a hundred souls in that Westside parish whose hearts had been savingly changed by the Lord. 'Their daily living is fragrant,' Mackay wrote; 'their fellowship blessed, their love vital and glowing – as beautiful a progeny of grace as one has ever seen.'[6]

A minister in Ness stated, 'Converts are growing in grace and are definitely an asset to the church and community.' He viewed the steady increase in their 'interest in spiritual things' in his parish as very encouraging.[7] Similar reports could be gleaned from numerous other districts.

Visitors were deeply struck with the impact that the gospel message had had on the community of Barvas, especially as a result of various community revivals. Campbell took one visitor from house to house to hear from the lips of the people themselves the confirmation of the things he had told him about the movement. 'I saw here,' the visitor observed, 'for the first time in my life, what might honestly be termed a Christian community.'[8]

Lingering Embers

While the revival peak may have been reached in the spring of 1952, embers from the Lewis revival continued to glow well after this date. The Rev. G. I. Thomas paid a visit to the island with Duncan Campbell in the early 1950s. By this time, 'there was no outstanding movement of the Spirit.' He nevertheless had two experiences which illustrated Campbell's emphasis on the awareness of God as being a key feature.

---

6. Peckham, *Sounds from Heaven*, p. 79

7. Wooley, *Channel of Revival*, p. 150.

8. Dwight Wadsworth, *The Pentecostal Evangel*, 01.04.1951.

His Presence Abiding

'One Sunday evening, while I was preaching, I believe that
God took hold of me and of my mind and lips, as I would say
He has not done on any other occasion. Thoughts flooded my
mind that were totally unprepared, and I just knew myself to
be borne along by the Spirit of God. I have rarely known so
moving an atmosphere as when I sat down and the people sang
the final Psalm. There was indeed an awareness of God that was
very wonderful.'[9]

Another night Thomas was disappointed to find only a small
number gather to hear him speak. Yet, 'in the midst of my
message – God came down. There was a moment when I left off
speaking and together we *felt* the silence. Yes, how dreadful was
that place. More than one present that night referred to that
moment in later days.' Campbell was not present at that meeting,
Thomas added, but 'God was there and in revival there is an
awareness of God.'[10]

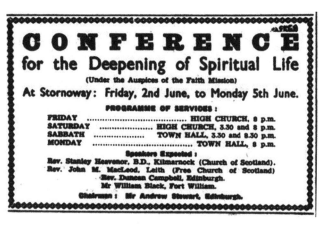

Stornoway Faith Mission Convention advert

One direct outcome of the revival was the Stornoway Convention,
which Campbell organised as an annual event – the first one

---

9. Campbell, *The Lewis Awakening*, Foreword, p. 9.

10. ibid.

taking place as early as 1950. Held in a different parish each summer with a closing gathering in Stornoway, it attracted big audiences, and there was often a marked sense of God's presence.

During the 1951 event, 'splendid open-air meetings' were conducted by fishermen's evangelist Jock Troup, which went on until almost midnight.[11] During the 1955 convention, one visitor praised the 'glowing witness' of the converts of the revival that she met, and remembered 'the sense of being in the presence of God, which was very striking.'[12]

Prayer Union

Faith Mission Prayer Unions were set up and carried on by the faithful few who stood with the pilgrims in their labours. Most groups were small in number – and were visited regularly by the District Superintendent. Most Lewis Prayer Unions began while the revival was in progress but were certainly in operation by the autumn of 1950.

In October of that year, Willie Black spoke of having had 'good meetings among the Lewis Prayer Unions ... The work is going on steadily and some are still finding Christ through the converts.'[13] As the P.U. Representative for Barvas, Kenneth MacDougall held prayer meetings in his home, sent donations to the Faith Mission and received the Faith Mission newsletter with updates of the work of the pilgrims.

The revival, while filling the Rev. Mackay's heart with joy, brought on an enormous additional workload for the Barvas minister, and he was frantically busy for its whole three-year duration. Indeed, his physical and emotional health began to gradually deteriorate over that period of time, and he broke down completely as the revival drew to a close in 1952. Mackay was forced to retire from the ministry and, along with his wife and

---

11. FM Report, 04.07.1951.

12. *Bright Words*, 1955, pp. 194–5.

13. Duncan Campbell, FM Report, 25.10.50.

three children, returned to the mainland. He died shortly after, in 1953.

Resurgence of Revival

It is most interesting to note something of a resurgence of revival in Barvas when Campbell paid a return visit to the island in the spring of 1955. There appears to have been a connection here to the national outreach mission conducted by American evangelist Billy Graham in Glasgow, during which Easter week live relay broadcasts were made to thirty-seven strategic centres across Scotland.

In Stornoway, the various Church of Scotland congregations hired the Town Hall, which was packed with folk from across the island wishing to watch the live relays. Although strong opposition to the Arminian methods employed by Graham came from the Free and Free Presbyterian Churches in Lewis, the Stornoway meetings were hailed a success, and several individuals made commitments of faith.

Donald & Morag MacPhail

In Barvas, Campbell found the revival converts of half-a-decade earlier to be 'growing in grace,' and noted that without doubt, 'the Spirit of God is moving again in the parish,' albeit amidst 'bitter opposition in high places.' Several house meetings Campbell noted as being 'full of the power of the Lord.'[14] Donald MacPhail was present at one, and proved again to be God's channel of blessing, for his prayer 'let heaven loose around us,' prompting Campbell to compare it to a similarly powerful meeting in the same parish at which the youthful prayer warrior had interceded in 1950.

Indeed, Campbell observed 'a spirit of expectancy abroad, and prayer meetings similar to 1949' occurring in Barvas (as well as in Bernera, where he found the unity and prayers among believers of both denominations on the island to be 'wonderful').[15] A month later, well after leaving Lewis, reports were still coming to Campbell 'of God moving again in Barvas.'[16]

Late Converts

Donald John Smith

Some Lewis residents influenced by the revival of 1949–52 weren't actually converted until a number of years after the movement had subsided. One such was Donald John Smith of Upper Shader. A teenager at the time of the awakening, Donald later moved to Glasgow, where he found employment in a large Singer factory employing over 10,000 workers.

Although affected by spiritual concerns, Donald was worried that by living through two powerful revivals in Lewis (1939 and 1949), yet still not being converted, he had perhaps committed the unpardonable sin (Matt 12:31), a doubt further exaggerated by the dramatic conversions of several others in his family (including his brothers, John Murdo Smith, one of the first revival converts in Shader, and William, the piper converted on his way to a dance).

---

14. ibid., 04.05.1955.

15. ibid., 11.05.1955.

16. ibid., 08.06.1955.

Dispirited, Donald went to hear Duncan Campbell preach in the city. Speaking privately with him at the close of the meeting, Campbell said he 'felt the power of the Spirit' around the young man in whose Shader home Campbell had spent many an hour during the revival. Smith, however, went through a particularly bad patch before being converted in 1962.

Donald John Smith, Shader

He shared the good news by letter with his father – then a deacon – in Barvas. Smith senior was one of the men asked to speak at a communion 'Question meeting' the following Friday; he chose as his message '*The prodigal son*.' Donald was the fifth member of the family to be converted, and understandably, both of his parents, as well as the Barvas congregation, were overjoyed with the news.

Donald Saunders
Another 'late' convert was Donald Saunders of Ballantrushal, who grew up during the 1949 revival. His father, an elder in the Barvas church, died of a heart attack while visiting a Christian friend in Stornoway shortly after the revival, in 1952. His sudden and premature death hardened Donald's heart further against the things of God.

Donald got married and they had a family of three. In April 1984, Donald's wife died of a brain tumour; aged just forty-eight.

As he stood by her bed, the Lord made it clear to him that He had taken her to be with Himself in heaven. Heartbroken and in a state of despair, for the first time in his life he cried out to the Lord from the depths of his heart. He had felt for some time that Jesus wouldn't accept him as one of His chosen, and he went through a terrible spiritual struggle. He prayed out loud, 'My Lord and my God,' asking the Lord to take him 'home' to be with his wife.

Donald Saunders

Instead, he sensed God spoke the words of Psalm 107, in Gaelic, to his soul:

They cried out to the LORD in their trouble,
*   and he delivered them from their distress.*
He led them by a straight way,
*   to a city where they could settle (6–7).*

Instantly, his soul was flooded with peace and joy; Donald was made a new man in Christ. The sudden death of his father had pushed him away from God; the death of his wife drew him towards Him. Throughout the days that followed, and despite his natural grief, the joy that now flowed through him was almost uncontainable, to the extent that he was afraid that those who saw him would think him mad! Donald continued to serve the Lord faithfully over ensuing years, and became an elder, of many decades duration, in the Barvas Church of Scotland.

Lasting Effects

By 1970 a minister visiting Lewis testified that everywhere he went he met people whose lives had been radically changed through Campbell's ministry during the revival twenty years previously.

The Rev. Aonghas Iain Macdonald served as minister of Barvas Church of Scotland from October 1973 until March 1981. He estimated that around a fifth of his communicant membership were converts of the revival (many others had moved away from Lewis or had passed away). 'The converts were extremely supportive and encouraging towards my ministry,' Aonghas noted. 'There was persistently a yearning, especially among the elderly, for a fresh outpouring of the Lord's presence.'

Aonghas recalls several abiding features of the spiritual impact of the '49 movement. 'First of all, these "special times" had deepened the prayer life of many in the congregation. They never lost their appetite for the word of God and true gospel proclamation. Secondly, those from that era as well as from earlier revivals continued to be influential in their spiritual encouragement of others – to believers and unbelievers alike.

'Thirdly, there was a communal effect through these awakenings, marking both believers and a majority of unbelievers (many of whom did not attend church). This effect was evident among the former in the significant concern and burden for the conversion of others that they experienced in their personal prayer life. Among unbelievers there was generally a respectful and sensitive attitude towards both the gospel and those involved with it.'[17]

---

17. Personal communication with the Rev. Aonghas Macdonald, 10.07.2020.

By the mid-1990s something of a cottage industry had developed, with a steady stream of visitors coming from all over to visit the church or speak with revival converts. According to the Rev. Ivor Macdonald, who served as minister of Barvas Church of Scotland from 1993 to '99, the legacy was mixed. It tended to result in 'an attitude that elevated revival blessing at the expense of ongoing evangelism and reformation,' he felt.[18] At the same time, while, naturally, the congregation always prayed for 'more' in terms of revival blessing, every new convert gained by means of the 'ordinary' activity of the church was warmly welcomed into the fellowship, and much rejoiced over.

Positions of Influence

Lasting results of the revival can be seen in other ways too. Around a dozen converts went into full-time ministry, mainly in the Church of Scotland. At least two were still in active service well over fifty years after turning to the Lord. The Rev. William Macleod was ordained and inducted to the Church of Scotland on the isle of Benbecula in 1957. He moved to Uig, Lewis in 1964, where he ministered for forty-two years before officially 'retiring' at the age of eighty in 2006. Even long after that date, he could regularly be found preaching in island pulpits.

The Rev. John Murdo Smith celebrated the sixtieth anniversary of his ministry in 2016, during which year he was also awarded a British Empire Medal in the Queen's Birthday Honours List for services to the communities of North and South Uist, on which island he was the hospital chaplain for thirty-two years, and where he set up the League of Friends for Lochmaddy hospital.[19]

---

18. Personal communication with the Rev. Ivor Macdonald, 22.06.2020. Also, Ivor felt that, being associated with the Faith Mission, the revival resulted in 'some people gathering around a certain church culture associated with the Mission.'

19. One colleague described Rev. Smith as a man who 'filled whatever gathering he was in with the impact of the personality of Christ' and of 'carrying Christ in an unselfconscious fullness, spreading Christ's fragrance

Rev John Murdo Smith

Several converts went into full-time missionary service. Several became home missionaries, spreading the good news of the gospel by differing means across the UK. Some joined the Faith Mission (two or three from Uig alone), through which ministry they had themselves been converted. Mary Peckham served with this organisation to help bring awakening to Tiree and North Uist in the late 1950s. Through the decades she also shared her own testimony in both word and song in countless locations across the world.[20]

Numerous converts went on to hold positions of influence in politics or other areas of impact. Allan Macarthur served his Lochcarron community in many ways beyond his role as local Church of Scotland minister. He was a member of Ross and Cromarty District Council, of the Crofters Commission and of a local Housing Society; he served on the Children's Panel and the local Parent Teacher Association, and was a Justice of the Peace.

---

in a beautiful way among the people of God and wider afield' (personal communication with Kenny Borthwick, 15.07.2017).

20. A number of years after the revival, Willie Smith calculated that across the island, just over twenty revival converts became ministers or (mainly home-) missionaries.

In South Uist, revival convert turned Church of Scotland minister Roddy Mackinnon served as chairman of the Social Work Committee on the Western Isles Council from its inception, vigorously applying himself to bring about improvement in services, until he accepted a ministerial transfer to Ross-shire in 1981. Here he also served numerous bodies, among them the Ross-shire Health Council, the BBC's Religious Advisory Committee and Highland Blindcraft.

Rev William and Margaret Macleod, 2019

Then there were individuals like Chirsty Macleod, a convert from Arnol, who, years after the revival, was employed in one of the Harris Tweed Mills in Stornoway. Yet, during communion seasons she found the time to help the minister's wife in every Church of Scotland manse across the island. She did this for a great many years; indeed, as long as she was physically able to – counting every opportunity to serve in this way as a blessing.

Nor must we forget the many who became office bearers in both the Church of Scotland and the Free Church, in this manner assisting their ministers and serving their congregations in a variety of ways over many years. Succeeding generations have also been touched; the sons of some converts going on to serve as full-time ministers in various districts of Scotland, while other descendants went out as missionaries to far-flung places. Indirectly, too, in many ways the revival is still reaping fruit, not least through the influence of reliable written, audio and video accounts of the movement.

The revival lives on in the lives of those converts who continue to offer their lives a daily sacrifice for Christ, breathing the air of humility and holiness. Of one revival convert, a visiting minister stated, 'I have never met someone who carries more of God. To be in her presence has always made me cry. I would sometimes cry when I didn't even know she was around! The presence of God would be sweet and beautiful to the point of unbearable. On each occasion, I turned around...and there was this lady! For me it is not superstition to say that whenever I visited her in her home I was on holy ground.'[21]

---

21. Facebook post, 12.07.2018.

CHAPTER 24

Revival Statistics

Recorded figures from the Church of Scotland Presbytery of Lewis show the following membership statistics for the years prior to, during and after the revival:[1]

1,371 in 1946
1,345 in 1950
1,449 in 1952
1,443 in 1953
1,429 in 1954
1,451 in 1955
1,382 in 1957

The figures show a gradual but steady decline in church membership over the period, with the years of the revival (1950–52) appearing as a dramatic but short-lived reversal of this trend. Thereafter, the figure immediately begins to decrease, so that, even if a number of revival converts joined their local congregations between 1952 and '53, their total was more than matched by deaths, membership transfers, etc.

Interestingly, there was a further (lesser) upward blip in 1955, presumably as a result of the earlier-noted 'revival resurgence' and the Billy Graham Scotland Crusade of March 1955. The downward trend continued over subsequent decades.

---

1. Figures from Church of Scotland Year Books, forwarded by Alister Murray, 19.08.2020.

The figure of 1,345 in 1950 was clearly recorded prior to the March communion, when membership increased dramatically in Barvas, Ness and several other parishes. Thus, the rise in the total number of communicants between 1950 and 1952 is a reasonably good representation of changes occurring during the revival. There were 104 overall additions to church membership across Lewis during these years. This does not include Harris (or Berneray), which forms part of the Presbytery of Uist.

The figure of 104 does not represent total professions of faith across Lewis during the revival period (because of deaths and membership transfers, etc). We already know there were 45 additions in Barvas during 1950–52; 29 in Ness and 13 in Kinloch and South Lochs, making a total of 87. I have not been able to obtain membership additions for Church of Scotland congregations of Carloway, Uig and Point, owing to records being lost or transferred to the National Records of Scotland.

The average annual decline in church membership across Lewis during the years 1946 to 1950 was 6.5. Taking this as a guide for subsequent years had there been no revival, we might assume a membership decline of around 20 for the three years 1950–52. This suggests that accessions to membership owing to the revival might have been around 118 (98 plus 20). Thus, total additions to membership for Carloway, Bernera, Uig and Point would approximate 31 (118 minus 87). Without seeing the actual church records for each parish, we know that this is only an approximation.

Epilogue

Revival Pilgrimage

In this book we have sought to distinguish between fact and fiction. Between events that happened and those that almost certainly didn't. Between the powerful moving of the Spirit of God and the wishful fantasies of man. Between the glorious revival that truly occurred and that which never did.

As early as 1965, pastor Mark Buch was holding special revival meetings in his home church in Vancouver following his 'recent thrilling visit' to the Hebrides, where he had attended meetings with Duncan Campbell and taken part in an all-night prayer meeting. His presentation included coloured slides of 'the house that God shook, the church at Barvas where the fire fell, and Cliff House, the home of Mary Morrison.'[1]

Every year, Hebrides Revival tours (often of American origin) take pilgrims to scenes connected with the Barvas movement. Hundreds more revival tourists make their own way to Lewis and Harris, intent on visiting the revival sites and meeting a few of those converted during the awakening. One or two islanders have been especially singled out, receiving visitors on an almost daily basis, names dutifully recorded in visitors' books.

In one fairly typical week in September 2001, Donald John Smith was visited in his Shader home by a group of Anglicans from Boise, Idaho; twelve intercessors from Glasgow, a team of believers from Colorado Springs, and a six-member prayer group from a church in Lanark. Donald John was even flown down to

---

1. 'The Sunday Sun', 16.10.1965.

London in June 1997 to speak on the Lewis revival before 50,000 Christians at an event in Wembley Stadium, organised by Noel Richards and Gerald Coates.[2]

Gerald Coates & Donald J Smith at Wembley

Many find a particular enchantment in visiting scenes of the Lewis revival. A New York pastor who was converted during a youth Pentecostal revival in his home town in his teens was fascinated with the concept of true revival and the fact that none of his western contemporaries had experienced anything resembling it. He took his wife and family on a world revival tour in 2019, intent on discovering the conditions that attract the presence of God.

The tour took him to seventeen locations where significant revival had been experienced, including scenes of the labours of George Whitfield and John Wesley in England; the South Wales town of Loughor; Cane Ridge, Kentucky; and Hernhutt, Germany. Yet he was unequivocal in stating that of all the revivals

2. Although introduced as having been 'converted at the age of thirteen during the revival,' in fact Smith wasn't converted till many years later (see Chap 23). The event was described as 'surely a forerunner for the forthcoming revival that is going to hit Britain.' Smith also spoke (along with Mary Peckham) at mass Christian gatherings in, e.g. Birmingham.

he had researched, 'what God did in the Hebrides' was what most interested him, and therefore Lewis was by far 'the place that moved me most.'[3]

The Lewis revival found its way into *The Word's Top Ten Revivals* (compiled by Towns and Porter), as did Duncan Campbell in a recent compendium of the world's most influential Christians, where he appeared alongside the likes of Columba, Martin Luther and John Wesley. Interest in the Lewis revival has never been stronger. I question if there are many revival sites in the world that receive more 'revival pilgrims' than does Lewis – all the more remarkable given its remote location.

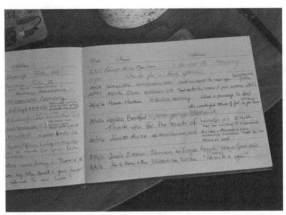

Agnes Morrison's visitors book

'The' Lewis revival?

Revivals vary in extent and duration; some being highly localised, confined to just one village or rural community; others extending across a wider region or even an entire country. A small minority become international in scope. Regardless of the magnitude, revivals tend to share similar characteristics – powerful Christ-centred preaching and an awareness of God gripping whole swathes of a community, followed by conviction of sin, repentance, a release of peace and joy, and so on. Stripped

3. Jon Tyson, Twitter posts, 2019.

of its sensationalist tales, which we have shown to be largely illusionary, the Lewis revival of 1949–52 was no different *in essence* from other revivals that have graced the island, or from awakenings that have occurred in other parts of Scotland, Great Britain or, indeed, the world.

One just needs to compare it to the 'Layman's revival' of ten-to-fifteen years previously on the same island. Some Christians who lived through both movements insist that the 1930s movement was the more powerful of the two. It might also be said to have been more organic, in that it started under the ordinary ministry of the parish minister rather than through an organised evangelistic mission. The '30s awakening, too, was widespread, despite it not requiring any prominent evangelist to transport it from one parish to another; rather, it spread spontaneously, from its starting point in Carloway, throughout much of Lewis.

The 1930s revival was more prolonged than the 1949 movement, extending for a remarkable six years (1934 to 1939), only drawing to a close with the outbreak of the Second World War. It, too, was characterised by dramatic testimonies, wonderful answers to prayer, bizarre manifestations and diverse stories of the supernatural – including strikingly accurate prophecies and a building shaking from its foundations! Church roll statistics were also impressive; Carloway Free Church alone added a formidable 105 new members over the course of the movement.

Yet the 1930s revival has never received anything like the attention that the later movement has. On the contrary, few people outside Lewis talk about it; few revival pilgrims have ever flocked to interview converts (or relatives of converts) of the movement; made their way to the Carloway church 'where it all started'; or to the site of the mission hall that shook. There has been a notable disinterest in the 'Layman's revival,' which, like all other Lewis awakenings, has been almost completely overshadowed by the '49 movement.

Indeed, the Lewis revival of 1949–52 has been accorded a sense of acclaim that has elevated it to a significance and prominence exceeding all revivals that have occurred on the island before or since. It is often viewed through a romantic lens that distorts reality and which affords it an ethereal aura of magic and mystique not given to other spiritual movements.

I well remember, a number of years ago, meeting with a small group of believers who had been privy to a remarkable outpouring of God's Spirit on the Lewis district of Callanish in the late 1960s. Most converts had connections to the Free Church and were young married couples. Preaching played a strong part and many were affected by the Word of God penetrating their souls. Hungry for fellowship, prayer and Bible study, believers gathered spontaneously in each other's homes house numerous times per week, meetings continuing till the early hours of the morning, with converts so caught up in the Lord's presence that time seemed to pass by unnoticed. There was said to have been next to no falling away among the new converts, who were quickly grounded in their faith and who advanced steadily in subsequent months and years. Many came to special fellowship meetings from other parts of Lewis, being impressed by the close fellowship of the Callanish believers, and by their depth of spirituality.

As I watched these believers become animated as they recalled the thrilling, life-altering experiences of those exciting days nearly five decades previously, I realised that I could just as well have been listening to converts of the Lewis revival of 1949-52 from any particular district affected, so comparable were their testimonies of God's profound blessings. The two revivals were different in specifics, but not in character.

Even while writing this book, I have felt an increasing unease referring without qualification to 'The Lewis revival.' Like all other awakenings on the island, this one requires context: 'The Lewis revival of '49-52', gives it that, though I have known those who prefer 'The West of Lewis revival', given that, though indeed it graced other districts, including Harris, it was predominantly a West of Lewis movement, and most stories that we've come to know and love in regard to it occurred on that side of the island.

Ultimately, one can only hope that a sense of perspective will prevail, one that will allow all revivals occurring before and after 1949 to find their proper, rightful place in the revival history of the island, while in no way detracting from the wonderful way in which the Spirit of God moved across Lewis and Harris between 1949 and '52.

Believing the Myth

A thirty-five-minute inspirational audio compilation released in 2005, entitled *Revival Hymn,* captures speakers such as Ian Paisley, A.W. Tozer, T. Austin Sparks and Leonard Ravenhill. The longest single clip (8 minutes) comes from Duncan Campbell, an old recording of him sharing stories from the Lewis revival. *SermonIndex.net* describes the recording as 'probably one of the most potent and powerful' of over 100,000 messages that fill their vast website. It has been downloaded over 134,000 times on that site alone.

One listener said the message 'radically changed my life. I have listened to it over fifty times.' Another said it 'changed both my husband and myself and we will never be the same and neither can we be … God bless you for making these truths available.' Ironically, Campbell's talk is peppered with *untruths*, accounts of events that were either greatly exaggerated or that never took place at all. How this matches with multiple testimonies of profound and lasting spiritual impact is curious, if not astonishing.

And yet, these testimonies parallel those of countless other individuals over the years who have been deeply inspired by the stories Duncan Campbell has shared of the Lewis revival. It is apparent that God has used these stories, exaggerated and distorted as some of them are, to impact the lives of thousands of people all over the world. Surely, this is a testament to the evangelist's integrity and sincerity – is it likely that the Lord would have blessed his public addresses so powerfully had he been culpable of overt dishonesty and deceit?

R. T. Kendall (centre) with Barvas revival converts (left to right): Donald John Smith, William Macleod, Margaret Macleod, Agnes Morrison, Stornoway Revival conference, 2019

Is it likely, further, that God would have used the evangelist in the striking way suggested by the following testimony? An unconverted teenager, while having lunch at Killadeas Camp Convention in Co. Fermanagh, N. Ireland, watched a man – a complete stranger – strolling along the disused airfield. The man was back-on to him, and although he couldn't begin to explain it, the teenager felt that he had 'a beauty for me that I craved … I never saw God until that day, and in the days that followed the vision lingered and haunted me.' The man taking an after-lunch stroll was Duncan Campbell, an invited speaker at the Convention. The awakened young man gave his life to Christ as a result of that encounter.[4]

---

4. Personal communication with Andrew Woolsey, 18.04.2023; Woolsey, *Channel of Revival*, pp. 177–8.

Despite the great care taken by the authors of *Sounds from Heaven*[5] to only relate what they knew to be true, that book's understandably subtle approach in regard to exaggerations and falsehoods hasn't ultimately achieved one of its intended objectives – to settle for once and for all the truth of the Lewis revival. Countless stories still get told in printed form, church sermons, conventions and Bible weeks, and endless blogs and websites – that are overflowing with exaggeration and distortion. Some people seem intent on peddling accounts of the Lewis revival that never was. As with *Donald's Bible,* a great many prefer to believe the myth.

When I shared a response to a popular YouTube video entitled *Donald's Bible* in 2020, stating briefly why the story was actually a myth, I received a reply saying, 'Oh, why spoil it for everyone!' The suggestion seemed to be that what I was saying might well be true, but why let truth get in the way of a good story! People are often happier believing the myth, not wanting their illusions to be shattered. Yet it's important to expose the myths. Because as they continue to get not only peddled but added to over the years – as with the recent *'Donald's Bible'* yarn, or the *'Fathers of the Revival'* tale in the mid-90s – accounts of the revival become increasingly distanced from reality.

The Lewis Revival that Truly Was
Some of the more extravagant tales of the awakening in Lewis are exciting to read about. Who wouldn't want to believe them? Exposing the revival that never was is unlikely to lead to increased popularity. Nevertheless, it will ultimately help us to construct a clearer narrative of what truly took place in Lewis and Harris between the years 1949 and '52. In so doing we discover a revival

---

5. Colin Peckham was 'suddenly and quietly called home' in November 2009; nine months later, Mary passed away following a stroke. Their book, *Sounds from Heaven* has sold all over the world, and went into four printings within two years.

just as exciting as the one it displaces. A revival that carries the ring of truth.

Even with the removal of fabricated and exaggerated stories, the evidence is overwhelming – a highly significant spiritual revival took place on Lewis and Harris between 1949 and 1952. It was a revival whose essence was powerful preaching, based on the truth of God's Word. A revival that exposed sin and revealed the life-changing truth of the gospel. A revival replete with remarkable, life-transforming testimonies, revealing the unbridled joy that relationship with Jesus brings.

It was a revival that led to a life of witness for hundreds of individuals, and full-time Christian ministry for many. It was a revival of supernatural occurrences, premonitions and prophecies. A revival that has stirred up faith and hope in the lives of thousands of Christians, not just throughout the British Isles but around the world, among believers hungry to see God move in their own communities.

The Lewis revival will continue to stir hungry hearts, build faith and inspire hope in believers. Revival tourists will continue to flock to the island and parish where it all began in December 1949, to visit the church where Duncan Campbell delivered his hellfire sermons, to be shown the site of the cottage where the saintly Smith sisters lived, the Shader meeting hall where the first conversion took place, the police station where many a powerful meeting occurred and the large Arnol house that allegedly shook.

There's great inspiration to be gained in such pilgrimage. Here's hoping such future visits are made on the basis of revival reality rather than revival fantasy. May the Christian world never forget, and never fail to be inspired and awed by the Lewis revival that truly was.

Appendix

Family Tribute

Margaret Heavenor, Duncan and Shona Campbell's eldest child, wrote this tribute shortly after her father's death in 1972.

Love and Loyalty

About a year before the death of my father, my husband and I visited my parents' home for the evening. Dad was expected home next day, but we had to return to Crieff that evening, so did not anticipate seeing him. About 10 pm we were just on the point of departure when dad appeared. An earlier flight from one of his many engagements abroad had brought him home a day early, and as he so often loved to give a pleasant surprise, he did so on this occasion.

We chatted to him for a short time but had to leave. Both he and my mother stayed at the door to wave goodbye. Then they closed the glass door. As we were driving off, we saw a shadow on the door, which, to me, symbolises the loving relationship between them. Dad wrapped his arms around my mother and kissed her lovingly.

Such affection would never be demonstrated publicly, or even to the family, but we all knew their deep love for each other, which made possible many sacrifices on behalf of my mother, and a confidence on the part of my father that home was a haven and the family in good hands when he had to leave on his many missions.

Duncan and Shona Campbell

One reads and hears of many who were influenced by either a father or mother. In the case of our family the influence of both father and mother was intertwined inextricably. One cannot think of one without the other. They supported each other in faith and practice; in love and loyalty; in adversity and in worrying times.

Now that dad has gone to be with the One he served, it is strange for us to see our mother on her own without him at her side, but '*he being dead yet speaketh*,' for he lives on in her. Our mother's example of courage, faith, peace and acceptance of God's will, more than convinces, if one needs convincing, that their pattern of life was based on a true foundation.

Bible Study and Prayer

From early childhood the Bible and family prayers were part of our lives. Each evening we all gathered together to read, each taking one verse, and then we knelt to pray, with mum and dad praying on alternate evenings. There the family realised that the Bible and prayer were no formalities, but an integral part of the daily routine, without which, like food or any other necessity of life, one's daily living would suffer.

I think it is true to say that later in life we all had to make personal decisions about our relationships with God. But as children no stone was left unturned to lead us to that decision. Never once had the family any doubt about their parents' view of the reliability of God's Word, their faith, or a belief in prayer. They lived entirely by faith, relying on God at all times, in joy and in sorrow.

Duncan Campbell's daughter, Sheena Vischer,
with the author, Haddington, May 2022

Dad was a very practical person about the home, and was in the best sense, 'head of the house.' If a job had to be done, he did it willingly, without complaint.[1]

A very early riser, he planned his day carefully, beginning, when most people were asleep, with his daily reading and prayer. He was excellent company, and had a flair for story-telling. One could relax in his company. Para Handy tales, tales of the Highlands, and war stories were among his favourite books when he took time to relax, especially in the years before he died, but

---

1. Sheena Campbell Visher added; 'Dad was indeed a very practical man. I've seen him on his knees, polishing the linoleum floor. I've seen him make pots and pots of soup. Oh, and he always made the breakfast. And I can remember going out fishing with him when I was small' (Personal communication with Sheena Campbell Vischer, 15.03.2020).

many of the stories he told himself, of happenings, both grave and gay in his own life, would make a fascinating book.

He told a story of one occasion when he was preaching and had trouble with a loose dental plate. The inevitable happened while he was in mid-sentence; the plate came out. But nothing daunted, and resourceful as ever, he turned round to replace it out of sight of the congregation, only to find he faced an amused choir! On another occasion, no doubt when tired, as he was leading the congregation in the Lord's Prayer, he forgot the words! But again, a diplomatic cough saved the occasion.

This One Thing I Do

As we grew up, our home was always open to all. People who came to help in the church, perhaps on a Mission, were immediately drawn into the family circle. Both parents were especially convinced that young as well as older people required teaching in the Word of God and the example of a Christian home.

Duncan Campbell relaxing

Dad's last days were spent in the company of young people. He disapproved of shallow attempts to influence youth, or to sugar-coat the message of the gospel. A very balanced person, he was too busy preaching Christ crucified and risen to indulge in complex theorising about prophecy or the Second Advent of Christ. He gave to the family, as my mother continues to give, a balanced Christian outlook, which has an 'instinct for what is vital.'

His one aim was to preach and teach the Gospel to as many as would listen, and this included his own immediate family. His life and work were intertwined in love, loyalty and service to God, and the influence of our mother's godly life was an important factor in his dedication, for they were both able to say, in all sincerity, '*This one thing I do*' (Phil 3:13).

The cumulative effect of his preaching and the example of true Christian parents have given his family something vital on which to base their lives. The family saw very early that they had the best interests of their children at heart. Their advice and affection have been an important contribution in shaping our lives.

Influence on Family

If we were asked to specify our father's influence on the family, it would be summarised briefly as:

a. Reverence for holy things.[2]

b. Clear moral values.

c. Respect for the Lord's Day and the Bible.

d. An example of hard work, which has left its mark. Although not a hyper-Calvinist, he picked out the best elements in Calvinism, including the belief that the faith must influence everyday work.

---

2. Archie Campbell noted; 'God was very real to my father. Even when he was at home, he seemed remote and almost in another world. And he was – his loyalty was 100 per cent to God, and he lived in constant communion with Him' (Personal communication with Archie Campbell, 18.10.2017).

e. The belief that all men are equal in God's sight, and a genuine disregard for snobbish values and material gain.

f. Practical kindness to others, often at a heavy personal cost. Dad never obtruded his own outlook on others, but witnessed with courtesy and respect. His deep humility was his most salient characteristic.[3]

To be in dad's presence was to be brought near to God. He truly was God's man. It should be said that this saintliness was not that of an anchorite, brooding in religious solitude. Here was a man, bustling, striving, organizing, speaking and preaching, with the dust and fire of the world on his clothes, but carrying his shrine with him everywhere.[4]

---

3. Sheena added; 'My father was marked by a deep love for people, and also by a sacred dissatisfaction, knowing that revival always begins with oneself' (Personal communication with Sheena Campbell Vischer, 15.03.2020).

4. Margaret Heavenor, *Tribute to Duncan Campbell,* unpublished paper, 1972.

Other books by Tom Lennie ...

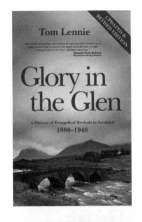

ISBN: 978-1-84550-377-2

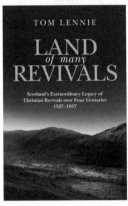

ISBN: 978-1-78191-520-2

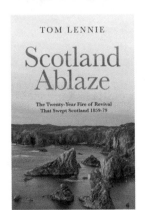

ISBN: 978-1-5271-0267-5

Christian Focus Publications

Our mission statement –

STAYING FAITHFUL

In dependence upon God we seek to impact the world through literature faithful to His infallible Word, the Bible. Our aim is to ensure that the Lord Jesus Christ is presented as the only hope to obtain forgiveness of sin, live a useful life and look forward to heaven with Him.

Our Books are published in four imprints:

CHRISTIAN
FOCUS

popular works including biographies, commentaries, basic doctrine and Christian living.

CHRISTIAN
HERITAGE

books representing some of the best material from the rich heritage of the church.

MENTOR

books written at a level suitable for Bible College and seminary students, pastors, and other serious readers. The imprint includes commentaries, doctrinal studies, examination of current issues and church history.

CF4•K

children's books for quality Bible teaching and for all age groups: Sunday school curriculum, puzzle and activity books; personal and family devotional titles, biographies and inspirational stories – Because you are never too young to know Jesus!

Christian Focus Publications Ltd,
Geanies House, Fearn, Ross-shire,
IV20 1TW, Scotland, United Kingdom.
www.christianfocus.com